Praise for *Coming Out Spiritually*

"De la Huerta whips up an enlightening, reverent, celebratory tome that refuses to deny the corporeal in order to celebrate transcendence. Full of words to live by, the scope and heartfelt intensity of this book should be required reading for every gay man as we approach the millennium."

—*Genre Magazine*

"*Coming Out Spiritually* is comparable to Jean Shinoda Bolen's *Goddesses in Everywoman* and Pinkola Estés' *Women Who Run with the Wolves*. It reveals how we may apply spiritual and archetypal wisdom relating to erotic and gendered diversity to enrich our daily lives."

—RANDY P. CONNER, AUTHOR OF *Cassell's Encyclopedia of Queer Myth, Symbol, and Spirit*

"*Coming Out Spiritually* is an encyclopedia of possibilities that make coming out politically and coming in spiritually easier and more joyous."

—ANDREW RAMER, AUTHOR OF *Two Flutes Playing* and *Revelations for a New Millennium*

'In Spanish, *huerta* is 'a large market garden as in an apple orchard.' In *Coming Out Spiritually*, Christian de la Huerta guides us through a large and fruitful garden of the soul. This is a rich sourcebook in spiritual discipline and diversity."

—MEL WHITE, AUTHOR OF *Stranger at the Gate: To Be Gay and Christian in America*

"Whether reclaiming or inventing, questioning or witnessing, testifying or envisioning, queer folks today are fomenting a dynamic spiritual renewal. With sympathy and insight, Christian de la Huerta surveys this burgeoning movement in all its diversity."

—WILL ROSCOE, AUTHOR OF *The Zuni Man-Woman, Queer Spirits,* and *Changing Ones*

"Written inclusively and warmly, *Coming Out Spiritually* expands the lineage of those of us who comprehend gayness as comprising positive, transformative attributes of spiritual office. This is a book to treasure and teach."

—JUDY GRAHN, AUTHOR OF *Another Mother Tongue*

"*Coming Out Spiritually* offers helpful new ways of thinking about queer people in society today. it is a hopeful book, encouraging as it is insightful."

—MARK THOMPSON, AUTHOR OF THE *Gay Spirit, Gay Soul,* and *Gay Body* trilogy

"De la Huerta's beautifully crafted prose and his passionate desire to help queers come out spiritually mark this book as an extraordinary achievement."

—*Publishers Weekly*

"*Coming Out Spiritually* is not only a wisely written book with valid affirmations about the human condition, but it is also a great compendium to help us achieve our better and best selves. De la Huerta's book is valuable to both gays and lesbians."

—*Gay People's Chronicle*

"A spiritual leader from the gay community offers an ambitious, optimistic view of the role gay people can play in the world, offering a fresh study of gay spirituality from an ecumenical, multi-religious perspective, and explains how gays can rebuild their spiritual connections. Original."

—*ALA Forecasts*

"Christian de la Huerta's book is an inspiring and ennobling look at our identities and purpose as gay people, and I recommend it highly . . . The book is worth reading."

—*The Los Angeles Times*

"De la Huerta often generalizes about the gay community and sees it as particularly prepared to bring about a spiritual change in our society. This argument and the chapter on sex are the unique aspects of de la Huerta's work, recommending it for the larger public libraries."

—*Library Journal*

Coming Out
Spiritually
The Next Step

Christian de la Huerta

With a Foreword by Matthew Fox

Jeremy P. Tarcher/Putnam
a member of Penguin Putnam Inc. New York

Most Tarcher/Putnam books are available at special quantity
discounts for bulk purchase for sales promotions,
premiums, fund-raising, and educational needs.
Special books or book excerpts also can be
created to fit specific needs. For details, write
Putnam Special Markets,
375 Hudson Street, New York, NY 10014.

The author is donating 10 percent of his profits to Q-Spirit.

Jeremy P. Tarcher/Putnam
a member of
Penguin Putnam Inc.
375 Hudson Street
New York, NY 10014
www.penguinputnam.com

Library of Congress Cataloging-in-Publication Data

De la Huerta, Christian.
     Coming out spiritually : the next step / Christian de la Huerta.
         p.   cm.
     Includes bibliographical references and index.
     ISBN 0-87477-966-9 (alk. paper)
     1. Homosexuality—Religious aspects.   2. Gays—Religious life.
I. Title.
BL65.H64D45   1999   99-12008   CIP
291.1'7835766—dc21

Printed in the United States of America
10   9   8   7   6   5   4

Book design by Ralph Fowler

ACKNOWLEDGMENTS

Thank you to all those gay and lesbian activists and visionaries who came before me, on whose shoulders I have stood. Thank you for your courage, your insights, your discoveries. Thank you for the freedoms, the choices, the rights you have made possible for us; and for the sacrifices you have made. Thank you for all the hard work.

Thank you to those whose thoughts and words I have distilled, synthesized, and woven, in particular: Mark Thompson, Judy Grahn, Randy Conner, Will Roscoe, and Andrew Ramer.

Thank you to all those whose direct support in this realm helped make this book possible, especially: Joel Fotinos, friend and publisher, for believing in me, and for not rushing me. I wasn't ready. I'm ready now; David Charlsen, for providing the cabin in the redwoods that made it possible for me to travel within. You are deeply missed; David Perry, for the gift of the Enterprise, which made it possible for me to travel to and from the Russian River; Dan Cane, for letting me use the house in the Keys; Roger Corless, for your comments about the comparative religions section; Kevin Bentley, for the insightful, caring, and sensitive editing; David Groff, for the editorial innovations; Maia Dhyan, former spiritual teacher, for an intense, unique, and transforming experience. What a trip!; my parents, for your steadfast love and countless sacrifices; my partner, Ian Ganze, for your generosity, compassion, and humor, but mostly, for holding steady—and for leaping; and finally, the Divine Choreographer, for weaving the magic together.

For my parents,

Raquel and Rene de la Huerta,

and in memory of

David Charlsen

CONTENTS

Several years ago there was a forty-one-year-old man in our master's program in creation spirituality who was living with AIDS. After graduating from our program, he spent the summer in the Bay area, and he, my dog, and myself would take frequent walks together. When his health deteriorated, I took him to the hospital where he lasted only a few weeks before he died. His death was very beautiful—nurses said a light and a presence hung about the intensive care ward for twenty-four hours after he left us. In our last conversation before he died, he surprised me when he said to me: "Tell the people that AIDS is a blessing. It is a blessing because the journey is so deep, and it is a blessing because it will help us to be more honest about sexuality."

Coming Out Spiritually in many ways represents the fruit of the ironic blessings that AIDS has brought about. It is an honest book and a candid one about sexuality and all aspects of life and living. It is made possible by the suffering of the AIDS crisis and how this has inspired friends and lovers and family of persons living with AIDS to explore the deeper aspects of compassion and grief, joy and gratitude. It is also inspired by the centuries of oppression of gay and lesbian people. It is a timely book and a necessary book.

We are, I hope, ready now to read a book that is as honest about sexuality as this book is. And that is honest about spirituality as well. For one of the important themes in this book is that we cannot do either of these realities justice in our lives without the other. Sexuality without spirituality becomes boring and addictive and even cynical; spirituality without sexuality becomes disengaged and diseased, that is, disincarnated.

Today the forces of homophobia, of hatred of people because they are homosexual, bisexual, or transgendered, are powerful and conspicuous. They are as conspicuous as the scarlet robes of Cardinal Ratzinger who occupies the Inquisitor's chair in the Vatican or the beating of a nineteen-year-old senior in a high school in Marin County, California, which included the painting of "fag" on his arm and chest. They are as open as the ugly murder of Matthew Shepherd, beaten and left to die tied to a fence in rural Wyoming. They are as evident as the full-page ads promising that Jesus can "cure" homosexuality. And they are as silly as the fulminations of self-styled "Christian" preacher Jerry Falwell who sees gay messages in "Teletubby" dolls. Clearly, the human capacity for projection is infinite when it is inspired by hatred and fear. How distant these attitudes are from those of Jesus, whom their proponents yearn to invoke but fail to imitate, because Jesus did not teach hate for God's children. Jesus, after all, sided with the outcasts, and we have not a single word of condemnation from him about persons who are homosexual. We do, however, have many words from him about persons whose righteousness drives them to hypocrisy and the condemnation of others.

This book is as important for straight people as it is for gay people, for we all need to learn more about spirituality today. Our survival and quality of survival depend on it. This book leads to deeper understanding of the inner life of a sexual minority and also to understanding spirituality and the spiritual movements that are coming to life in our time. Ultimately, spirituality is a concern to us all. In a culture where the *external* gets raised to levels of idolatry, spirituality—the quest for the essence of things—is important medicine. Consider these facts: America has 4 percent of the world's population, but it consumes over 64 percent of the world's illicit drugs. Is the search for what drugs can give us not a search for transcendence? Are addictions not, in St. Thomas Aquinas's words, "a quest for the infinite"? The addiction menace in our culture attacks gays and straights, blacks, whites, Hispanics, Asians, Native peoples. The grounding that spirituality can bring to our lives is medicine for this plague in our midst. With so much folly happening today at the hands of humans destroying self, others, and the planet with our great powers of technology and greed and resentment, it is indeed important that we "come out of the closet spiritually" as this book advises.

In this book, Christian de la Huerta offers substantive theory *and* useful practices to get spirituality moving in the souls of gay and lesbian and bi peoples. In doing so, he touches what the late Dr. Howard Thurman, who was Martin Luther King, Jr.'s, mentor, called *common ground:* Soul issues *are* common-ground issues between gay and straight, old and young, educated and uneducated, black, white, brown, and red peoples. When they are ignored, addiction sets in. Addictions are dictators (they come from the same root word)—they rob us of our freedom. They are also, in theological terms, idols: they substitute themselves for the real experience of Spirit, creativity, and encounters with the Creator. The gay population knows first-hand about the plethora of addictions and addiction peddlers in American society: the peddling of drugs and drink, of money and power, of luxury living and sex, of self-hatred and outer bigotry. Spirituality is medicine for the soul. It cuts through denial and offers an alternative to self-hatred, a cleansing, a return to origins. It helps us to unfold our wings so that we can soar to the divine like the eagle does or the great goose of the Celtic peoples. When homophobia poisons a culture, spiritual leadership is lost and moralizing substitutes for spiritual living. Therein lies the death of soul for a people.

In response to moralizing, some people rise up in anger to say "There is no morality. Anything goes." But that, too, is impossibly simplistic and immature. Humans *do* have to learn to "bridle our passions with a bridle of love" as Meister Eckhart put it six centuries ago. Adults do need to learn to take responsibility for our powers and our actions, and among the greatest is the responsibility to mentor the young by example as well as by instruction in both understanding and wisdom. While moralizing is to be eschewed, morality still calls us to our better selves. When, for example, adults teach hatred and bigotry—as homophobia does—then they are creating the kind of scandal to youth that Jesus warned against when he suggested that such a person put a stone around their neck and plunge in the water. In her book *Prayers for Bobby,* the mother of a young gay man relates the sad story of her son's suicide at nineteen years of age and how her negative attitudes toward homosexuality, espoused by her minister and church, actually drove her son to self-loathing and despair. His death woke her up to her blindness and, in that sense, was redemptive. It could wake many of us up. Bobby's mother is now very active in groups that instruct parents of gay and lesbian children to love their kids. There are many stories I have heard over the years as a teacher and a priest about the awful price people have paid because they were homosexual. I think of the man I know from the Philippines who, being gay, felt that his reality would so shame his family that he moved to Africa for several years when he was in his twenties and then to America. He had to leave his home and country because he felt he could not be honest about who he was.

Christian de la Huerta offers many paths to "bridling our loves" in healthy ways. He gifts us with a veritable *Source Book* of spiritual practices we can choose and centers we can visit, where we can learn inner technologies for our healing and our heart development. He draws on traditions old and new, East and West, and he offers sound judgment of movements available to us all today. He also brings together deep and critical reflections of his own and others that gift us at this time of need with prophetic insight.

I have little doubt that at the heart of homophobia and at the heart of internalized homophobia on the part of homosexual and bisexual persons *there lies the issue of creation.* And the highest-degree demonization of homosexuals and people who are different is found in those religious traditions that, in their arrogance and superiority, have ignored creation. The issue of our sexuality is an issue of creation: How diverse is it? Are other species homosexual? (De la Huerta says at least fifty-four have been identified, and he tells a moving story of his study of nesting birds during a college assignment as a young man where he first realized he was studying an all-male couple building their nest.) Homosexuality is about creation. People are created with their sexuality. Do we accept creation as God-given and as God-intended it or do we feel we are so in control that we have the right and mandate to condemn those different from us in order to remake God's creation. The Dutch theologian Father Edward Schillebeeckx warned years ago that Christology without creation is "pure projection." So much of the religious animus against gays and lesbians comes from persons with a Christology but no cosmology, that is, people without creation as an integral part of their experience of Christ. Thus, all the projection (including Tinky Winky of the "Teletubbies" characters). As humorous as Jerry Falwell's war with Tinky Winky is, we should not underestimate the seriousness of religious folly. Neither Matthew Shepherd's death nor that of Bobby who committed suicide because he was gay can be explained without the reality of conscious and unconscious homophobic messages passed through our society and religions.

Paul's epistles have some unkind things to say about homosexuals, but readers of Paul should remember the message that Howard Thurman's grandmother, who was an ex-slave, left her grandson. Do not read Paul, she would caution. He supported slavery. Christians who invoke St. Paul to support homophobia should remember that St. Paul also instructed slaves to obey their masters. He, like the rest of us, was deeply influenced by the cultural period in which he lived. Surely we have learned something more about creation and sexuality (as well as slavery) than Paul and his contemporaries knew two thousand years ago. St. Thomas Aquinas says that "a mistake about creation results in a mistake about God." Today we know that to see homosexuality as "unnatural" represents a mistake about creation. (Aquinas, who lived in the thirteenth century, did not know this.) We now know that a given percentage of every human population is gay as is that of non-human populations as well. (Also, a given percentage of every race and every religion is homosexual.) The God of homophobia is a mistaken God, one that hates part of the Divine creation. Such an image of God will not last. To worship such a God is to blaspheme the God of creation.

There is much about homosexuality that we do not yet know. There is much about spirituality that we have forgotten or do not yet know. But one thing we do know from the teachings of Jesus is this: "Love your neighbor as yourself." If you are heterosexual, learn to love your homosexual neighbor. And vice versa. And learn to love yourself, however you have been created. It is all a glorious creation, a making in God's image. What we know is this: It is time to *stop the hatred of homosexuals including self-hatred.*

I find both hope and excitement in reading this book. This book gives evidence that the human race *is* beginning to grow up around issues of sexuality and reconnecting sexuality and spirituality—lessons we need to relearn from indigenous peoples but also from the *Song of Songs* in the Hebrew Bible. Many people experience the theophany that happens in love-making. Sexuality, like the rest of creation, is sacred in its being and in its actions. We can be grateful to Christian de la Huerta for the inspiration he brings to the deep research he has brought together in these pages. There is hope, too, from the many rich citations that the author brings together from the bountiful and growing literature about gay and lesbian experience and history. Learning is a powerful antidote to bigotry and projection. This book honors the many thinkers and researchers—to say nothing of just plain livers—who have dared to explore the shadow side of western life: that of both spirituality and sexuality and homosexuality.

In the ancient tradition of creation spirituality there lies a special invitation to all people to learn to love themselves well and to love all of creation well. Homosexuals are welcome in this tradition and, as de la Huerta points out, have often been leaders in areas of spirituality. Perhaps the homosexual so often dives deep into the life of the Spirit because he or she has to learn to forgive at an early age: forgive oneself, forgive others, forgive nature, forgive God. And the homosexual is driven to create and give birth in many forms. Creativity follows from diving into one's pain and learning forgiveness and also from paying attention to what is deeply within and wants to come out.

This is a courageous book. The author tells some simple but telling stories that reveal his courage in speaking out at conferences such as that on United Religions about the issues between religion and homosexuality. Courage is an important sign. For me, it is one of the signs that distinguishes spirituality from mere religious posturing.

The late Benedictine monk, Father Bede Griffiths, who ran an ashram in southern India that served both Christians and Hindus for about fifty years, was asked late in his life about sexuality. His answer was as simple as it was profound. Sexuality, he said, is far too powerful to repress and keep down, and it is also too powerful to allow to run totally unbridled. "The only solution is to consecrate it." There lies the ultimate statement about our sexuality and our spirituality. Sexuality is sharing in such immense powers of the Divine generativity and playfulness that the proper response to it is to consecrate it, that is, to give it special status in the world of the sacred. We thank Christian de la Huerta and the ancestors he invokes for carrying on this important work in these pages. And we pray that the new millennium will be more successful at marrying sexuality and spirituality than the late Piscean age and the recent modern age have been.

—Matthew Fox
   University of Creation Spirituality
   Naropa Institute Master's program in Creation Spirituality
   Oakland, California

Matthew Fox is an Episcopal priest and author of twenty-three books on spirituality and culture, including *Original Blessing; The Coming of the Cosmic Christ; The Reinvention of Work,* and his new book, *Sins of the Spirit, Blessings of the Flesh: Lessons on Transforming Evil in Self and Society.* He is president and founder of the University of Creation Spirituality in downtown Oakland and co-director of the Naropa Institute's master's program in creation spirituality in Oakland.

Where one falls in the spectrum of *essentialist* versus *social constructionist* is a cause for heated debate and controversy among historians, anthropologists, and queer theorists. Simplified, the argument goes something like this: The former believe that enough evidence indicates that queer people have always existed throughout the world, even though they may not have called themselves by a specific name or even had a separate sense of identity. The latter point to the fact that the word *homosexual* did not even exist until 1869 (exactly one hundred years before Stonewall), when it was first used by Dr. Karoly Benkert, a Hungarian physician. Adding that the concept of *gayness* was not even developed until the mid- to late-twentieth century, social constructionists argue that gayness, or homosexuality, as a means of self-identification, is an invention of modern-day Western culture. In fact, they affirm, many non-Western societies still have no concept or word for homosexuality, even if some of their members exhibit same-sex sexual behavior. To project onto other cultures or historical periods our concept of gayness, they claim, is wrong.

I am certainly not a historian or an expert in these matters. Although I understand the argument for social constructionism, it seems to me that regardless of what they called themselves, or whether they self-identified in a particular way or not, there is substantial evidence that throughout our short tenancy on this planet a certain percentage of humans have expressed their sexual desire and explored their sexual passion with others of the same sex. And furthermore, in contrast to what ex-gay ad campaigns would have us believe, far from needing to "recover" from homosexuality in order to have spiritual grace, it appears that throughout history and across different cultures queer people have not only been spiritually inclined but may have actually been respected and revered for assuming roles of spiritual leadership. Many enact those same roles today.

In the ultimate sense, all human beings are the same. We come from the same place, and are here for the same reason. We all have the right to live, to blossom, to follow our dreams, to become who we really are and fully realize our human potential. Obviously, that is not the case in the world at this time. I believe in the oneness of all humanity, and our relatedness to all other life forms, to all of nature, to all the universe. I believe that we are all manifestations of the Great Mystery which we call by a myriad of names. Viewed in this context, is a book on spirituality for gays and lesbians a paradox?

In the process of human individuation and spiritual evolution, the ego, our separate sense of identity, needs to be fully developed before it can be transcended as a person reaches high states of enlightenment or realization. Similarly, it is important for the gay community to develop a deep sense of identity, and an awareness of who we are, before moving beyond labels—frames of thinking about ourselves which can perpetuate the illusion of separateness. My purpose in writing this book is to support that development and help deepen that awareness. *Coming Out Spiritually* hopes to catalyze the reader beyond detached study and into practical experimentation with his or her expression of spirituality. In this sense, it is a call for us to reclaim our rich spiritual heritage.

My desire is to inspire a sense of wonderment, purpose, service, and mission in the gay community. It is now time for us to consciously reclaim and reinvent the roles we have played. It is time for us to look inside, to do or intensify the work of self-discovery and self-healing, of acknowledging and stepping more fully into our archetypical roles of teachers, healers, prophets, artists, visionaries, mediators, messengers, entertainers, priests and priestesses, conveyers of beauty and Spirit.

In a sense, it doesn't matter whether homosexuality is a matter of nature or nurture, genetics or the environment, essentialism or constructionism—whether it's a choice or not. What does matter is that we are, that we always have been, and that we always will be. That is the reality. The question, then, becomes, What am I going to do about that reality? What are *you* going to do about that reality? What is the queer community, and the world at large, going to do with that reality?

Many gay people struggle with the words we use to refer to ourselves. While acknowledging that many find the word "queer" offensive, in reality it is probably here to stay for at least a while because the younger generations have owned it. We have to deal with it until we come up with a better term. That term will be used throughout this book, and will alternate with others like "gay" and "lesbian," and "GLBT" (gay, lesbian, bisexual, transgender). Clearly, enumerating these would soon prove tiresome for both reader and writer. At times, the word "gay" will be used in a collective sense; it will even be employed in a transhistorical and transcultural context. Also used are more accurate terms such as "sexually fluid," "third gender," and Randy Conner's phrase, "homoerotically inclined or gender-variant people."

Tragically, most recorded history has a predominantly male focus and bias. In spite of the dearth of research about women, I attempt to include a fair number of references to women's issues. Although my perspective is clearly that of a gay man, I try to incorporate a feminist perspective, and the voices of lesbians, bisexuals, and transgendered people.

We all know there is racism and sexism in the queer community, on all sides. There is transphobia, and prejudice against bisexuals, whom many think are "just gay and haven't fully accepted it yet." That may be true in some cases, but I believe there are genuinely bisexual people, and suspect that more and more will begin identifying that way. If Kinsey's numbers even remotely represent reality, that is the biggest closet there is. We need to develop awareness of one another's issues. In particular, I feel that gay men need to become more sensitized to the issues confronting lesbians, women in general, bi, and trans people.

I don't believe in separatism. I feel that the times call for something beyond that. Separatism is the old paradigm response. We need to discover ways of working together, ways to heal the separation, ways to help empower women, gays, and everyone else to become fully who they are, to assume their rightful roles of power and leadership. The world is in desperate need of enlightened leadership.

Coming Out Spiritually presents a well-synchronized and diverse chorus of GLBT voices from a wide spectrum of spiritual beliefs and traditions. In it you will hear from queer Buddhists, Christians, Jews, Muslims, Taoists, Hindus, Wiccans, Druids, and New Agers. You will hear from gay people of Native American, Latino, African, European, and Asian descent. You will hear young voices and mature voices. You will hear from amazing thinkers, explorers of consciousness, and radical transformers. You will hear from queer meditators, yogis, Sufi dancers, ritualists, teachers, bodyworkers, breathwork practitioners, and other healers. You will hear from an impressive array of artists, politicians, students, volunteers, authors, priests, ministers, rabbis, sheiks, sex teachers, and successful business people who are living and practicing their spiritual beliefs. You will feel their idealism, passion, depth of thought, and commitment to making a difference in the world. This woven tapestry of voices, perspectives, and modalities creates a powerful image of a queer community that is wise, loving, creative, and insightful. The book tells of a growing movement of people who are exploring what it means to be gay and spiritual in a wide variety of ways.

The book is divided into four parts. Part 1 presents ten spiritual roles, functions, or archetypes sexually-fluid and gender-variant people have fulfilled and continue to enact. No matter what path we're on, or even if we're not on a conscious spiritual path, in Part 2 we discuss the importance of coming in, of learning how to go inside. It exposes the reader to a variety of different practices—such as yoga, meditation, breathwork, and ecstatic dancing. In recent years, the gay men's community has been polarized by controversy around sexuality—its limits and varieties of expression. Part 3 takes this crucial discussion to the next level, by placing it within a spiritual context. In Part 4 we come back out again and explore ways of contributing and making a difference in the world. Appendix 1 provides a snapshot of the different spiritual traditions with specific attention to their policies, attitudes, and teachings about homosexuality. Appendix 2 is a Resource Guide including national and regional organizations, retreat centers, and schools with a spiritual focus. Appendix 3 provides a bibliography of gay-related books plus video and audio material.

Freeing ourselves requires self-awareness. My greatest hope is that this book helps you on your journey of liberation.

1

Walking Between Worlds

Introduction: Reclaiming Our Spiritual Heritage

I looked up at the room filled with two hundred delegates from all over the world, many dressed in their religious or cultural garb. Slowly, I lifted the pieces of hand-written, ruled paper and realized my hands were shaking. Yet I knew that there was no going back—I had crossed the point of no return. I began to read, a little nervously at first, but then with increasing power, emotion, and conviction.

Just a week before, I had received an invitation to take part in a global summit for the United Religions Initiative, an effort spearheaded by Bishop William Swing of the Episcopal Diocese of Northern California. During the previous year, he had traveled all over the world and met with dozens of spiritual leaders in a campaign to create the United Religions, an organization parallel to the United Nations with the purpose of establishing dialogue and peace among the world's religions. I was invited to Grace Cathedral to meet with Charles Gibbs, the president of the Initiative, who informed me that my name had been given to him as someone who might be interested in attending the conference and possibly writing about my experience. I responded that I would be honored to participate, with the understanding that I would be representing Q-Spirit, a nonprofit organization which I had founded to promote personal growth and spiritual development in the gay/lesbian/queer community. Gibbs's response was immediate: "Sure. Come on down."

Over the next couple of days, as I prepared for the conference—packing, completing projects, and rescheduling appointments—I kept thinking about a story Gibbs had told me about the regional conference in Buenos Aires, Argentina, which had taken place a few months prior. Apparently, the issue of sexual orientation had become a prominent focus of discussion and controversy during those proceedings. Somewhere in the back of my mind I thought that perhaps, if the opportunity presented itself, I would need to address that issue. But only if no one else tackled it first.

The procedure each morning was the same. We'd start out with an invocation, prayer, or meditation led by representatives from different traditions. That morning, Masankho Banda, a young man from Africa, engaged us with a song in his native tongue. By the time he finished, the entire room was enlivened and energized. Five or six others moved toward the front of the room to make announcements. John Hamilton, the conference production manager, began by saying, "Now we move from the spectacular to the mundane," and proceeded to share with us some logistical information about our day. As I waited nervously, allowing the others to go before me, one of the organizers zoomed in on the papers I was holding, leaned over and asked, "You *are* going to make an announcement, right?" To which I replied, "Yes." The gatekeeper pressed, "And it's going to be brief, right?" Again I replied, "Yes," adding to myself, "Well, brief *is* relative." Finally, the last person spoke. The moment of truth had arrived. I stood up, grabbed the mike, and walked slowly to the center of the room. I unrolled the papers in my hand and raised them up to eye level. The papers, unsupported by a podium, were shaking. The choice had been made. There was no turning back. I said, "Now we move from the spectacular to the mundane to the controversial. I am going to make an announcement, but before doing so I feel it necessary to read a few words." And I began:

> First of all, let me be very clear in stating that I am aware that the most important priority of this conference is—and should be—the creation of a United Religions working together toward world peace. That is why I'm here. However, there is another reason I'm here, and I would not be true to myself if I didn't take this time to address an issue which I feel needs to be acknowledged in this conversation.
>
> Just a couple of days ago, I was told a story about the Buenos Aires Regional Conference, which preceded this Global Summit. In one of the small group processes striving to design the mission and values of a United Religions charter,

a discussion ensued about tolerance—about who should or should not be included in a United Religions. As the participants came back together for the large group reports, the elected speaker, a minister from the Metropolitan Community Church in Buenos Aires, reported that his group had reached consensus that no one should be excluded because of their faith, their ethnicity, their national origin, their gender, their age, their political beliefs, etc. In fact, there was only one area where they had been unable to reach agreement—and that was sexual orientation. He then handed the microphone to another representative from their group, who stood up and said that his religion did not allow him to entertain that possibility, but that in discussing it, his mind had been expanded and now had new material to consider. I think that's great, even hopeful, but from my perspective, it's just not good enough.

I am here as an unofficial ambassador from a tribe of people belonging to every culture and faith in the world—people who share a love for others of the same sex—those who in the West call ourselves, gay, lesbian, bisexual, or simply, queer. There isn't another group of people in this world which has been, and continues to be, as universally maligned, as universally repudiated, as universally excluded, as universally condemned, as universally excommunicated, and yes, even eliminated by some of the religions of the world.

The ironic, and tragic, thing is that before patriarchal times, back when women and the Divine Feminine were honored, before we entered this present period of our history several thousand years ago when, somehow, we got this mistaken idea that there was only one name for the Creator, one way to speak with and worship the Divine—and that we were entitled to use violence and military power to impose our beliefs on the rest of the world, that we were entitled to kill each other in the name of God—before these times gay and sexually ambiguous people were often spiritual leaders.

We were the shamans, the healers, the visionaries, the mediators, the peacekeepers, the "people who walk between the worlds," the keepers of beauty. The *berdache* or Two-Spirit people of the Native American tribes—the *winkte* of the Lakota, the *nadle* of the Navaho, the *minquga* of the Omaha, the *hwame* of the Mohave—as well as the *isangoma* of the Zulu and the "gatekeepers" of the Dagara in Africa, the *hijras* in India, the *galli* priests of the goddess Cybele in ancient Europe and the Middle East, and many others, were honored, respected, and even revered for the spiritual roles they fulfilled.

I am here today to remember the tens of thousands and probably millions of women loving women and men loving men who have been killed throughout history because of who they were. I come here, though, not from a place of victimization, but rather, one of empowerment. I am here to announce to you, as representatives of the world's cultures and religions, that we are reclaiming our natural, our sacred, our archetypal, and yes, our God-given role of spiritual leadership.

Today at lunch a group of us will sit together in the dining room. We would like to invite anyone—regardless of faith, ethnicity, national origin, gender, age, or sexual orientation—to share a meal with us.

I had no idea what to expect. To say that I was surprised by the response could not begin to capture the drama of the moment. Suddenly, I was being embraced and kissed. I looked around briefly and realized that some people were clapping, others were crying, and some were beginning to stand. The statement was receiving the first, and the most intense, standing ovation of the entire week!

DeAnna Martin, a beautiful, bright, twenty-one-year-old bisexual from Seattle with whom I'd connected a couple of days earlier, was one of the first. As we held each other, we both burst into tears. A young man in his twenties, whom I sensed was dealing with sexual-identity issues, also embraced me. As he pulled away, he pecked me very subtly on the cheek, whispering, "Thank you. You'll never know how much you helped me." And there was Rosalía Gutierrez, from the Cholla tribe in Argentina, who came over in her multi-color Indigenous dress and long black braids: "Thank you for doing what you did; you created the space for others to do the same. When you go out and tell others about this experience, ask them to remember us Indigenous people. Ask them to stop the evangelization. Tell them that we don't wish to be evangelized. For if you do away with our traditions, who will tell you about the Earth or remind you of nature?"

Later, I was told that about 80 percent of the audience had stood, while 20 percent remained sitting and did not clap; one person actually walked out and left the conference. My personal experience was one of overwhelming support—no one approached me directly with any negativity. I was a bit concerned about how Bishop Swing would respond, since I had somewhat derailed the process that morning, and possibly, in his eyes, opened a can of worms. That evening I bumped into him as we waited in line to get something to drink at the closing reception. Having gotten his drink, he turned around, and suddenly we were looking into each other's eyes, no more than a foot apart. "Oops," I thought. With piercing blue eyes staring right into mine, he said, "Young man, what you did this morning required a lot of courage; I could see your hands trembling. I want you to know that I'm very glad that you were here and did what you did. I also want you to know that I've probably ordained more gays and lesbians than the rest of the Anglican church put together. And if you ever want to be a priest, call me."

Back home in San Francisco, I soon realized that in some fundamental way I'd never be the same. I also understood that the occasion would likely prove to be pivotal for Q-Spirit. The vision for the organization was expanded, its impetus augmented. Initially, I had hoped it would assist gay men to explore different spiritual paths by creating a forum where we could come together and learn from each other. Then the mission grew to include the queer community as a whole. Our hope was, and is, to increase our collective level of self-acceptance, while alleviating our collective internalized homophobia, by helping us to reclaim our spiritual heritage and giving us a sense of hope, a sense of our history, a sense of our self-worth. As a result of the URI experience, I saw that Q-Spirit could also serve as a vehicle for change in the world at large. The organization could potentially fulfill more of an activist role by helping to educate people globally about our heritage and our cause. Given that most of the roots of homophobia lie in religion, this felt like an important effort.

What is lacking in the queer community—both among individuals and collectively—is a real sense of self. It's no wonder, given the rejection, ostracism, and abuse many of us have experienced becasue of the homophobia still rampant in the world. But while we must continue to relentlessly chip away at the strongholds of sexism, racism, and homophobia, complete societal acceptance, if at all possible, is still years away. Addressing the internalized homophobia at the root of many of our emotional problems and dysfunctional behaviors is now crucial. We can no longer afford to look for acceptance only in external sources but must first find it in ourselves. We must take care of ourselves and of our own.

One of the reasons why so many in our community lack a sense of identity is because we have attempted to reject intrinsic parts of being human, parts essential to a sense of wholeness. Many gays and lesbians have attempted to reject their sexuality—a tragic and fruitless endeavor as ludicrous as waking up one day and deciding that one no longer needs to breathe, because someone, somewhere, decreed that breathing is an evil, sick, sinful, or immoral act. Many have also tried to shed their spirituality, an act equally ludicrous, for our spirituality is as innate a part of being human as breathing and as natural as our sexuality. To quote a saying common these days in spiritual circles: "We are spirits having a human experience."

One problem is that so many confuse religion and spirituality. And no wonder gays and lesbians have turned off to religion: Throughout history we have been condemned, excommunicated, tortured, even burned at the stake for our sexuality. Even today, in the expanded consciousness of the late twentieth century, many "religious" folks still regard queer people as pariahs and abominations. Fear of the "homosexual agenda" is constantly invoked by unscrupulous and hypocritical preachers in order to extend the insidious grip of their ministries and to line their pockets with untold millions of dollars. Sadly, in modern-day America, political careers are still made or broken depending on where a politician stands on the "issue" of homosexuality.

Because of the prejudice, intransigence, and abuse we have experienced in churches, temples, and mosques, many queer people have felt compelled to radically break away from the traditional religions in which we were raised. Attempting to define our identity and find a place for ourselves in the world, we have often thrown the baby out with the baptismal water. Many of us have rejected our inherent spiritual natures along with the religious traditions we felt forced to disavow in order to accept our sexual nature.

Now we must in turn reclaim our spiritual natures. Realizing that spiritual life is simply part and parcel of all human experience, we need to rediscover, reframe, and reinvent ways to express our spirituality, ways that are appropriate and right for us. Being spiritual can be radically different from being religious. The former implies a personal connection with something greater than ourselves, whether we call that something God, Goddess, Spirit, the Universe, the Tao, Allah, Buddha, Higher Power, Higher Self, or one of the countless other names used by people all over the world. To many, the latter smacks of social and historical manipulation, and the abuse of power and wealth. It reeks of politics and lies.

Evidence abounds that historically, particularly before the rise of the patriarchy, queer people formed an intrinsic part of religious structures, often assuming roles of spiritual leadership. That was one of our functions in early tribal societies, and among Indigenous peoples even up to the present. It is time for us to educate ourselves about those traditions, reclaim our innate right to spiritual experience, and reinvent its expression.

Where do we come from? What are we? Where are we going? These questions were the title of a Tahitian-themed 1897 painting by Paul Gauguin, and were later echoed by Harry Hay: "Who are we as gay people? Where do we come from, in history and in anthropology, and where have we been? What are we for?"[1]

What I know is that each and every one of us holds within him- or herself indescribable potential, and that our community as a whole contains vast, untapped resources. We must search deeper than we ever have before, and reach higher than we ever have before, to discover who we really are, what we are here for on this planet, and what contributions we are here to make. The time is now. As the forces of freedom and oppression, of love and fear, continue to polarize the world, we must each choose who we are and how we want to be.

. . .

The first step in discovering who we are as gay people is to look back throughout history and attempt to determine who we have been and what roles we have played. Among many Indigenous cultures, homoerotically inclined or gender-variant individuals were recognized, honored, and occasionally even feared for their roles as spiritual leaders. These humans were considered to bridge the male and female worlds and were at times thought of as a third gender, believed to be imbued with special powers. They were also said to walk between the worlds of matter and spirit.

I have distilled and synthesized the following roles that gay people have fulfilled for millennia, which could all fall under the broader category of "spiritual functions." Some are variations of each other and occasionally overlap.

1. Catalytic Transformers: A Taste for Revolution
2. Outsiders: Mirroring Society
3. Consciousness Scouts: Going First and Taking Risks
4. Sacred Clowns and Eternal Youth: A Gay, Young Spirit
5. Keepers of Beauty: Reaching for the Sacred
6. Caregivers: Taking Care of Each Other
7. Mediators: The In-between People
8. Shamans and Priests: Sacred Functionaries
9. The Divine Androgyne: An Evolutionary Role?
10. Gatekeepers: Guardians of the Gates

Catalytic Transformers: A Taste for Revolution

> Queer people often function as catalysts, acting as agents of change, helping to bring about reform, inciting social movements, and supporting the advancement of humanity.

A catalyst is an "agent that stimulates or precipitates a reaction, development, or change."[2] At first reminiscent of auto mechanics, I use the term "catalytic transformer" to refer to the propensity among many queer people to function as catalysts, to bring about reform, to incite social movements, to transform society, to be instruments or agents of change. How can social activism be classified as a spiritual role? Social activists often propel the evolution of humanity toward a more enlightened, evolved, and compassionate way of being.

As Jesus exemplified, the role of spiritual teacher sometimes involves bringing down the "sword of truth" and smashing ignorance, lies, injustice, and social conditioning.

Even a brief analysis of recent history yields an appreciation of how involved queer people have been as catalysts for social evolution. The feminist movement, to begin with, is deeply indebted to lesbians, who comprised an integral part from its inception. As such, lesbians have played an indispensable role in helping to bring about the beginning of the reversal of thousands of years of misogyny and oppression of women. Some of the founding mothers of the suffragist movement were women-loving women, of which Susan B. Anthony and anthropologist Ruth Benedict are examples. An early leader of the women's movement and an advocate for many other social causes, Eleanor Roosevelt represents another prototype of the queer social activist.[3]

From the '50s to the '70s, the Beat movement had a distinct gay presence. According to Cassell's *Encyclopedia of Queer Symbol, Myth, and Spirit,* during the Beat scene "bisexuality or homosexuality became interwoven with radical left politics and a spiritual vision linking elements of Buddhism, Hinduism, Christianity, Judaism, and Sufism." Among the gay or bisexual "beatniks" were William S. Burroughs, Allen Ginsberg, Neal Cassady, Jack Kerouac, and Peter Orlovsky.[4]

Likewise, the hippie culture of the late '60s was influenced by gay people. Originating in San Francisco's Haight-Ashbury neighborhood—then a neighborhood with a substantial gay presence—the "flower children" were unquestionably impacted by the gay culture of the time. For example, Judy Grahn indicates that expressions such as "'straight,' meaning not us, others; 'blow your mind,' meaning to produce an altered state of consciousness through hallucinatory drugs; and 'what a drag,' meaning bad time or bad happening," penetrated the hippie language via gay tongues.[5]

Many gays and lesbians were also intricately involved in the civil rights movement. In fact, it was a gay African-American, Bayard Rustin, anti-nuclear activist, pacifist, folk singer, and one of Martin Luther King, Jr.'s closest advisers, who organized the momentous 1963 March on Washington for Jobs and Freedom, which culminated in the historic "I Have a Dream" speech.

And although many consider their *modus operandi* controversial, few would dispute the effect Act Up! has had in the battle against AIDS.

Additionally, many gays and lesbians are involved in the ecology movement. In fact, it was a lesbian scientist, Ellen Richards, who helped institute the science of ecology and was instrumental in the passing of the Pure Food and Drug Act. Marine biologist Rachel Carson, whose innovative work triggered significant environmental legislation, is also considered one of the pillars of the environmental movement. Her books, such as *Silent Spring*, exposed how the abuse of insecticides desecrates the environment.

More recently, Seattle resident Ruth Baetz wrote *Wild Communion*, an inspirational and practical guide—particularly for urban dwellers—urging them to develop or deepen their relationship with nature, even while living in the frantic pace of city life. Baetz believes that gay people have a particular need to learn how to commune with nature, because so many of us have become disenfranchised from our families, societal support structures, and organized religions. As she toured the U.S. promoting her book, she experienced a disproportionate number of gay people showing up at her events and sharing a deep concern about environmental issues.

Of particular interest here is Andrew Ramer's "channeled" information that one of the sacred functions of gay men in prehistoric times was that of "Guardians of the Trees." As a young child, Ramer began hearing voices in his head, and fairly soon realized that not everyone heard them. Not only that, but he discerned that those who did were considered "crazy." While coming out as a gay man in the '70s, he began a process of spiritual self-discovery, as he sought answers to the perpetual questions of "Who am I?" and "Why am I a man who loves men?" After years of unsuccessfully attempting to quiet or ignore the voices in his head—voices he eventually identified as those of spirit guides and angels—he once again tuned in and began to discover answers to many of the questions that had plagued him. Whatever one may think about the source of channeled materials, there is much in Ramer's work that rings true. Ramer suggests that trees mirror gay men energetically, not the least of which is the fact that trees embody both female and male aspects—that they are, in fact, androgynous. Through one of his spirit guides, Ramer extols gay men to "take the lead . . . in becoming foresters, reforesters," to plant trees and join organizations that plant trees as "part of our work in the healing of the planet."[6]

Poet James Broughton brings our role as social activists and revolutionaries explicitly into the spiritual realm: "That is why we have to start a revolution. And soon! Not a revolution that waves banners and assassinates presidents. Ours will not be a revolution that marches into the streets or blows up public buildings. This is an inner uprising and overthrowing; this is the revolution in the souls of all of us. This is the realization of our oneness, our love, and our strength."[7]

In Part 2 we will explore different practices and techniques for "coming in," ways through which we can support that "inner uprising" of which Broughton speaks. In order for us to fully enact our role as catalytic transformers and sacred revolutionaries, it is important that we first clean up our own side of the street, looking within and seeing what areas are in need of attention. In Part 4 we will "come back out" and explore different avenues for action, ways in which we can make a difference in our lives and in the world.

Outsiders: Mirroring Society

As outsiders, queer people help society to more accurately perceive itself. We reflect diversity and help society determine its limits and boundaries.

The second role we often play is that of reflecting diversity, holding up a mirror so that in its reflection society can better see itself. Judy Grahn believes that society does in fact use gay people for this purpose: "We are closely watched to see what constitutes the limit of a thing—too far out, too much, too low, too bad, too outrageous, too soft, too dangerous, too rough, too cultured, too aggressive, too sexual . . . We are essential to them knowing who they are."[8]

In order to serve this important reflective function, and have perspective on a given situation, one must have a certain distance from it. Having "outsider status" is thus intrinsic to being able to see the bigger picture, the forest from the trees. This quality is what makes so many queer people good observers and chroniclers of society, why we excel as writers, filmmakers, historians, and journalists.

How often we read in the news about ways in which gay men and lesbians are testing the limits. We always seem to be pushing the envelope, seeing how far we can take things. Even within our community, this creates controversy. When a couple of retail shops in the Castro designed sexually explicit window displays for Halloween in San Francisco in the fall of '97, a heated discussion took place about pornography, decency, and the right to freedom of speech and self-expression. One store flaunted a poster featuring, in full-frontal majesty, the erect penis of a well-endowed porn star advertising an event. The same image had also been dispersed all over the Castro in the form of thousands of promotional cards. Another had placed a couple of Billy Dolls, also very well endowed, in a variety of graphic sexual positions. What later became known as the "Great Penis Debate" was triggered by an editorial written by the straight editor of a local gay publication, expressing shock at being bombarded by penises all over the Castro as she walked to work. The controversy intensified when the principal of the Harvey Milk Elementary School in the Castro wrote a letter to the owners asking them to cover up their window for their students' annual walking tour of the Castro's Halloween window displays. In San Francisco, where the concept of political correctness can sometimes be taken to the extreme, what followed was a barrage of letters to the editor from both sides—those advocating "decency," concerned with how this would reflect upon the gay community at large, and those fiercely defending freedom of expression. Eventually a community meeting was called to discuss the issue, and the controversy was picked up by the mainstream media. On one level we can interpret this as yet another example of the assimilation versus liberation debate; on another, we can see how the discussion prompted society to look at an issue and attempt to delineate what constitutes societal limits.

Anthony Turney, former Executive Director of the Names Project and ordained deacon at Grace Cathedral Episcopalian Church in San Francisco, compares gays to lightning rods, in the sense that we force the world to look at things that it usually doesn't wish to deal with, and in the process attract attention and controversy. But it is above all in the sexual arena that we force the world to evaluate itself. Legitimizing homosexuality, by extension, makes *all* sexuality valid for its own sake rather than for procreative purposes only. That is but one of the reasons why we are so controversial and why the road to equality and acceptance has been and will likely continue to be a tortuous one.

Besides helping to define sexual limits, other areas in which we are currently prompting reexamination are the institutions of marriage and the military. The possibility of gay marriage is forcing society to ask some pertinent questions about that practice. Is marriage merely a heterosexual, patriarchal construct, developed out of the need to establish paternity and property, including that of wife and children? If so, how will the function marriage serves be impacted as our society moves back toward gender equality? And what about polygamy—the "next, you'll have to accept that too" argument used by opponents of gay marriage to instill fear of the impending collapse of civilization should gay marriages come about? These are profound and—to many—scary questions, with important social, religious, economic, and political implications. No wonder gays are feared and despised. We truly represent a threat to the status quo simply by being who we are.

In nature, and in all of life itself, we witness constant cycles of birth, death, and rebirth, what Robert H. Hopcke, author of *Jung, Jungians, and Homosexuality,* describes in terms of building up and decaying or breaking down. He points out that the breaking down or destructive process is a crucial one, one without which new life or growth could not occur. His thesis is that "the outsiders, the androgynes, the people who break the boundaries—

in other words, gay people in our culture—serve a very vital function in that second half of the cycle, in the breaking down and dissolution." It is because of that, he asserts, that lesbians and gay men are often found at the vanguard of creative pursuits, "since we are the people who break down and let something new come in. That's the function we serve and that's why we're here."[9] The down side to that role, however, is the risk of becoming associated with the cycle of death and decay. He cites the merging in much of the world's mind between gay men and AIDS, in spite of the fact that there are many more heterosexuals infected with the virus. But because gay people are the ones who "dissolve the various myths in our culture," we are threatening to and attacked by many fundamentalists and other reactionary and dogmatic enemies of change.

Jamake Highwater's *The Mythology of Transgression* is a brilliant and eloquent analysis of the phenomenon of outsiderhood—of people who stand outside of society's boundaries for whatever reason: their appearance, ethnic heritage, beliefs, or the book's specific focus, sexual orientation. The author weaves together a wide range of sources, from physics, biology, and anthropology to psychology, literature, and the arts, as well as his own triple-outsider status (as an orphaned Native American gay artist) to explore how mythologies—both past and present—have tinted the way our society views issues like normality, alienation, and social transgression.

> People who exist at the margins of society are very much like Alice [in Wonderland]. They are not required to make the tough decision to risk their lives by embarking on an adventure of self-discovery. They have already been thrust beyond the city's walls that keep ordinary people at a safe distance from the unknown. For at least some outsiders, "alienation" has destroyed traditional presumptions of identity and opened the mythic hero's path to the possibility of discovery. What outsiders discover in their adventures on the other side of the looking glass is the courage to repudiate self-contempt and recognize their "alienation" as a precious gift of freedom from arbitrary norms that they did not make and did not sanction. At the moment a person questions the validity of the rules, the victim is no longer a victim.[10]

Outsider status can serve to clarify one's perceptions and deepen one's ability to understand and empathize with others. Indeed, Highwater confides that he has "always seen [his] separateness as the basis of a cherished freedom from constraints, preconceptions, and social expectations."[11]

There are at least two challenges presented to an outsider. Falling beyond the margins often results in a "unique and powerful vision of the world inaccessible to insiders,"[12] but there is also a risk involved. As Highwater points out, learning to turn alienation into something positive, dealing with hatred without letting it turn into self-contempt, is not an easy task.

We don't need to be astute observers of human behavior to realize that many in the gay community carry old wounds and internalized self-hatred, which can manifest as bitchiness, "attitude," ostentatiousness, and pretense. Often, these are defense mechanisms, ways of compensating for feelings of inadequacy, self-contempt, and internalized homophobia. This is one of those areas where we obviously have our work cut out for us. Though perhaps understandable, attacking each other and failing to take care of our own, rather than supporting each other and standing together in the face of external and very real adversity, is tragic, to say the least. As most of us know or at least intuit, acceptance and compassion begin at home: Our ability to accept others is a direct function of the degree to which we accept ourselves.

A second challenge to our outsider role, which a number of queer thinkers and leaders have pointed out, is the danger inherent in "assimilation." As we become more and more accepted and assimilated into the culture, perhaps one day even becoming part of the mainstream, do we risk losing the edge and perspective provided by our outsider status? As psychiatrist Richard Isay, author of *Being Homosexual: Gay Men and Their Development,* expresses it, "Being gay is an adventure because there are no guidelines for living our lives. We make them up as we go along. Sometimes I wonder what will happen when society is more accepting. Will we then become bound by convention? Life wouldn't be as challenging. I like being a renegade."[13]

Consciousness Scouts: Going First and Taking Risks

One of the traditional roles we have played throughout history has been discovering new paths, searching out new answers, being "consciousness scouts"—those who go first to see what lies ahead.

Did you ever wonder why it is that queers tend to be trendsetters when it comes to music, fashion, or the arts? Or why we are usually the ones to "discover" the best restaurants or neighborhoods? Take, for instance, a partial list of trendy neighborhoods which queers discovered, fixed up, rebuilt, and which then experienced a renaissance: Miami's South Beach, San Francisco's Castro, New York's Chelsea, Atlanta's Midtown.

The work of Edward Carpenter, English writer, visionary, and proto-gay rights activist, sheds some light on this concept of going first. Carpenter believed that the importance of the "homosexual temperament" in early human history is the fact that the "nonwarlike man and the nondomestic woman . . . sought new outlets for their energies . . . different occupations." So, he theorized, they became the "initiators of new activities," especially when it came to the arts and crafts, spirituality, shamanism, and the priesthood.[14]

These early outsiders needed new ways to express their talents, energies, and interests. By virtue of being different, they were forced to reflect upon themselves in an attempt to understand their differentness and, by extension, the world in general. As a result, they would become some of humanity's first visionaries: "They became students of life and nature, inventors and teachers of arts and crafts, or wizards . . . and sorcerers; they became diviners and seers or revealers of the gods and religion; they became medicine men and healers, prophets and prophetesses; and so ultimately laid the foundation of the priesthood and of science, literature and art."[15]

Because these "intermediate types" or "Uranians," as Carpenter referred to us, merged the qualities, powers, and experiences of both genders, he concluded that they would consequently exhibit greater ability than other members of the tribe—"making forward progress in the world of thought and imagination, [they] would become inventors, teachers, musicians . . . and priests; while their early science and art—prediction of rain, determination of seasons, observation of stars, study of herbs, creation of chants and songs, rude drawings, and so forth—would be accounted quite magical and divinatory."[16]

According to Andrew Ramer, author of *Two Flutes Playing,* "because we live on the edge of gender and on the margin of society, we are consciousness scouts."[17] The function of the scout in a tribe is one of great importance, going first to see what lies ahead, then returning and sharing the findings with the rest of the tribe. This concept of consciousness scouts helps to explain why so often the music we hear in gay clubs or the fashions we wear eventually wend their way into straight society months or years later.

In his writings, Harry Hay, considered the father of the modern gay movement, outlines the differences between the genders. To him, the first gender fulfilled the role of "warriors/herdsmen/hunters/farmers/husbands/fathers—the inseminators and protectors of the bloodline." The second gender was comprised of women serving the role of wives and mothers, who also assumed responsibility for maintaining the homes and tending the gardens and fields. And then there were the third-gender people, whose responsibilities entailed "discovering, developing, and managing the frontiers between the seen and the unseen, between the known and the unknown."[18]

In my own family, and among my circle of childhood, high school, and college friends, I certainly fall under the guise of consciousness scout. Consistently, I struck out in a different direction. In my own search for meaning I rejected a comfortable and "successful" life in search of something more, something greater. The challenges of my spiritual journey have strengthened me and heightened my perception of life, the benefits of which I often share with friends. Furthermore, in my travels across the United States and other parts of the world, I have attended countless meetings and listened to a myriad of spiritual teachers and leaders exploring the reaches of the mind and the outer edges of consciousness. Often, on both sides of the dais, there were gay and lesbian people. I also know many, like Ram Dass, Andrew Harvey, and Tami Simon, president of Sounds True Audio, who have taken spiritual journeys to India, Nepal, and other places in the Far East, spending time in ashrams and with gurus.

AIDS represents another area where we have gone first, an act whose value the world has yet to recognize. The rest of the world has an opportunity to benefit from our experience not only in a medical sense, since many gay men have been the first guinea pigs for a variety of treatments, but also in terms of education and prevention. The sacrifice of countless gay lives will surely prove to be an invaluable contribution to the field of medicine and humanity in general, in terms of the new knowledge being discovered about the workings of the immune system and its repercussions in the treatment of many other diseases. According to James Broughton, "Gay men are at the vanguard of [the AIDS] tragedy; they are the martyrs to the sickness of their destructive society. We all hope that their suffering may help the finding of a cure that will save the rest of mankind. What would be most rewarding to their memories: if they effected a real change of heart in the body politic."[19]

Going first, being consciousness scouts, has its inherent challenges and dangers. Sometimes the risk taker makes a mistake, takes the wrong turn, or takes a fall for the others who follow. And there's always the risk that having taken the plunge, no one will follow, or that we will be left alone with no one to soften the fall. Going first, taking the chance of being different, always entails the risk of rejection or ridicule, of being ostracized. And particularly when it comes to deep-rooted societal change, those who play out the role of consciousness scouts, who push out society's boundaries, become a threat to the status quo and sometimes must pay a price for transgressing. Because of this tendency to go first and our willingness to risk being scouts of consciousness, gay people evoke the hatred and wholesale rejection of much of our culture. As a result, we are often mistreated, unappreciated, and even punished for being who we are.

Sacred Clowns and Eternal Youth: A Gay, Young Spirit

Queer people seem to embody a spirit of humor and youthfulness, qualities that often bring entertainment, sustenance, and a refreshing sense of joy to the world.

Humor, in its many manifestations, is one of the best means of support, encouragement, and even survival for outsiders, and so, for lesbians and gay men. Humor functions as a salve, softening the pain we sometimes feel as a result of the rejection, judgment, and discrimination we encounter in the world. The ability to laugh at life's often nonsensical nature reminds us not to take it—or ourselves—too seriously. One of the most universal acts of being human, laughter brings forth our commonality and softens the hard edges around our differences.

Paul Monette observed that

gay and lesbian people who have fought through their self-hatred and their self-recriminations have a capacity for empathy that is glorious and a capacity to find laughter in things that is like praising God. There is a kind of flagrant joy about us that goes very deep and is not available to most people. I also think that something about our capacity to live and let live is uniquely foreign—that we have learned in the crucible of the discrimination against us how broad our definitions must be for us to be fully human.[20]

Because of its very universality, humor also wends its way into people's minds and hearts, enabling them to hear messages that perhaps would go unheard if delivered by more confrontational methods, such as in-your-face demonstrations and anger-filled diatribes (which also have their time and place). Humor defuses defensiveness, allowing the mind to open and the heart to soften, thus serving as a dynamic educational tool. Humor and irony have been effectively used in literature and the arts to challenge the status quo and advance new social or political theories.

Camp is our unique and distinctive brand of humor, and the unquestionable domain of drag queens. By unmasking and confronting society's basic premises about gender while spoofing them, camp serves a definite social function. It is perhaps this that Will Roscoe was alluding to when he characterized gay humor as "the sword of truth, the great equalizer."[21]

José Sarria, known as the Widow Norton, epitomized the role of drag queen during the '50s in San Francisco. Sarria became well known for his solo performances, outrageous take-offs of operas like *Aïda* and *Carmen*. In an interview by Mark Thompson, he illumines the underlying meaning of camp: "Our humor is our key. If we lose that we're dead. The cross-dressing was part of our humor. Yes, it was our camp. I dressed at the Black Cat to show some of the absurdities expected of women. I poked fun to make gay people laugh, but when they started to laugh too hard I turned the joke on them. I played one against the other. I wanted the queens to see how ridiculous they were, too." Sarria may have thus embodied the archetype of the "fool, the trickster, the *contrary one,* capable of turning the situation inside out." Thompson explains that "often cross-dressed or adorned with both masculine and feminine symbols, these merry pranksters chase throughout history, holding up a looking glass to human folly."[22] Here, as in Sarria's statement, we find a reference to the outsider function of reflecting society's shortcomings back to itself.

A more recent example are the Sisters of Perpetual Indulgence, a politico-spiritual "order" founded in San Francisco in the late '70s. In 1998, the Sisters attained unexpected national recognition when they were used as a weapon by certain right-wing senators to accuse presidential appointee for ambassador to Luxembourg and gay community stalwart James Hormel of being "anti-Catholic." In a ludicrous and thinly disguised discriminatory act that sought to prevent his nomination from even going to the full Senate for a vote, the senators in question camouflaged their homophobia in their expressed concern about Hormel's "religious intolerance." The only basis for their consternation was the fact that he had been captured on film during a Pride parade, appearing to laugh at the Sisters' antics.

Composed of gay men donning the robes and, to some degree, the office of nuns, the Sisters personify the tradition of "religious parody."[23] Interviewed in *Gay Spirit,* one sister confided that "our ministry is one of public manifestations and habitual penetration. Our motto is 'Give up the guilt.' And we're going to do that through any form at our means—theater, dance, spiritual expression and therapy." Her testimony yields further insight into the philosophy beneath the Sisters' acts: "Humor and sexuality are at the root of spirituality. . . . They are the transcendental experiences that take us beyond morality. Through humor and sexuality we can realize visions and feelings beyond everyday life. The truest religion in the world is theater, or ritual. On a broad philosophical range, we are being religious in the truest sense, but merely by definition. Being nuns is a practical application of our spiritual feelings as gay men."[24]

Like Sarria and other drag queens (and kings) of past and present, the Sisters continue to push the envelope. They remain deeply involved in community service and over the years have volunteered countless hours and raised many thousands of dollars for nonprofit organizations.

Robert H. Hopcke points out another connection between humor and outsiderhood when he writes that "any outsider is a Trickster figure: Coyote, Hermes, Loki, the thief. There's a certain kind of trickster function that gay men and lesbians serve in this culture. . . . the Trickster's function is to grab people from inside the circle and pull them out, to help people become outsiders and therefore gain spiritual enlightenment."[25]

Besides identifying trickster as a "complex character type known for his trickery, buffoonery, and crude behavior, but also as a creator culture hero, and teacher," Randy Conner, David Sparks, and Mariya Sparks also point to his ability to shift shapes, and its connection with transgenderism and/or same-sex eroticism. Uncle Tompa, for example, is a trickster figure from the Tibetan Buddhist tradition. Known for his shape-shifting abilities, he occasionally metamorphoses into a woman in order to contact or seduce members of either sex.[26] In Germanic/Scandinavian mythology, Loki, another trickster deity, is a prankster "who delights in mockery, gossip, scandal, and social chaos." Loki is also able to transform into a female or an animal, another shamanic characteristic. Like other tricksters, he is associated with homoeroticism, and, in his case, particularly with anal eroticism.[27] Usually portrayed as hairy and masculine, Hairy Meg, a female brownie, or British fairy, is an example of a female trickster.

Coyote: Native-American Trickster

Featuring prominently in the stories and myths of many Native American tribes, Coyote is perhaps the best-known trickster figure. A powerful and spirited shape-shifter, in one tale Coyote transforms into a god-like "tall, regal, and handsome man" in order to seduce Tehoma, the guardian of the smoking mountain and a rather flawless specimen himself. Their thunderous wrestling match turns into steamy, passionate lovemaking, until they fall asleep exhausted. So profoundly were they sleeping that they failed to notice the fire blazing inside the mountain. Tragically, the "smoking mountain" erupts and Tehoma is never again found, but was said to have gone to the stars, leaving Coyote so disconsolate that he can still be heard crying out to his lover at night.[28] In another story, Coyote turns himself into a woman to lure Not Enough Horses, an attractive man he sets his eyes on. After tricking the object of his desire into marrying him, Coyote's deception is eventually exposed when he delivers twin coyote-infants.[29]

A related character is that of the jester, or fool. These *sots,* as they were called in medieval France, were wandering performers who traveled throughout Europe well into the Renaissance. Their dress, exemplified by Harlequin, consisted of tights with different-colored legs (usually green, yellow, or red), a cap, and a scepter with a doll's head on top. Their performances, or *sotties,* reveled in sex and other sensual delights in a rather burlesque fashion. The *sots* were associated with gender variance and same-sex desire, particularly in France, where they were classified into an elaborate system of "homoerotic activities and relationships." The *sot,* for instance, was considered more feminine and assumed the receptive role, while the *galant* was more masculine and fulfilled the active role. The *fol,* or fool, generally represented a bisexual male. The *sots* were also thought to be pagans and involved in the worship of *Mère Sotte,* a figure which may have been connected to the goddess Cybele.[30]

Like most everything else, gay humor has a shadow side which can reveal itself as viciousness, bitchiness, backbiting, sarcasm, and plain old nastiness. In the poetic and direct way that typifies his writing, James Broughton declares that

> Gaiety is a great moral good and a high spiritual value, as well as being a key to the universe. . . . God was certainly merry when he played around making giraffes and volcanoes and octopi and comets and toucans. The cosmos is full of great silliness. But it gets along with itself, it loves its games, it enjoys its mutations and upheavals. If it didn't like what was going on, it would fall apart. In human relationships the lack of love is destroying God's beautifully wacky world. Man's vandalism of the earth is similar to the way he treats fellow creatures: bilking, raping, destroying, using living beings as objects of greed and exploitation. So much of human society is resentfully loveless, no wonder it is violent and guilt-ridden. All power seekers want to make slaves of other men; hence they create abusive relationships. . . . Lovingness is the essence of gaiety.[31] . . . Gaiety makes us gods, said Frederick the Great. And love is what enriches gaiety. Nothing works well without love, and anything done without love is irrelevant or drab. Nietzsche called the practice of lovingness "the gay science." Rumi said love was the first thing God created.[32]

Broughton seems to be calling us to become more gay, to embody more fully the qualities of joy and humor with which we are often gifted, and, at the same time, to temper them with love. We use that gift/power positively when we use our humor as a means of creating change and generating joy and compassion in our relationships, and negatively, when we make it a weapon of combat, a defense mechanism, a compensation for our own woundedness and feelings of inadequacy incurred at an early age.

The other archetype relevant to this section is that of the Divine Child. Mark Thompson writes in *Gay Body* that "as an ageless wunderkind, the Divine Child does not grow into adulthood. This eternal youth, or *puer aeternus,* flies irreverently in the face of death and decay."[33] According to James Broughton, "We are the Peter Pans of the world, the irrepressible ones who believe in magic, folly and romance. And, in a sense, we never do grow old. That's part of what being gay signifies: innocence of spirit, a perennial youthfulness of soul. The gay spirit is a young spirit. Which is why the world needs us. We refuse to become dowdy and old, we refuse to dwindle into the doldrums, and we never die."[34]

Gerald Heard was an English-born philosopher, writer, anthropologist, and lecturer, who relocated to Los Angeles and is considered to have been a major influence on the likes of Christopher Isherwood, H. G. Wells, Stravinsky, Aldous Huxley, and others. A follower of Vedanta, a Hindu-influenced spiritual path, Heard believed that gay people, whom he called *isophyls* (meaning "lovers of the same"), "best represented the biological concept of neoteny—prolonged youth. Our neotenous nature allows gay people to be open and growing and mobile and exploring long after our heterosexual age peers have been forced to settle down into the specialization and stability required of parenthood and so-called maturity."[35]

In spiritual terms, the importance of the Divine Child archetype is best illustrated by Jesus' suggestion to "become like children." We are being asked to cast off the cynicism, sadness, and disillusionment, the years of conditioning, the lies we've been told, the ideas, judgments, and prejudices we've formed about life and other people, the rigidity in our thinking, the fear-based defensiveness, and return to a wide-eyed state of innocence and wonderment, an openness to new ideas, a more flexible, playful, and joyful state. We are being asked to return to a realm where we allow ourselves to freely feel our emotions rather than stifling them out of fear of conflict or social recrimination and suffering their festering for years at a time. In so doing, we can more quickly return to a condition of love and forgiveness, no longer bitterly and self-righteously holding on to grudges.

Of course, the danger with this archetype lies in the propensity to become stuck in an immature stage. For many of us, feeling like we never had a real childhood or that we were robbed of our innocence, coming out represents a reclaiming of that lost childhood. However, some get caught in cycles of ceaseless and unrestrained partying characterized by the abuse of drugs and alcohol; the shirking of the responsibilities of adulthood; the feelings of invulnerability and denial of mortality typical of adolescence, often leading to reckless behavior; and the inability to forge meaningful and longstanding relationships. Additionally, many gay men have an obsession with physical youth and a cult of male beauty, which can be as oppressive as Western society's advertising-driven emphasis on the type of female beauty idealized by anorexic supermodels.

Jungian psychotherapist Alzak Amlani clarifies that Jung's *puer* archetype has two aspects: the Divine Child, symbolized by creativity and innocence, and its shadow side, "characterized by the unwillingness to grow up, and sexual acting out. The *puer* has a hedonistic tendency, and is drawn to the drug, sex, and beauty scene. One has to find the balance between these for oneself. Because we are missing good mentors, grown-ups who have faced their inner dragons, and because we don't have regular responsibilities of raising children, this stage tends to last longer with gay people." Again, Thompson brilliantly captures this shadow side of the Divine Child archetype when he writes that "we live in a state of protracted adolescence, with all its wildness and curiosity. Our innocence emboldened us. Invulnerability was never doubted. And, to a point, we were transformed. But then we were confronted with mortal reality, including death in the form of an unstoppable virus."[36]

Keepers of Beauty: Reaching for the Sacred

> Throughout history, queer people have been responsible for creating, promoting, and supporting much of the world's art and beauty, and have done so disproportionately to our numbers.

As a psychology student at Tulane University, I took a couple of independent studies courses observing animal behavior at Audubon Zoo, near campus. One semester, I studied the mating behavior of the scarlet ibis, a wading bird common in marshes and estuaries. Like other species of birds, the ibis is seasonally monogamous. For weeks, I watched seven pairs go through the process of nest-building, courting, and mating. Right on schedule, all but one pair stopped sexual and nest-building behavior within days of each other, settling in for the incubation period. My interest was piqued by the behavior of one particular pair that kept building their nest, as well as mating.

A couple of weeks passed and their nest continued to grow. One day I thought I saw the bird I had identified as "female" mounting the male, but I did not record the behavior, thinking that I must have gotten confused. More time passed, and by now the nest was absolutely stunning—about twice the size of the others, and much more beautiful—it was a perfect nest. Then I saw it happen again; my birds had switched roles while mating. At this point I went to my professor and told him what was going on. His rather nonchalant response was "Oh, sure, it's very likely that they are both male. Homosexuality is common among certain species of birds." "Of course," I thought to myself, "leave it to the gay birds to have a fabulous designer nest!"

This anecdote helps introduce the archetype of creators of beauty. But first we need to establish that the pursuit of beauty and the creation of art are spiritual expressions. English poet John Keats wrote in *Ode on a Grecian Urn:* "Beauty is truth, truth beauty—that is all / Ye know on earth, and all ye need to know." Modern dancer Martha Graham referred to dancers as "athletes of God," and according to Wallace Stevens, in *Adagia,* "The poet is the priest of the invisible."

All artistic pursuits—in fact, all acts that seek to create and express beauty—are attempts to give expression to a need deep inside most humans to reach higher, to capture the ethereal essence, and express the ineffable nature of the sacred.

Parenthetically, this generates another question, which modern art has been weighing since the turn of the century: Is the purpose of art only to create beauty? Many movements, such as cubism, fauvism, and abstract expressionism, have shattered previous conceptions of beauty and forced us to reexamine what art is all about. For our purposes here, I simply acknowledge that the debate has been going on and maintain that a connection exists between art and spirituality.

The artistic process forces us to look inside, to search deep within in an effort to clarify what we value, and then attempt to articulate it. That process of inner scrutiny at times feels and looks like the "dark night of the soul" that many spiritual seekers describe—a time when preexisting beliefs and personality constructs are shed, released, or destroyed, and new ones emerge to replace them. The interim period between one state of being and the next is often characterized by confusion, lack of clarity or direction, and even depression.

In his *Maxims,* Marcel Proust wrote that "only through art can we emerge from ourselves and know what the other person sees." In most cases, an artist has first undergone a rigorous process of self-examination to understand clearly what it is that he/she sees, before being able to share that vision with the world. That process is a deeply spiritual one—dealing with questions of values, purpose, and meaning—even if it is not described in those terms. Moreover, the ability and willingness to express one's sensitivity and innermost thoughts, feelings, and dreams is a sign of courage, for each time artists share their expression they take a risk and put themselves on the line. Indeed, the word *courage* originates from the French *coeur* for "heart." Having courage—and heart—is a founding block for spiritual development. Artists refuse to censor their imaginations and thus fill our otherwise drab lives with beauty, humor, color—and spirit. Perhaps this is what gay poet Allen Ginsberg was alluding to when he said that "the only thing that can save the world is the reclaiming of the awareness of the world. That's what poetry does."

Human beings exhibiting a certain fluidity in their sexuality have always been at the forefront of the arts throughout history. Greek poet Sappho's name is now used as an adjective (sapphic) to connote love between women, and the legacy of her island home, Lesbos, is the word *lesbian*.

Native American attorney, artist, and modern-day Two-Spirit, Clyde Hall explains that gays are in fact "keepers and creators of beauty. It's something that Spirit gives you when you're born. These powers and talents are an integral part of a way of being. They have to manifest one way or another because that's what we were given to do in the world."[37]

Similarly, Andrew Ramer observes that we are in the "business of making beautifulness. . . . If there's theater, we're doing it. If there's art, we're doing it. If there's music, we're doing it. If there's writing, we're doing it. If all of us decided to stay home for a week, the entire cultural life of the planet would grind to a complete halt."[38] Florists, fashion and interior designers, hair stylists, window-display artists, graphic designers, and other makers of beauty also fall in this category.

Some of the greatest artists in history have exhibited desire and love for members of their own sex. The list is both exhaustive and impressive, and includes names like Leonardo da Vinci, Michelangelo, Caravaggio, Keith Haring, Robert Mapplethorpe, Frida Kahlo, Andy Warhol, David Hockney, Juan Gonzalez.

In letters: Audre Lorde, Adrienne Rich, Walt Whitman, Virginia Woolf, Jean Genet, Elsa Gidlow, Arthur Rimbaud, Paul Verlaine, Jalal al-Din Rumi, Henry David Thoreau, Oscar Wilde, Wu Tsao, Tony Kushner, Dorothy Allison, André Gide, Edward Albee, Tennessee Williams, Alice Walker, Armistead Maupin, May Swenson, Thom Gunn, Paula Vogel, John Ashbery, Emily Dickinson, E. M. Forster, Maria Irene Fornés, James Baldwin,

Christopher Marlowe, William Shakespeare, Edith Hamilton, E. Lynn Harris, Chrystos, Rita Mae Brown, Terrence McNally, Paul Monette, Reinaldo Arenas.

In film: Jean Cocteau, Pier Paolo Pasolini, Bernardo Bertolucci, Derek Jarman, Marlon Riggs, Christine Vachon, Rainer Fassbinder, Colin Higgins, Dorothy Arzner, Gus Van Sant, Pedro Almodovar, John Schlesinger, Monica Treut, Deborah Chasnoff, John Waters, Pratihba Parmar, George Cukor, Tony Richardson, Tomas Gutierrez Alea, Edith Head, Robert Epstein and Jeffrey Friedman, Vito Russo, Barbara Hammer, Todd Haynes, Rosie Troche, Gregg Araki, Paul Rudnick, Clive Barker.

In music: Benjamin Britten, Peter Tchaikovsky, the Indigo Girls, Melissa Etheridge, k.d. lang, Elton John, Ani DiFranco, Boy George, Janis Joplin, Cole Porter, Leonard Bernstein, Noël Coward, Kay Gardner, Michael Tilson Thomas, Janis Ian, Lou Harrison, Laura Nyro, Stephen Sondheim, Michael Bennett, Wende Persons, Michael Callen, Paula Kimper, Brian Asawa, Liberace, Freddie Mercury, Rob Halford, George Michael, Neil Tennant, Skin, Rufus Wainwright, Meg Christian.

In dance: Sergei Diaghilev, Vaslav Nijinski, Rudolf Nureyev, Merce Cunningham, Paul Taylor, Bill T. Jones, Michael Bennett, Alvin Ailey.

Perhaps there is something to scientific discoveries indicating that the *corpus callosum*—that part of the brain connecting the right and left hemispheres—is larger in gay men than straight men. It would certainly make sense that greater communication between the left (logical or analytical) brain and the right (conceptual or creative) one would yield an increased aesthetical sensitivity and ability to translate ideas, feelings, or dreams into form. Unfettered by the need for stability and tradition, third-gender people are much more apt to discover, invent, and create. In fact, Harry Hay asserts that "creativity is a hallmark of gay nature. . . . Under its own autonomous development, gay nature develops a gay window through which to critically examine the workings of tradition, to create new ways for shaping the culture, and to adapt to changing conditions."[39]

It is this function that prevents stagnation and helps keep human thought in a fluid, creative state. How ironic that one of the most universally rejected and despised groups in the world has been so disproportionately responsible for bringing so much beauty to the world! And how dreadfully boring and drab the world would be if they had succeeded in eliminating us "abominations"!

Judy Grahn notes that gay involvement in all aspects of theater—used here as a broad term inclusive of all the performing arts—is a "natural inheritance, for theater began as the ceremonial dramas and rites whose purpose was the reenacting of spiritual events for the benefit of tribal and village people." Drawing a clear connection between the theater and spirituality, she asserts that "it was the Gay shamanic/priesthood who was in charge of these ritual dramas." In fact, the word *theater* stems from *Thea,* the Greek word for "goddess." According to Grahn, "formal traditional theater retains much of its original purpose as rite, the reenactment of transformation. The curtain, or veil of consciousness, opens to display a second world, a state of being different from the everyday one."[40]

Perhaps it's from that different state of being that an artistic sensibility emanates, from the same place as the inclination, which also reveals itself among many queer individuals, to "take care" of other people and things. Maybe they are two sides of the same coin.

Caregivers: Taking Care of Each Other

> Gay people have fulfilled the function of healers, teachers, and caregivers of all types—from physicians to massage therapists, from counselors to flight attendants, and in all forms of the service industry.

The category of caregiver is a broad one encompassing a wide variety of specific roles such as flight attendants, food servers, events coordinators, and other hospitality industry workers. One example is the stereotypical gay butler portrayed in films and television as the consummate and fastidious but ultimately trustworthy, loving, and self-sacrificing caretaker.

Another version of the caregiver includes counselors, at all levels of mental-health practitioners, as well as financial advisors, hair stylists (who play the dual role of producers of beauty and nurturing coaches/counselors/confidants), and healers of all types ranging from physicians to chiropractors, massage therapists, and personal trainers.

Teachers can also be said to be caregivers, providing knowledge and, ideally, facilitating their students' transition into their next phase of maturity. The large membership of organizations like GLSEN (Gay, Lesbian, and Straight Education Network) and GLAMA (Gay and Lesbian Medical Association) provides some indication of the numbers of queer caregivers. (Note: Q-Spirit is compiling a resource guide for queer healers of all kinds. Those wishing to be included should contact the organization. See Appendix 2 for contact information.)

Joseph Kramer is a healer who is focusing his gifts specifically in the area of sexuality. A former Jesuit, he founded the Body Electric School in Oakland, which combines techniques of bodywork with breathwork and Taoist sexual massage. Through his work, thousands of men all over the world have been assisted in integrating their sexuality and spirituality. Kramer contextualizes his healing work in terms of "weaving." At the level of the individual, the "shaman-weaver" helps bridge and intertwine conflicting aspects of a person into a complete human being. In a larger sense, another function of the weaver is what Kramer refers to as the "weaving together of people to spark evolution"—creating community by bringing together its often discordant members. We will soon investigate more carefully this mediating and peace-keeping role, which clearly has a component of caregiving.[41]

Profiled in the nationally televised and award-winning program *In the Life,* Dr. Kate O'Hanlan embodies both archetypes of healer and social activist. A dedicated and compassionate gynecologic oncologist, she also founded the Lesbian Health Fund, and is actively involved in an educational campaign to reduce homophobia in the medical establishment.

Andrew Ramer posits an interesting theory about gay men fulfilling a role he calls "Midwives for the Dying." According to the beliefs of this "tribal mythologist," women are "midwives of birth and men are the midwives of death." Just as the role of one is to cut the umbilical cord and facilitate a person's entrance into this world, the other severs the cords that tie us to this realm and facilitates our passing into the next world. The problem is, according to Ramer, that men got a "little bit confused" and got carried away in expediting people's crossing into the next world—a possible, if euphemistic, explanation for the wanton violence and killing perpetrated mostly by males on this planet. "Standing at the closing door made men feel like it gave them the power to push people through it very quickly, before their time." He concludes that it is up to gay men to be the "guardians of death, who now stand at that door. Because we live between the genders, we also live between matter and spirit, between this world and the next. In a very ancient way, we have the capacity to sit with someone when they're dying and shepherd them across."[42] In recent years, the AIDS epidemic has played a dramatic and catalytic role in compelling us to reclaim the role of midwives for the dying. Many of us have sat by and witnessed the heartbreakingly premature transition of countless loved ones, many of them shunned by families and healthcare professionals. As a result, many of us have become proficient at compassionately facilitating people's transitions into the next realm.

In the face of AIDS, many lesbians have stepped up and provided a solid support system both for individuals and on a community level. Others have shouldered key roles in running AIDS organizations or spearheading fund-raising efforts to combat the plague. According to Ramer's mythology, in ancient times lesbians, also considered a scouting tribe, were referred to as the "Holds Together people, for they were connected to the primal creative energy of the Mother, as guardians of the animals, of birth and growth and keepers of the rites of passage for all the people."[43] This certainly feels like a fitting title, one congruent with the premise of caregiver: Lesbian sisters have undoubtedly fulfilled their mission and have held the community together during this time of crisis.

In *Gay Spirit,* Mark Thompson captures the essence of this quality of caregiving, while, at the same time, helping to introduce the next function: mediators.

> I would define gay people as possessing a luminous quality of being, a different-ness that accentuates the gifts of compassion, empathy, healing, interpretation, and enabling. I see gay people as the in-between ones; those who can entertain irreconcilable differences, who are capable of uniting opposing forces as one; bridge builders who intuit the light and dark in all things. These people who seem to spring from between the cracks, these androgynous alchemists, have a certain and necessary function for life on this planet.[44]

Mediators: The In-Between People

> Gay people have often served as mediators or "go-betweens," particularly between the genders as well as between the physical and spiritual realms.

Experts suggest many cultures believe that third-gender people have been instrumental in transferring knowledge or power from one world into another. In some cases, as in tribal settings, we fulfilled that through the shamanic role, by actively exploring other realms of consciousness and bringing back information and revelations to share with the rest of the tribe.

Others further theorize that we played a pivotal role in facilitating the shifting of power that occurred between the matriarchal societies of ancient Europe and Mesopotamia and the rising patriarchal military states of Greece and Rome. Judy Grahn writes that the "gay function has been to make crossover journeys between gender-worlds, translating, identifying and bring-ing back the information that each sex has developed independently of the other. . . . Gay culture acts as a buffer and a medium between clashing worlds and helps effect the transitions of power and knowledge from one sex to the other."[45] In the case of gay males, the crossing over resulted in the transfer of knowledge of certain areas which were previously the exclusive arena of women: agriculture, religion, astrology, midwifery. Because of their affinity to women, sexually- and gender-fluid men were the only males allowed to enter the temples to take part in temple rituals, which were conducted by women. Over time, they learned the secrets and skills developed by priestesses and other women and imparted that crucial information to other men.

The role of mediator between worlds is one for which gay people are innately equipped. The fact that we lie somewhere in between both sexes, embodying and expressing traits of both, places us in a unique position to attempt to bridge the gender gap.

During World War II, which preempted a large percentage of the male population, women were forced to leave home and take over the operation of many of the factories and industries which supported the war machine. Since that time, lesbians have often led the way as women crossed over and blazed inexorable trails in arenas previously considered to be the exclusive domain of men: business, sports, politics, science, technology. In recent times, significant inroads have even been made by women in what is, ironically, one of the last bastions of patriarchy: religion.

One of the corollary effects of the shift toward male domination was the creation of a system that rewarded the most aggressive, militaristic, and violent displays of behavior. Power, therefore, came to be wielded by those males exhibiting the most violent, sexist, and homophobic traits. Based on control over other humans, other species, and all of nature, and established on a foundation of heartless greed, fierce competition, and the relentless search for profit, the patriarchal system has resulted in the precarious situation in which we presently find ourselves—one in which unacceptable numbers of human beings lack the most basic resources, and one which has dramatically imperiled our planet's intricately balanced ecosystem.

In order to complete the transition of power, such a system had to diminish and eventually nullify the influence and status of women. History is a witness to that process, and as examples we need only mention the burning of "witches" in medieval times, and the horrifying incidence of female genital mutilation still practiced in many parts of the world.

In the first case, we will see later how the annihilation of "witches" coincided with the rise of modern medicine, which for hundreds of years has been controlled by men. In order to shift the balance of power, the village midwives and healers, mostly women, had to be removed. Their demonization as "witches" and subsequent genocide was fueled by political and financial motives.

The case of female circumcision, a barbaric practice by any definition, is one of the most extreme and gruesome examples of male domination and possession over women. Each year, an estimated two million young girls or women (about six thousand per day) have their clitorises, or portions thereof—as well as their ability to enjoy sexual pleasure—removed. Worldwide, the number of girls and women who have been subjected to this procedure approximates 135 million. Commonly inflicted on girls as young as three predominantly throughout Africa and the Middle East, this practice is often performed without the benefits of antiseptics or anesthesia. The result is infection, untimely death, and, more recently, HIV transmission. Although defended by practitioners as a cultural tradition, the bottom line is ensuring paternity and exerting control over women's bodies and sexuality.

Of significant interest is the high correlation throughout history between the oppression of women and the repudiation of homosexual men. Most societies which negate or oppress women also view gay men as a threat to their system. Any organization or society with the implicit goal of maintaining hegemony of one sex over the other, of upholding an unfair imbalance in terms of political, economic and social power, and responsibility, will have a vested interest in minizing the communication between the sexes, and will try to keep them separate. It then becomes necessary to silence, exclude, discredit, and demonize the main conduits of communication between the sexes: gay and lesbian people.

Arthur Evans corroborates this theory in *Witchcraft and the Gay Counterculture:*

> And so the story of human history in the West has been the sickening spectacle of increasing patriarchal power, first gradually in the Bronze Age, then with a sudden leap in the triumph of Christianity, and finally overwhelmingly with the onrush of industrialism. Corresponding to this rise has been a fall, first in the status of women, then of rural people, then of Gay people, then of non-white people.[46]

It makes sense, then, that as the pendulum swings back toward the feminine—a most welcome and timely change, to be sure, and one which will hopefully result in a more balanced and equitable state—it will be lesbians who lead the way in facilitating the transition. As we have already seen, through their involvement in the feminist movement many lesbians have been influential in educating and catalyzing women to reclaim their power.

The notion of balance is of particular interest when we consider the original meaning of the word "dyke." According to Grahn, the word *dike* originally stood for "balance." Stemming from the name of the Greek goddess Dike, the word also meant "the way, or the path."[47] Dike, whose grandmother was none other than Gaia, the Earth Mother, was responsible for maintaining balance among natural forces, a function which feels remarkably similar to Ramer's concept of "holding things together." So perhaps lesbians, who have been critically involved in the environmental movement, have an even more specific role in restoring balance to our natural world. People like Ruth Baetz, by teaching us the importance of communing with nature, and how to relearn that capability, are embodying that role.

Wouldn't it be appropriate for gay men to now assume leadership in modeling a more balanced way of living for our straight counterparts? If, as many spiritual teachers claim, the Divine Feminine is on the rise again—and will find expression not only in women but among men as well—who more appropriate to demonstrate how to balance masculinity and femininity? Who more appropriate to redefine and expand masculinity to encompass more traditionally feminine qualities like compassion, nurturance, gentleness, sensuality, equalitarianism, cooperation instead of competition, "build and nurture" instead of "search and destroy" or "fuck and kill"?

In many Native American tribes, the *berdache,* or Two-Spirit people, were considered the "go-betweens." Most tribes, particularly before the relentless and often violent impact of Christianity, considered them special, and honored them as recipients of special powers because they were in between the sexes, and could therefore perceive and understand both realities. In *The Spirit and the Flesh,* Walter Williams writes that the

> *berdache* received respect partly as a result of being a mediator. . . . Since they mix the characteristics of both men and women, they possess the vision of both. They have double vision, with the ability to see more clearly than a single gender perspective can provide. This is why they are often referred to as "seer," one whose eyes can see beyond the blinders that restrict the average person. . . . By the Indian view, someone who is different offers advantages to society precisely because she or he is freed from the restrictions of the usual.[48]

In one well-known Navajo creation story, after First Man and First Woman quarrel, the men of the tribe move across the river and set up camp over there. They only decide to do so, however, after consulting with the *nadleeh* and realizing that the *berdache* was capable of fulfilling many of the functions of the women. After several years of separation, both camps were getting desperate, and upon receiving advice from Owl, the men ask First Man if they can go back. Again, it is only after deferring to the *nadleeh's* advice that First Man gives his approval.[49]

Another important aspect of the mediator archetype concerns the mediation between the physical and the spiritual realms. Mitch Walker believes that queer people are born with an "innate sense that [the] universe, [the] world, is as much a world of the spirit as it is a physical and material world."[50] Like the *berdache,* who were revered for mediating between the realms of flesh and spirit, it seems that by our very natures modern-day queers are able to embody opposites within ourselves. This ability finds expression through the mediator archetype. In a real sense, the mediating function is connected to the spiritual function, and many of us are gifted intermediaries to the divine realms.

Shamans and Priests: Sacred Functionaries

> Throughout history, and across many cultures, queer people often have assumed roles of spiritual leadership, and have been honored, respected, and revered for doing so.

An analysis of historical research yields clear indication that throughout many epochs and widespread across different cultures, homoerotically inclined and gender-variant individuals have directly fulfilled spiritual functions, assuming the role of shamans, healers, seers, diviners, spiritual teachers, priests, priestesses, and sacred prostitutes.

Looking first to the African continent, the Lugbara tribe of Eastern Africa honors gender-variant mediums of both genders. The *agule* ("like men") are women spiritual functionaries who serve as intermediaries or mediums, and the *okule* ("like women") are their gender-bending male counterparts.[51] Among the Zulu, the male *isangoma* experiences a brutally demanding initiation process before attaining the role of shaman or "diviner." Having survived the initial phases, he is eventually taken in by other *izangoma* to heal and begin to experience the process of gender transformation as well as same-sex erotic activities. The female *izangoma* also stand apart from other women in the tribe; besides engaging in activities usually associated with men, such as carrying a spear and shield, and eating meat and drinking beer, they are also considered "active" and "masculine."[52] Another example is found in the fifteenth-century writings of Leo Africanus, where mention is made of the *sacahat,* the sacred diviners or "women witches" of Morocco who were said to be seducers of young women.[53]

In ancient Mesopotamia, the Goddess Innana (also known as Ishtar) was considered the patron of the *sinnisat zikrum,* a class of gender-variant and possibly lesbian priestesses. Likewise, she was also honored and served by the *kalbu,* gender-variant male priests, which included the *assinu* and the *kurgárru.* Both male and female functionaries wore androgynous attire combined with sacred vestments and were considered to hold special powers. It was believed, for example, that the simple act of touching an *assinu*'s head would lead to victory in battle, while the mere sighting of a *kurgarru* was thought to bring good luck.[54]

The Canaanite Goddess Athirat was also served by a class of gender-variant priests, called *qedeshim* (the "holy ones"), who were responsible for the up-keep of temple grounds and the creation of ritual objects. They were said to engage in sacred temple prostitution and may have used sexual practices as a way to induce enhanced states of consciousness. Conner notes an interesting connection between the multicolor garments of the *qedeshim* and Joseph's "coat of many colors," which, at least based on Andrew Lloyd Webber's portrayal, was fabulous.[55] Although Conner's mission is not to "out" Joseph, he presents other clues which make one wonder, such as the fact that Potiphar, the man who bought Joseph from his brothers and brought him to Egypt as his servant, was actually a eunuch priest of a pagan goddess. Furthermore, the interpretation of dreams was one of the qualities for which the *qedeshim* were known; and, indeed, biblical writings reflect that prophetic dreams were commonplace with Joseph. In fact, it was because of his accurate explanation of the Pharaoh's dream that Joseph eventually became the Pharaoh's right-hand man. His translation of the dream of the seven "sleek and fat" cows which were devoured by the seven "ugly and gaunt" cows as representing seven years of great abundance followed by seven years of famine was right on and resulted in Joseph's being placed "in charge of the whole land of Egypt."[56]

Ancient Greece and Rome likewise yield several examples. There are various accounts indicating that many gay or bisexual men, including Roman Emperor Hadrian and his lover Antinous, were involved with the Eleusinian Mysteries honoring Demeter, Goddess of the Grain. After Antinous committed suicide by drowning himself in the Nile—probably as a ritual act of sacrifice intended to prolong the emperor's life—Hadrian, disconsolate, instituted a religious cult dedicated to his young lover, whose beauty was legendary.[57]

The goddess Astarte, otherwise known as Aphrodite, was identified in Sappho's poetry as the patron of lesbians. In her manifestation as Aphrodite Urania, she was considered the patron of "gay" men—a fact which in the late nineteenth century inspired Karl Ulrichs, a gay German attorney, to coin the term "Uranian" or "Urning" to refer to homosexuals. Astarte also enjoyed a retinue of gender-variant priests, called *kelabim* (the Goddess's "dogs") who wore androgynous dress, served as sacred temple prostitutes, and were thought to be soothsayers.[58]

Greek Goddess of the hunt, nature, and the moon, Diana is often depicted as a lover of women. *Melissae* ("bees") was the word used to identify her priestesses, whose leader was, by extension, referred to as their queen.[59] While acknowledging that the existence of the Amazons is controversial among some historians, Conner points out that Diana, also known as Artemis, may have also been served by a retinue of Amazonian priestesses distinguished by their "rejection of marriage, love of hunting, skill as a warrior, hatred of traditionally masculine men, a sense of comradeship with gender-variant males, and a desire to remain in the company of women." As with other manifestations of the Goddess, Diana was also served by gender-variant male priests, alternatively called *essenes* (a reference to male bees) and *megabyzoi*. The *megabyzos* was often depicted as wearing a feminine hair style, a combination of men's, women's, and sacerdotal garments, and a shaved and powdered face. Interestingly, the *megabyzoi* were also known for the special purple dye of their garments.[60] According to Grahn, one of the purple dyes of the Greeks was actually called *paideros*, a word which also meant "lover of boys."[61] Grahn goes on to give a compelling analysis of the meaning of the color purple and its connection to homoeroticism. Originally, purple was associated with the spiritual power of the shaman/priest; its power and significance was later transferred to the royalty and the Christian clergy.

Probably the most famous of Diana's devotees was Alexander the Great, the Macedonian king who, as a very young man, defeated Egypt and Persia, creating an empire which extended to India. Tutored by Aristotle, and known for his love of men as well as for his dazzling exploits in the battlefield, Alexander's story was fictionalized by Mary Renault in *The Persian Boy.* Alexander was said to appear in public dressed as Diana, and was also known to be on close terms with the *megabyzos* at Ephesus.[62]

In our day, Diana/Artemis has been reclaimed by the burgeoning Women's Spirituality movement, particularly through the practices of Z Budapest, author of *Grandmother Moon* and *The Holy Book of Women's Mysteries,* Diane Stein, author of *The Women's Spirituality Book* and *Essential Reiki,* Celeste West, author of *A Lesbian Love Advisor,* and other lesbians.

The *galli* were a class of transgendered functionaries who worshiped the Phrygian (from what is now Turkey) goddess Cybele, whose Greek and Roman equivalents were Rhea and Magna Mater respectively. From available descriptions, the *galli* were known for their cross-dressing, outrageous makeup, flamboyant hairstyles, ritual ecstatic dancing, characteristic mannerisms, and the gift of prophecy. Wandering mendicants, they were found all over ancient Europe and the Middle East. Evidently, many engaged in ritual castration.

In ancient Russia, the *enarees* ("the unmanly ones") were third-gender priests who worshiped the Goddess Artimpasa. Similar to the *megabyzoi* and the *galli*, they may have practiced ritual castration, and, like them, dressed in a mixture of androgynous and sacerdotal clothing. They appear to have been deeply respected by their people, the Scythians. Of particular interest is archaeological evidence indicating that the *enarees* may have used *Cannabis* as part of their rituals in order to induce altered states. From the historian Herodotus we learn of one of these rituals: "On a framework of three sticks, meeting at the top, they stretch pieces of woolen cloth . . . and inside this little tent they put a dish with red-hot stones in it. Then they take some hemp seed, creep into the tent, and throw the seed on the hot stones. At once it begins to smoke. . . . The Scythians howl with pleasure."[63]

Another Indo-European group, the Celts, are said to have actually preferred homoerotic relations over heterosexual ones. Women in general, and gender-variant women in particular, seem to have been highly respected in their culture as reports about their warrior women, the *gwiðonot*, reveal. Among other deities, the Celts worshiped Cernunnos, a Pan-like deity, and Macha, androgynous goddess of athletics and war.[64] Interestingly, halfway across the world, the Mapuchi Indians of Chile identify their shamans as *Machi*. According to some reports, the Machi are lesbians who often engage in relationships with their female apprentices.[65] Additionally, in Cuba and other Spanish-speaking countries, the slang word *macha* or *marimacha* is commonly used to refer to lesbians. The Celts may have also honored the *fil-idh*, a gender-variant combination storyteller, bard, singer, poet, historian, soothsayer, and spiritual functionary reminiscent of the medieval French *sot*.[66]

In ancient China, *shih-niang* ("master girl") was the term ascribed to gender-variant shamans, who fused together mixed gender and priestly elements in their dress. Around 300 B.C.E., Qu Yuan, thought to be one of China's first important poets, was also a shaman who reportedly enjoyed an intimate relationship with the King of Huai.[67] In the 1800s, Wu Tsao, a Taoist priestess, excelled as a poet and wrote beautiful, passionate poetry about her female companions.

In India, the archetype of gender-variant spiritual functionary was (and continues to be) fulfilled by the *hijras*, many of whom practice ritual castration and are therefore considered to be transgendered. Even though they are occasionally the object of jokes in modern-day India, they are still respected and even feared as conveyors of magical powers, and are said to be able to attract wealth or rain.[68]

Among the Polynesians, the Hawaiian *mahu* is connected with shamanic and healing functions, as well as with the performance of the hula, the traditional dance form which evolved out of native Hawaiian myths. Another gender variant functionary, the *manang bali* of the Iban Dayak people in Borneo, was endowed with the ability to heal the sick using prayer, crystals, and soul-retrieval from the spiritual realms.[69]

In North America, the *berdache,* or Two-Spirit, were well known and highly respected as third-gender spiritual functionaries. The French term "berdache" was originally ascribed by European explorers and missionaries to male members of the Indian tribes who assumed the work and dress of women. Later, the term included female tribe members who rejected traditional female dress and activities and chose to engage in male roles such as chiefs, healers, guides, hunters, and warriors. Will Roscoe, author of *Changing Ones,* clarifies that rather than assuming the dress and identity of the opposite sex, the *berdache* was more accurately assuming an in-between or androgynous role—an alternative gender mixing elements of both male and female. In fact, several of the native terms used to describe them directly point to this. For example, the Lakota word *winkte* translates as "half and half people," or "halfman-halfwoman," which is also what the Cheyenne word *he man eh* means. The Crow referred to their *berdache* as *badé,* translated as "not man, not woman," and the meaning of the Cree word *ayekkew* is "neither man nor woman," or "man and woman."

The *berdache* were usually thought to have special powers—for which they were both feared and respected—and played key roles in certain tribal ceremonies. They were associated with the gift of prophecy and the implementation of rituals, and were said to possess healing powers, intelligence, and to provide either spiritual protection or curses. According to Roscoe, "you didn't ever want to get one mad at you because their curses had an uncanny way of coming true."[70] The sacred names with which they gifted certain males were considered extraordinarily good fortune and a blessing. As "go-betweens," they were eagerly sought after as matchmakers (mediating between the sexes) and were responsible for facilitating funeral arrangements (mediating between worlds). Many of the tribes held them as sacred beings; for example, the Lakotas use the word *wakan,* which means "very sacred or holy," to describe their *winkte.*[71]

Roscoe's *The Zuni Man-Woman* is a fascinating account of the life of We'wha, the Zuni *lhamana* who is probably the best known *berdache* in

American history. An expert potter and weaver whose artwork achieved considerable renown, We'wha was actually invited to the White House to meet President Grover Cleveland during his six-month visit to the capital as the guest of a close friend and advocate, anthropologist Matilda Coxe Stevenson. Officially representing the Zuni people, We'wha was highly respected and feted as a "Zuni princess" by the highest echelons of Washington society; his real identity was not discovered by most until later, even though he measured a towering six feet. In his capacity as spiritual functionary, We'wha was reportedly observed making prayer sticks and reciting prayers—both traditional male roles—as part of various ceremonial events. In one of her reports, Stevenson writes that "owing to her (We'wha's) bright mind and excellent memory, she was called upon . . . when a long prayer had to be repeated or a grace was to be offered over a feast. In fact, she was the chief personage on many occasions."[72]

Mohave women referred to as *hwame* were known to be masterful healers and shamans. Reports exist of a Kutenai woman who, after claiming a sex transformation, changed her name to *Kauxuma Nupika,* or Gone-to-the-Spirits, and achieved notoriety as a powerful warrior, peace mediator, and guide for her shamanic powers of prophecy and healing. In line with other legends describing the *berdache* as having special protection which made them difficult to kill, *Qa'nqon,* as she was later known, was eventually killed by a group of irate Blackfeet whose ambuscade she had outsmarted. According to the story, after being shot several times and then slashed repeatedly with knives, she kept fighting, her wounds mysteriously healed. Only after one of her enemies actually cut her chest open and removed a portion of her heart did she succumb. It was said that in deference to her shamanic powers not even wild animals would approach her corpse.[73]

After the colonization, decimation, and Christianization of Native tribes, the *berdache* role almost disappeared. In many instances, they were the first to be killed by the invading white frontiersmen bent on disempowering Native culture. It is logical that one of the first tactics of a colonizing force is to subvert the religious backbone of a people. Most often, among Indigenous tribes, it is the spiritual leaders who are the repository of culture, power, and meaning. Surviving Two-Spirit people were forced to go underground, hoping to protect themselves and the rest of the tribe.

Today, however, many Native Americans are revitalizing their traditions and reclaiming their Two-Spirit roles. Beth Brant, a Mohawk writer interviewed in *Gay Spirit,* believes that "if there is a spiritual awakening for Indian people, it may be the gay Indians who are seeing the visions,"[74] while Randy Burns, a Northern Paiute and cofounder of Gay American Indians (GAI), asserts that the gay Indian today is likely to be "more traditional and spiritual and more creative than his or her straight counterpart because that was the traditional role we played."[75] In 1997, the International Two-Spirit Gathering celebrated its tenth anniversary. The gathering is an occasion for attendees to affirm their identity as Indigenous people and to strengthen their spirituality through workshops, talking circles, pow-wows, sweat lodges, and other ceremonies.

One further aspect of the *berdache* and other third-gender spiritual functionaries which merits mention is what could be categorized as ritual-making. Among the Lakota and other tribes of the Plains, for instance, it was the *berdache* who were responsible for conducting many of the rituals surrounding their most important religious ceremony, the Sun Dance.[76] A review of the literature easily leaves the impression that if a ritual was needed—whether it involved a funeral, a marriage, a thanksgiving ceremony, a naming ceremony, a performance of some sort, or a healing ritual for the sick—a *berdache* would be involved in its production, and most likely, not in an incidental role. Another recurrent theme we encounter among third-gender spiritual functionaries across culture and time lines is the propensity to use dance and sacred hallucinogenic substances as a means to induce trance or altered states of consciousness.

I find both of these of particular significance since *we* all know gay people throw the best parties and have the best dance clubs. Oftentimes, dancing at a gay club invokes a real sense of tribal ritual. The constant, rhythmic beat, the theatrical interplay of music, lighting, decor, and the amorphously sensual mass of bodies moving, gyrating, prancing, touching, and cavorting in seemingly wild abandon, can actually induce a trance state or even a transcendent experience. Needless to say, this is often heightened by many through the use of mind-altering substances. I know of several men who frequent circuit parties and translate their experiences in spiritual terms. My comments here are intended neither as a blanket defense of circuit parties nor a glorification of drug use, which, sadly, is most often partaken unconsciously and indiscriminately. I believe that drugs are intrinsically neither good nor bad; their effect, instead, depends on the substance, the user, and how they are used. Obviously, the abuse of drugs leads to serious physical breakdown as well as personal, family, work, and social dysfunction, even destruction. Nevertheless, I find it interesting that many modern-day gays share a heritage with the ancient Russian *enarees,* the *galli,* the Aztec *cihuaollo,* and many other "sacred partyers" who used dance and/or mind-expanding substances to attain transcendent and ecstatic states.

As queer people engage in a conscious process of reinventing ways of expressing our spirituality that are congruent with who we are, an awareness of the need for bringing a sense of celebration back into spirituality is important. Spiritual expression need not be staid, passive, and boring, and can incorporate elements of music, dance, movement, theater, and other artistic manifestations. In San Francisco, Q-Spirit is launching periodic "techno rituals"—drug-free celebrations involving dance, music, live performances, ritual, chanting, introspective and interactive processes, and other artistic media. These events were inspired by Matthew Fox, who is blazing new trails by reinventing worship for the twenty-first century. His Cosmic Masses, which have been covered by *People Magazine* and *The New York Times,* attract hundreds of participants of all ages, colors, and sexual orientations.

Cross-cultural research, then, shows that gay people—or to be more accurate, homoerotically-inclined and gender-variant people—have played an important spiritual role throughout the world: as healers, priests and priestesses, mediators, prophets, diviners and seers, trailblazers in the arts and crafts, makers of ritual and magic. But why do these spiritual leaders and ceremonial functionaries often appear to be androgynous? What about "butch" gay men and "femme" lesbians; do they share this propensity toward spirituality?

Mark Thompson observes that "there's a historical precedent of effeminate men being spiritual leaders all over the world. . . . When a man is feminine and a woman masculine, I think that person is more in touch with the total range of human experience. They are more receptive, they have a broader range of sensibility and awareness. It goes far beyond the boundaries of sex roles."[77]

The practice of ritual cross-dressing, according to the experts, signified entrance into "magical states" which involved the personification of a deity's qualities.[78] In thus embodying the qualities of the Goddess, for example, the priest or priestess was said to become her representative and conduit; through sexual relations or other ritual functions they became a passageway through which others could access the divine.

Yet others indicate that it is a misconception that all the *berdache,* for example, were effeminate or cross-dressed. Clyde Hall points out that "some were very valorous warriors, since to have a berdache along on a war party was considered good luck. This person was in great communication with Spirit."[79] In *Changing Ones,* Roscoe describes the life of Hastíín Klah, the best known Navaho *nadleeh.* Much is known about Klah as a result of his friendship with traders Arthur Newcomb, his wife Franc Johnson, and their friend Mary Wheelwright. His contributions and innovations elevated weaving to an art, and his sandpainting tapestries now hang on museum walls, particularly at the Wheelwright Museum for the American Indian in Santa Fe, which he cofounded. Klah, who retained his masculine identity and attire, was also known for his selfless generosity and attributes of holiness, as well as for his powers as a medicine man. Roscoe includes a wonderful story from Franc Newcomb's biography of Klah, which persuasively illustrates his impressive powers. Once, while traveling together, Klah and the Newcomb family suddenly found themselves in the direct path of a rapidly approaching tornado. Terrified, the huddled family watched in awe as Klah walked directly toward the tornado, picking up bits of earth and plants, which he put into his mouth. Suddenly, he "held up both hands and raised his voice to a loud chant. The column stood still for a moment and then divided in the center of the hourglass, the upper part rising to be obscured by the low hanging clouds and the lower half spinning away at right angles to its former course like a great upside-down top."[80]

Issues of gender are constantly being redefined in our times, as our society attempts to sift through the false and calcified notions of masculinity and femininity that we have inherited. Perhaps gay men will be able to reinterpret and model for straight men a more compassionate, open-hearted, humor-filled, and tolerant masculinity. Maybe lesbians will continue to stretch the boundaries of what it means to be a woman, assuming the vanguard in that necessary process of emancipation and empowerment.

In the words of Jason Cromwell, a self-described transman, "issues of gender are deeply spiritual issues—crucial to who and what we are." Undeniably, the trans community is taking questions of gender to their limit and prompting all of us to reexamine these constructs.

The Divine Androgyne: An Evolutionary Role?

> The sacred writings of several spiritual traditions include references to the concept of "holy androgyny"—the marriage within each person of both female and male aspects of the psyche, which could have evolutionary significance.

Several writers have speculated about possible roles fulfilled by the homosexual in terms of humanity's evolutionary process. The fact that we're still around—despite nature's relentlessly unforgiving evolutionary thrust and man's destructive and homophobic bent—begs the question of whether, in fact, we serve an evolutionary purpose. Since, for argument's sake, homosexuals generally tend not to reproduce, and when they do, as is ever more often the case, they don't bear or "raise" homosexuals, how, then, do they contribute to the survival of the human species?

According to some researchers, an inverse correlation exists between a society's emphasis on population growth and their attitude toward homosexuality. The more importance placed on reproduction, the less tolerance exhibited toward nonreproductive sex, particularly homosexuality. This theory has been utilized to help explain the early Hebrews' negative attitudes toward same-sex relations, which may have stemmed from their contemptuous beliefs about "spilling the seed." In Russia during the time of the Bolshevik Revolution, when there was little concern about population expansion, laws prohibiting both abortion and sodomy were abolished. Later, in the 1930s, population growth was heavily emphasized, and Stalin reintroduced antiabortion laws and conducted countless arrests of homosexuals. Japan, as well, during the earlier part of the 1800s, enjoyed very open attitudes toward homosexuality, at a time when overpopulation was such a concern that abortion and infanticide were used to curb population growth. And, in America, where population growth has been strongly advocated since the country's beginning, it wasn't until the 1960s Sexual Revolution that sexual freedom and nonreproductive sex were actually championed. Not surprisingly, it was then that the gay liberation movement was born.[81] This theory, however, fails to explain why in modern-day China, a country claiming one sixth of the world's population and which has strict population controls, homosexuality is still denied and suppressed.

But, surely, are we not more than just an effective population-regulating mechanism? E. O. Wilson, considered the founder of sociobiology, theorized about the "strong possibility that homosexuality is a distinctive beneficent behavior which evolved as an important element of early human social organization." Homosexuals, he claimed, may be the "genetic carriers of some of mankind's most altruistic impulses."[82] Questions about our possible evolutionary significance may or may not be satisfactorily answered at some point. In a deeper sense, however, in terms of social and spiritual evolution—the evolution of consciousness—is there a purpose served by being gay?

Edward Carpenter, author of *Intermediate Types Among Primitive Folks,* was quite open about his homosexuality even when many of his contemporaries concealed their true natures. Carpenter visited America to spend time with Walt Whitman, with whom, he would later acknowledge, he had intimate relations. He believed that the integration of masculine and feminine qualities increased personal power and possibly created a "higher order of consciousness" and "a further degree of evolution," which could "lead to the development of that third order of perception which has been called the cosmic consciousness."[83]

In what could easily qualify as one of the most unabashed endorsements of homosexuality, he wrote (with an enthusiasm and style bordering on naïve and amusing, yet evoking a resonance of truth) that

> Uranian people may be destined to form the advance guard of that great movement which will one day transform the common life by substituting the bond of personal affection and compassion for the monetary, legal, and other external ties which now control and confine society. . . . The instinctive artistic nature of the male of this class, his sensitive spirit, his wavelike emotional temperament, combined with hardihood of intellect and body; and the frank, free nature of the female, her masculine independence and strength wedded to thoroughly female grace of form and manner may be said to give them both, through their double nature, command of life in all its phases and a certain freemasonry of the secrets of the two sexes which may well favor their function as reconcilers and interpreters. . . . It is probable that the superior Urnings will become, in affairs of the heart, to a large extent the teachers of the future society.[84]

Gerald Heard, the English writer and philosopher, wrote about the importance of the "open mind" as a prerequisite for evolution. He felt that even more than intelligence, the quality of "resiliency," or flexibility, was imperative for evolution to occur. Because of our innate constitution, he concluded that "isophyls" enjoy the "openness of heart and mind without which toleration disappears, progress is arrested, and society declines into tyranny."[85]

Heard, like Carl Jung, believed that the "'great hermaphrodite' was the aim of human evolution."[86] He further theorized that because the isophyl preserves such childlike or "neotenous" qualities as "uncrafty geniality and trusting friendliness," she or he is ideally disposed to excel in the intellectual realm, and to advance the "frontiers of the mind and in the diplomatic or anthropological services working toward the federalization of mankind."[87]

A discussion about the possible evolutionary significance of the queer person invokes the archetype of the Divine Androgyne. Among the sacred writings of several spiritual traditions we find references to this concept. In ancient China, for instance, Lao Tzu, considered the founder of Taoism, wrote that "he who knows the masculine, and at the same time keeps the feminine, will be the whole world's channel. Eternal virtue will not depart from him, and he will return to the state of an infant." The Christian tradition yields the following passage in *The Gospel of Thomas:* "When you make the two into one, and when you make the inner like the outer and the outer like the inner, and the upper like the lower, and when you make male and female into a single one, so that the male will not be male nor the female be female . . . then you will enter the kingdom."[88]

Finally, in Hinduism the term *Trititya Prakriti,* or "third nature," is used to refer to third-gender or transgendered persons. Alain Daniélou writes in *While the Gods Play* that "once a certain level of androgyneity develops in living beings, it is called the Third Nature."[89]

Born to English and Indian parents, modern-day mystic Andrew Harvey's passionate quest for the divine has allowed him to integrate both Eastern and Western traditions. Asserting that God is both male and female as well as "beyond both," this author and editor of many books such as *The Essential Gay Mystics* and *Hidden Journey,* explains that human beings should strive to attain a "holy androgyny"—the marriage within themselves of both female and male aspects of the psyche—thus becoming "at once as immanent and transcendent as the Divine itself. When the male and female aspects of the inner being fuse they give birth to the child, the Divine Child, the complete being at one with all the yin and yang forces, free from conventions, barriers, burdens, and definitions. I think the homosexual, by virtue of his or her makeup, may have a greater chance of realizing this androgyny and its end in divine childhood."[90]

As we transition out of the patriarchal era and collectively find our way into a more balanced state of homeostasis, a good question for both women and men to contemplate is how to balance the inner male and the inner female. Who more appropriate than queer people to undertake this exploration and teach others how to do it? Again, one is reminded that the meaning of the word "dike" is balance. If, in fact, a more androgynous state of being is the way of evolution, as gay people we seem to have an innate advantage—a head start, so to speak. Let us not squander it. In the words of Maia Dhyan, author of *A Call to Greatness,* let us "take advantage of our advantage."

Gatekeepers: Guardians of the Gates

> According to some traditions, gay people have a "higher vibrational level" and are uniquely suited for the role of "gatekeepers," or "guardians of the gateways, with the spirit world."

Among the Dagara tribe in Africa, people who in the West we would call "gay" play a very interesting and important role—that of gatekeeper. The Dagara believe that gender is determined more by "vibrational frequency" than by actual anatomical differences, thereby making it a much more fluid construct than what we generally think of as gender in the West. The Dagara also believe that the Earth has certain gateways, or points of higher vibrational frequency, which allow contact to the spiritual realms. According to their traditions, because gays have a "higher vibrational level," they are uniquely suited for the role of "gatekeepers," or "guardians of the gateways with the spirit world."

Malidoma Somé is a Jesuit-educated Dagara who came to the West with his wife Sobonfu on a mission to disseminate the wisdom of their people, a process he began with his book *Of Water and the Spirit.* Somé believes that Western "gay" people have been tragically cut off from our true purpose, and that for society to define our identity by sexual orientation alone is very limiting, even harmful. He blames a "dysfunctional" society for the disenfranchisement of gay people from our life purpose: "This is not justice. It is a terrible harm done to an energy that could save the world, that could save us. If, today, we are suffering from a gradual ecological waste, this is simply because the gatekeepers have been fired from their job." Gay people are said to come from the "Otherworld," and our purpose is to keep the gates to the Otherworld open "because if the gates are shut, this is when the earth, Mother Earth, will shake—because it has no more reason to be alive, it will shake itself, and we will be in deep trouble."[91]

Somé believes that because of its emphasis on an afterlife and on removing the divine from the Earth and placing it "out there" in Heaven, rather than here and now, Christianity has helped (as have other religions) to create a schism between body and spirit, between humanity and Mother Earth. Pointing to a system that demands that people go through Christianity in order to make contact with the divine, he argues that "the real priests and priestesses are out of a job," and concludes that this is "the worst thing that can happen to a culture that calls itself modern."

In *The Spirit of Intimacy: Ancient Teachings in the Way of Relationships,* Sobonfu Somé writes that "the gatekeepers stand on the threshold of the gender line. They are mediators between the two genders. They make sure that there is balance and peace between the two genders." They also "live a life at the edge of the two worlds—the world of the village and the world of spirit." Gatekeepers are said to be the "keepers of the keys to other dimensions" and are responsible for keeping both worlds aligned.[92]

Scott Balderson is an openly gay psychotherapist who completed a year-long program with the Somés. He has found a deep wealth of information and enrichment in the Dagara tradition. Besides mediating between the physical and the spiritual worlds, he says that the gatekeepers are "the ones you go to when you need spiritual protection, renewal, or for any spiritual problem; they are very highly regarded." Along with seventy other people,

Balderson participated in a three-day initiation with the Somés that culminated in a grief ritual. A large, egg-shaped ellipse had been created outdoors, its boundaries demarcated with ash. The bottom part of the egg, where a bonfire had been set, symbolized the village. The top side of the egg had been marked off with a line of ash. It symbolized the Otherworld, the place people who had left this realm now inhabited. Four people had been chosen to stand at the boundary—two lesbians and two gay men (Balderson and another therapist, "Alex"). Taking turns, each pair assumed the tribal role of gatekeepers. Much discussion and explanation had been necessary to explain to the group why it had to be gay people who assumed those roles. "You don't understand," one insistent person was told. "You can't do it; you are not physically equipped to assume that role." After hours of preparation and drumming, participants would go to the boundary line between the two realms and ritually express their grief. The gatekeepers stood at the line of separation; sometimes people would become so upset that they literally tried to hurl themselves across to the other side, something which, according to the Somés, could be very dangerous spiritually. The gatekeepers' job was to support the grieving participants, protecting them—both physically and spiritually—from going over to the other side. According to Balderson, they sometimes had to restrain, even tackle people, "to keep them from going over to the other side." "Alex" reported having been profoundly moved by the experience: "It was one of the most powerful experiences of my life, and it made very real for me at a cellular level the fact that gay people have played important spiritual roles in many cultures."

The tragedy is that while we have been gifted with this innate ability to fulfill the role of mediators, peacekeepers, communicators, and facilitators, for quite some time we have become disenfranchised from those traditions. We have forgotten our roles, and the culture in which we exist refuses to acknowledge, much less honor, our contributions, which too often remain dormant and unexpressed. The time has come for us to reclaim that heritage, both for ourselves and for the sake of the world at large. The world, though it may not know it, desperately needs us to step back into our traditional roles. Torn by strife, violence, and ecological destruction, the world needs our mediating, transforming gifts now more than ever.

2 Coming In

Introduction: Religion vs. Spirituality

One of the main reasons why so many people today have a problem with spirituality is because the word has become associated with and inseparable from the word *religion,* with all of its connotations of an established, organized, controlling hierarchy with a restrictive, punitive, and authoritarian moral code. In particular, many queer people, keenly aware of the treatment we have received and continue to experience at the hands of most organized religions, scoff or simply turn away at the mere mention of spirituality. On occasion, when at a party or other social function, I am asked the inevitable, "What do you do?" it is with detached interest, even mild amusement, that I observe the reaction when my response includes the dreaded "S" word; sometimes I could almost swear a curtain falls behind their eyes.

But religions of hate, power, greed, and torture—those which seek to control, convert, exclude, condemn, and judge—are aberrations of true religion. In fact, most did not start out that way. The actual origin of the word *religion* stems from the Latin root *religare,* which means to rebind (presumably to the divine, or the ultimate source of things). However, even framed in a positive context, "rebinding" can still have an uncomfortable sense of restrictiveness to it.

In contrast, the word *spirituality* comes from the Latin *spirare,* which means to blow or breathe. To me, its feeling is one of life-giving, energizing, limitless, flowing breath—one of grace. According to Webster's, spirituality refers to the "animating or vital principle held to give life to physical organisms," and the "activating or essential principle influencing a person."[1] The word spirituality stands free, unfettered from any exclusive affiliation to a specific religion. It is about our own connection to our deepest selves, and to the Divine. One could certainly be spiritual while belonging to an organized religion, and one could be equally spiritual without subscribing to any systematized doctrine. Obviously, one could also be religious, adhering to a structured system of dogma, and be completely out of touch with one's spirituality.

According to Matthew Fox, "longing" is the difference:

> Spirituality allows room for longing, for desire, for a yearning for the Divine and touching it. Religion tends to get preoccupied with itself and with sociological form; religion readily succumbs to all the shadows of institutions everywhere. Mystics do come along regularly, though, to drive the money lenders from the temple, and they generally pay a rather dear price for that work. . . . Spirituality is about awe and wonder, grief and letting go, creativity and birthing, compassion as justice-making and celebration. When religion can embrace these elements as constituting the heart of its presence in the world, then it is doing its real job, which is to connect people to their real Source.[2]

For Penny Nixon, co-pastor of MCC San Francisco, spirituality is about inclusion, rather than exclusion. Spirituality is "your way of seeing the world, and relating to the Divine Mystery or Universal Force," she added in a 1997 lecture. "I don't know if there's a place for us [queers] in religion, but there is definitely a place for us in spirituality." Spirituality, she believes, is about developing an authentic relationship to the divine, dropping social conditioning, and re-imaging God beyond gender constructions.

For Rabbi Eric Weiss, director of Ruach Ami, a Bay Area Jewish organization which gives spiritual support to people who are ill, dying, or grieving, "religion is more about institutions, and has not been good to women, people of color, gays and lesbians." He adds that "spirituality is connected to the experience of awe—however you define that, and wherever you find it. Whether it's in the ocean, in sex, or whatever, awe is the locus of spirituality. When you name your awe Jesus or the Buddha, you enter into religion." Weiss believes that religion provides a structure, a language, and a cyclical nature, or calendar, to help us experience and express that awe.

Religions tend to set themselves up as intermediaries to the Divine, even establishing elaborate hierarchies of priesthood. Intercessors, though, no matter how holy or qualified, can still prevent direct access to the Divine. A certain dependency may be generated that is sometimes evident among followers of gurus, for example—a certain false comfort or lack of initiative stemming from the (often subconscious) belief that all they have to do is hang around their teacher to find "enlightenment." This type of relationship can remove a sense of responsibility or a feeling of urgency to establish a personal connection with the Divine.

In his book *From Queer to Eternity,* Peter Sweasey acknowledges that the word spirituality is often used as a alternate to religion by people who feel uncomfortable with the latter, even in an effort to distance themselves from it. A contributor to his book writes that "religion is trying to make you what you're not. Spirituality is trying to make you who you are." Another one asserts that spirituality is about "inner landscapes" rather than "external journeys." After defining spirituality as what provides a deep sense of identity for humans, as well as a context for all of life with all of its big existential questions, Sweasey adds that "religion is sometimes our enemy, but our spirituality cannot be colonized. Our sense of being cannot be taken away from us."[3]

Until that time when someone takes up the mission of reclaiming the word religion, and purifying it of its negative charge, I think we're better off sticking to spirituality.

Choosing a Spiritual Path

What should a queer person look for in choosing a spiritual path? Clearly, we need to connect with a tradition or group that at least attempts to understand us; that does not exclude us, or have a separate set of rules for us; one in which we may find openness, friendship, and support; one which provides both spiritual sustenance and opportunities for discovering our essence and becoming better human beings. One which will offer a sense of community and encourage service and selfless giving. One which will help create a context for our lives, and a sense of cosmology, of belonging to something bigger than ourselves. One which will engender a sense of responsibility for others, of stewardship for other humans as well as for the Earth itself. One which does not deny our essence or treat us as second class. One that does not judge us or try to change us. One which will be receptive to our perspective and the unique gifts we have to share.

As we search for spiritual growth, there are many paths we can take. No matter what path or combination of paths we choose, the destination remains the same: spiritual growth; reestablishing or deepening a sense of connection with the Divine; becoming better human beings; rediscovering who we are; deepening our sense of self; becoming real, authentic, and fully human; developing a sense of purpose; cultivating those personal attributes that will enhance the quality of our relationships with ourselves and others—compassion, equanimity, a sense of justice, and generosity, among others.

Bob Barzan, former Jesuit priest and author of *Sex and Spirit,* says there are two important and practical ways by which he gauges any spirituality: 1) How does it support his relationship to himself, that is, his process of self-discovery and the development of a strong and authentic sense of self? and 2) How does it aid what he terms the "development of virtue," his relationship to other people and the rest of nature? For Barzan, "a healthy spirituality encourages love, compassion, truth, generosity, forgiveness, tolerance, peace, and courage. It increases my active concern for the environment and for the welfare of the human community. I know what I am doing is off track when it fosters hate, intolerance, greed, fear, envy, jealousy, waste, injustice, war, and a lack of compassion." This practical approach is reminiscent of Jesus' wise saying, "By their fruits, ye shall know them." We can gauge the fruits of our spiritual endeavors by the results we may see blossoming in all areas of our lives. The best advice is "follow your heart."

It is also important to remember that spirituality is not a separate and compartmentalized aspect of who we are. Rather, it imbues *all* of who we are. In fact, the word "integrity" stems from the Latin *integer*—as in a whole number. As we become integrated—that is, whole—beings, spirituality will be reflected in all of our relationships, interpersonal ones as well as those to work, money, the environment, and leisure. When we attain that level of integrity and wholeness, our separate life components (personal philosophy, work expression, relationships, etc.) are no longer fragmented, disjointed, or at odds with each other. Ultimately, everything that we do is an expression of our spirituality.

To Deify or Not to Deify?

According to some experts, through our various religions humanity has anthropomorphized (attributed human qualities to) the ultimately mysterious and transcendent experience of the Divine, often creating complex mythologies and entire pantheons of Gods and Goddesses, and a host of other supernatural beings such as angels, fairies, and demons. Other religions, such as Buddhism and most forms of Taoism, are not deistic at all. In choosing a spiritual path, how do we reconcile such essential questions?

Quite possibly, each religion is a piece of a great puzzle, revealing a different facet of the Unknown. Perhaps all of them together point to a much bigger mystery that is nameless and beyond our abilities to comprehend. This is a big question that is ultimately answerable by each individual's personal experience.

In the final analysis, I feel that it does not matter whether these entities or deities are real or simply metaphors to describe the ineffable. The bottom line is whether they assist or impede our spiritual progress, improve the quality of our lives, and help make us better human beings.

More and more, we are finding that in our rapidly shrinking world, people are incorporating practices of one tradition with the beliefs or deities of another. Particularly in the West, we are seeing Christian yogis, Sufi-dancing Taoists, "JewBus" (Jews who embrace Buddhist practices), Transcendental-Meditating Wiccans, neopagans incorporating Native American sweat ceremonies, and altars displaying images of Jesus or the Virgin Mary right next to one of Buddha, Isis, Ganesh, or Yemayá.

The Spanish word *mestizo* refers to a "half-breed"—one of mixed blood, particularly, of mixed European and Native American ancestry. In her foreword to *Cassell's Encyclopedia of Queer Myth, Symbol and Spirit,* Gloria E. Anzaldúa, a Chicana lesbian and author of *Borderlands: La Frontera: The New Mestiza,* describes this new "spiritual *mestizaje"* which "involves the crossing of borders, incessant metamorphosis. It is a spirituality that nurtures the ability to wear someone else's skin, its central myth being shapeshifting. In its disturbance of traditional boundaries of gender and desire and its narratives of metamorphosis . . . as well as in its traversing of cultural and historical borders, Queer Spirit qualifies as a kind of spiritual *mestizaje.*"[4]

Here we find themes we have already encountered as queer spiritual archetypes: weaving together, crossing borders, shapeshifting. Our outsider status predisposes us to, and perhaps even gives us a head start in, this trend toward spiritual fluidity.

To Stay or Not to Stay?

Some gay people wonder why any self-respecting queer would wish to stay within the confines of organized religions that refuse to acknowledge us and have so often let us down. Particularly, Christian lesbians are often met with derision by feminist friends who cannot fathom why they would remain in such heavy-duty patriarchal settings. Even though I don't belong to any particular tradition, I have had very spiritual friends ask me outright why I am wasting my time with the United Religions effort. To them, such religions are part of the "old paradigm," and it is only a matter of time before they either implode or are forced to make radical changes in order to keep up with the rest of our rapidly shifting society. I believe that if there is the slightest chance that the UR can contribute to peace on our planet, it is worthy of support. Besides, I don't believe in "accidents" or "coincidences," and have a clear sense that I became involved with this organization for a reason, and that my purpose there is still unfolding.

"We need to claim God and morality, rather than let it be used oppressively against us," says Malcolm Boyd, author of *Gay Priest* and *Are You Running with Me, Jesus?*[5] Penny Nixon believes that it important for us to stay inside these religious organizations in order to change them, adding that "activism within the church is hard work but yields fulfillment." Rabbi Eric Weiss agrees: "We must not underestimate the power of the laity, because it has been largely responsible for most real change in the Jewish tradition." He does not find it necessary to throw out all of the tradition, nomenclature, wisdom, and sense of context that lies within organized religions. And according to Toby Johnson, editor of *White Crane Journal,* "If religion is one of the biggest problems the gay community faces, then we'd do well to encourage and support the transformation of religion."[6]

Others point out that not all religions are our enemies, and that we can already be found among most, if not all, religious bodies. They report being inseparably identified with the religions in which they were raised, and do not find it necessary to forsake their sense of community, culture, or tradition, or their enjoyment of the rituals, sacred music, and art associated with some religions.

By choosing to stay inside, queer religious folks are personifying the role of activists for social change, as well as the pioneering role of consciousness scouts helping to expand the boundaries of existing institutions. They are also enacting the outsider role to effect change from inside, often forcing the redefinition of archaic rules and beliefs; at least, by their very presence they are compelling many of these groups to look at issues which would otherwise remain in the closet. And, of course, many, including rabbis, priests, nuns, ministers, and monks—some openly and some not—are assuming the role of spiritual functionaries within these institutions.

There are probably many queers who have stayed because of fear or an inability to step outside of or question the religion of their upbringing. No doubt, challenging, stepping out of, or renouncing such intrinsic aspects of our lives can be an arduous and difficult thing to do, nothing less than a huge existential confrontation. It certainly was for me. Who is to say what is right for someone else? Discovering what is right for ourselves is often challenging enough. Rather than sitting in judgment on those who stay, those of us for whom the traditional religions no longer work might be better off extending to them the benefit of the doubt and acknowledging their often heroic efforts.

Before casting the first stone, let us remember, in the words of Matthew Fox, that "it is not only religion that has been cut off from its essential purpose for existence. Haven't we also in our culture separated learning from education and justice from law and stewardship from commerce and art from community healing?" Perhaps we should all focus on our own lives, careers, relationships, business practices, and consumer habits, and strive to reincorporate these essential elements, which are ultimately based on spirituality, into our lives and our community.

As we will see later, Appendix 1 offers a quick guide to what both traditional religions and alternative spiritual paths have to say about homosexuality.

Whether we stay in a more traditional religion, or launch off in search of meaning through less tamed paths, it is crucial that we develop our own sense of spirituality, our own connection with the divine. Regardless of which path or paths we choose, inner work—developing or deepening our connection to ourselves and to the divine—is crucial to our spiritual growth. In addition to the established paths we have described, there are other teachings and practices which can be explored concurrently or which may be undertaken independently as paths to the Divine. Among them are psychotherapy, meditation, prayer, yoga, dance, and other forms of movement, contemplation, reading, spending time alone in nature, gardening, breathwork, bodywork, Tantric or sacred sexuality, and conscious relationships. (These last two will be covered in Part 3.) Most of these require active participation and even discipline. In spirituality—as with most everything else—without conscious effort, little progress will be made.

Psychotherapy

Simply defined, psychotherapy is a process through which we may heal our mental and emotional damage or resolve psychological conflicts in intimate interaction with a professional counselor. One of the psychotherapist's primary roles is to help us get in touch with and communicate our problems, in order to help us clarify and gain insights into them. Ideally, the therapeutic process results in personal growth, deepened self-awareness, optimized functioning, improved mental health, or changes in behavior.

Psychotherapists emphasize the importance of delving into and facing down whatever may be lurking inside our psyches. Unless we do that, they caution, our feelings and behavior may often be driven by subconscious and often self-defeating motives based on past experiences.

According to Mitch Walker, author of *Visionary Love,* therapy is about "helping us to regain a healthier connection with [the] psyche." The process also includes a spiritual component "because when you connect with psyche, you are connecting with the spirit world."[7] In fact, the Latin word *psyche* stems from the Greek *psukhe,* which means soul. Although much of modern psychology tends to focus exclusively on the mind, the word actually refers to "the study of the soul."

Psychiatrist Richard Isay, author of *Becoming Gay: The Journey to Self-Acceptance,* also acknowledges the spiritual component to therapy: "Power comes from dealing with . . . pain in a psychological or spiritual way. . . . Clearing away the roadblocks to loving first ourselves and then others takes both a psychological and spiritual healing."[8] In this case, power refers to personal power, which, like creativity, can be activated by the experience of emotional pain and woundedness common to many gay people.

In a 1998 article in *The Advocate,* Marian Jones reported on a University of Washington study which revealed that in the process of searching for a therapist, 46 percent of gay men and lesbians came across a homophobic therapist. An additional 34 percent encountered therapists who either refused to recognize their sexual orientation or "dismissed it as a fad." And a shocking 10 percent reported experiences with therapists who tried to "'cure' them of their homosexuality."[9]

Compounded by all the horror stories we have heard, read about in news magazines, or seen on TV sitcoms about incompetent or abusive therapists, these statistics demonstrate that finding a therapist can be a daunting process. It is important to research or "shop around" before committing to a therapist, and to undertake the process consciously, fully aware that you are at choice every step of the way. Feel free to interview prospective therapists by telephone, and ask all the hard questions, such as their feelings toward, formal training in, and actual experience of working with gay people. Remember also that you are free to change therapists if the process does not feel appropriate to you, or if you are dissatisfied with your progress. It is important to be vigilant, however, of subconscious desires to sabotage the therapeutic process, particularly when confronting or closing in on scary or "hot" issues.

Sheppard and Kathryn Kominars, Ph.D., the gay father/lesbian daughter co-authors of *Accepting Ourselves & Others,* offer simple ways of differentiating between the several kinds of therapists.[10] When you are deciding on a therapist, I would further recommend finding someone who is compatible with your personality and individual preferences. In my case, for example, that would mean someone who would incorporate a holistic approach, taking into account all areas of my life: physical, emotional, mental, and spiritual. I would look for someone who would be spiritually connected and open to different traditions. Additionally, this therapist would have to be someone who would exhaust other options before recommending medication. I would look for someone who could help me get clear about objectives, and outline a possible course of action and an estimated length of treatment, since I would like to feel that there was a foreseeable end to the process. Other qualities important to me would be compassion and sensitivity, balanced by sufficient intelligence, clarity, and skill so that he or she could point out fallacies in my thinking or patterns of behavior needing correction. In other words, I would want someone willing and able to call me on my stuff. Another personal preference would be active responsiveness, as opposed to a more passive psychoanalytic approach (where the therapist basically remains quiet, allowing the client's free-flowing conversation), or a philosophy of exclusively reflecting questions back to me and never expressing advice or feedback. (Incidentally, this is not to put down any of these methods but simply a statement of preference.) Besides credibility and trustworthiness, I would look for someone who also was on a conscious path of personal evolution, who had done their homework and struggled with their own demons, and who had no vested interest in the outcome other than my highest good.

Again, the most valuable advice is: trust your heart; trust your instincts; trust your intuition; trust your gut. Your inner guide knows. However, we do need to be very aware of our own fear and resistance, which is to be anticipated, since any type of counseling work will be confrontational to the ego mind. We need to learn to discern between a normal fear response and our own intuition or guidance. In my experience, the voice of fear tends to be louder and will likely come up with a thousand "logical" reasons not to do something: "He seemed fine and I liked him, but he didn't go to the right school"; "She seemed open and competent, but I think I'll wait until next fall, when I have more time." Needless to say, although issues of time and money are the most common excuses, they certainly can be realistic concerns.

The voice of guidance or intuition is usually quieter, and comes from a deeper place, usually emerging as a feeling, rather than a thought-out process. The "inner voice" is usually the first one on the scene, although it tends to be softer and less contentious than some of the ones who follow. Winning arguments or presenting a conclusive case is not its style. Its answers tend to be simple and, often, straight to the point: "That feels right." "Don't do it." "I have a funny feeling about that which won't let me alone." We all know what that feels like. We have all had moments when we knew exactly what was right for us but instead overrode the feeling and decided to do something else, usually having to "pay the piper" and suffer the consequences. Often our inner voice's whispered advice will make us uneasy, which is a good sign, because when we're too comfortable, it means we're not growing.

Clearly, some conditions and diagnoses are more complicated than others and require a longer period of treatment. Some people develop a trusting relationship with a therapist and drop in periodically throughout their lives for a few sessions when they need support. Others feel they need to go more regularly, and for longer periods of time. It is important to remain vigilant about the possibility of developing a dependent relationship with a therapist. In most cases, the goal should be to get you healthy, fully functional, and out of therapy as soon as possible. Assessing our progress is important and should be done periodically. According to the Kominars, "perhaps the single-most important guideline indicating success and progress is whether we are feeling empowered to be healthier, happier individuals."[11]

Therapists use many different techniques to help us access our innermost thoughts, feelings, and memories, or to modify our behavior. Among these are hypnosis, free-association, guided imagery, neuro-linguistic programming, dream study, primal screaming, role playing, and many more. Most are geared at facilitating self-knowledge, and understanding our patterns of behavior so that we may choose to change them.

Alzak Amlani, Ph.D., practices psychotherapy in the Bay Area. Combining elements of Transpersonal and Jungian psychology, his approach involves connecting psychological and spiritual issues. In his work, Amlani incorporates the concept that "all of life is spiritual, a journey of awakening, a journey of finding the self," and within that context creates a stage where the person "looks at life issues as opportunities to become more whole or reclaim more of the self." Amlani has found that, in some ways, that process is harder for gay people. "As children there was a certain amount of rejection, ridicule, and marginalization—whether conscious or unconscious—because of the gay identity. The self then goes into hiding, not daring to express a large dimension of who we are." If this does not get worked out, he points out, as we grow older it gets "introjected"—and then shows up as compulsive behaviors, addictive tendencies, heavy self-criticism, low self-esteem, and psychosomatic illness.

For Vilma Longoria, a Missouri-based psychotherapist, spirituality is implicit in her work. "As a therapist, I am very respectful of whatever religious or spiritual beliefs a client has. During the first session, as I gather information on physical, emotional, and psychological symptoms, I also find out about spiritual beliefs. Just as I encourage the client to take better care of their physical, mental, and emotional bodies, I also encourage that better care be taken of the spiritual body." Longoria often recommends meditation, yoga, or breathwork, if the client is open to those types of practices. She finds that most clients come with a "spiritual yearning, a confusing longing for something they feel is missing from their lives." Part of her role as a therapist, she feels, is to "facilitate developing a better connection with Spirit; often this involves working through shame, stigma, and dogma." With gay and lesbian clients, the process frequently involves examining religious beliefs acquired from their families, beliefs which too often lead to self-hatred and condemnation. The healing process requires facing that self-hatred and releasing it, a process which is easier said than done, Longoria points out. "It involves sorting through belief systems, keeping what feels true, and letting go of what is condemning. In my experience, the deeper the pain and wounding in an individual, the deeper the potential for spirituality, compassion, and love. As this potential develops, there is a blossoming. Our strength comes from Spirit, and without it there is very little healing. The fountain of self-love and acceptance is in Spirit. That is where we find our truth—the truth of who we really are and what our purpose is in this lifetime."

Like Amlani and Longoria, countless other queer psychotherapists are fulfilling the role of healers and caregivers. For many people, counseling is an important prerequisite for embarking on a spiritual path.

Meditation

All human beings are spiritual, simply by virtue of being human, even if not all of us are equally in touch with that part of our nature. So how can we develop or deepen an awareness of our spiritual nature? Barring such phenomenal or revelatory occurrences as near-death or hallucinogenic-induced experiences, probably the best—and maybe even the only—way to really discover this is in solitude and silence. In these days of multi-media, hi-tech, sensory overload, it has become increasingly important that we consciously seek out time and space to spend alone. Otherwise, we risk feeling disconnected and alienated, trapped in the superficial challenges and dramas which life will inevitably present. Probably the single most important thing we can do to break out of the rat race—the never-ending, vicious circle of demands from work, creditors, lovers, family, and friends—and begin to regain a sense of ourselves is to simply stop, even for twenty minutes a day and retreat to the quietude inside our minds. Needless to say, we all know from experience that our minds are not inherently quiet; in fact, their incessant chatter is so loud and intrusive that we sometimes keep ourselves busy as a means of avoiding what is going on inside them. It is sometimes easier to remain stuck in the ceaseless cycle of getting up in the morning, rushing to get ready for work, working long days—usually at tasks that are not fulfilling—going home, exercising, eating, watching TV or reading, finally falling asleep exhausted, only to start all over again the next day. What a way to live! No wonder many of us suffer from existential exhaustion. As with anything else, incorporating meditation practice into our busy lives will first require a choice on our part: Have we had enough of the craziness?

Why Meditate?

Meditation is one of the most effective ways to improve our well-being in every sense of the word: mentally, emotionally, physically, and spiritually. Meditation involves observing aspects of ourselves—our own deepest dimensions—that too often remain hidden and ignored. Meditation is about developing an alert and one-pointed, yet peaceful and relaxed, inner focus. It can facilitate self-awareness and the discovery of our essential nature.

One of the first goals of meditation practice is to learn how to quiet the mind, how to temporarily release its thinking, analytic, and problem-solving functions. Instead of allowing it to continue compulsively to rehash the past or fantasize and project (i.e., making stuff up) about the future, the goal is to anchor its attention in the present moment. So when we meditate we are consciously striving not to worry about or attempt to solve our problems; we are trying to eliminate or, more realistically, move past the constant strategizing and planning of our days and lives; we are taking a break from the never-ending and often aimless succession of our thoughts and daydreams. Rather than concentration on outside events, meditation is about inner focus, inner awareness, inner attention. It is about slowing down and quieting the mind and achieving one-pointed attention. This might sound like hard work and intense concentration. Sure, it takes discipline and effort, especially in the beginning, but it can also be quite pleasurable, relaxing, and, at times, even ecstatic.

Besides providing a peaceful respite from its constant, stress-inducing preoccupations and machinations, a quieted mind yields other benefits: increased clarity of thinking, as well as occasional insights, brilliant ideas, or unexpected solutions to problems. Studies measuring the brain's alpha waves indicate increased levels of alertness during meditation. Other studies point to increased levels of comprehension and increased ability in focusing.

There are emotional benefits as well. Once we learn to observe our thoughts and feelings from a place of detachment—what some refer to as "witness consciousness"—this skill can be utilized to more appropriately deal with emotions that pop up during our daily interactions with others. Meditation engenders a type of equanimity which can assist in preventing the quick-fire, shoot-from-the-hip, emotional reactivity, which too often characterizes the majority of our interpersonal relations. Becoming more aware of our emotions means increased choice in how we respond to others. This, in turn, results in less turbulent, more functional relationships, and by extension, lives that work better and flow more gracefully. Studies have also shown reduced levels of anxiety, depression, and anger among meditators.

People who meditate regularly enjoy added physical benefits: the reduction of stress often results in improved health and an overall rejuvenating effect. Other outcomes are perhaps not easily measurable, but many meditators attest to an increased ability to handle life's challenges with equanimity, as well as heightened relaxation, productivity, creativity, clarity of thought, and well-being. In his best-selling book *The Seven Spiritual Laws of Success,* Deepak Chopra designates daily meditation as the first law.

All of these benefits, however, are not the goal, but the icing on the cake. The main purpose for meditating is attaining awareness, understanding, and wisdom—spiritual insight into our essential nature—thereby uncovering who we really are. According to experienced practitioners, meditation cuts through illusion and denial and gives us a glimpse into our inner reality. Eric Kolvig, a gay Insight Meditation instructor living in New Mexico, says that "as people go deeper into their consciousness through meditation, the internal toxins come to the surface and they have to deal with them. I've seen people get beyond their homophobia and start to generate genuine self-acceptance."[12]

Many religions—most notably Buddhism and Hinduism—utilize meditation as a vehicle to the Divine. In fact, Sogyal Rinpoche, author of *The Tibetan Book of Living and Dying,* describes it as a practice that "cuts through and soars above cultural and religious barriers, and enables those who pursue it to establish a direct contact with the truth of their being. It is a practice that at once transcends the dogma of religions and is the essence of religions."[13] Meditation helps us contact that ineffable place of peace, centeredness, and union which is alternately called God, the Higher Self, Samadhi, or Nirvana. What we call it is ultimately unimportant; it exists, and through careful practice, we can access it through meditation.

Ram Dass, an openly gay, world-renowned spiritual teacher, in his classic meditation guidebook, *Journey of Awakening,* addresses the question "Why meditate?" His answer: "To live in the moment. To dwell in the harmony of things. To awaken."[14] In the words of Sogyal Rinpoche, "the gift of learning to meditate is the greatest gift you can give yourself in this life."[15]

Types of Meditation

There are two basic approaches to meditation: one could be called the *concentration* method and the other, *mindfulness* meditation. An example of *Shamatha* or *Samatha* (Calm Abiding) meditation is the repetition of a mantra or sacred sound as a means to direct, calm, stabilize, and quiet the mind; the intent is to develop concentration, defined as "the ability to maintain the focus of attention one-pointedly but without undue exertion on a chosen object."[16]

In *Vypashyana* or *Vipassana* (Insight or Higher Vision) meditation, deliberate observation of the breath, thoughts, or physical sensations becomes the focus. The skills cultivated through the concentration meditation are put to use as tools of self-observation and inquiry. In either case, by providing the mind with a single purpose, object, or focus, we make it possible for it to cease its other familiar and fatiguing functions.

Concentration

Ram Dass says that concentration is the "root skill of all meditation practices."[17] The goal is to keep the mind completely focused on a particular object (such as a flower, mandala, or other sacred image), task (such as breathing), or body part, for a predetermined period of time. Thoughts, sensations, or other distractions are allowed to occur, but our attention is gently brought back to the object of concentration. The image is held in the place of concentration, generally, the third eye area right between the eyebrows. If using an actual object, the eyes will obviously be open. An example of this technique is a flame meditation, where one's attention is fixed on the flame of a candle.

The purpose of this method is to achieve one-pointed attention, thus freeing the mind from its association with thoughts and physical sensations. With practice, the number and frequency of distractions diminish, along with our attachment to or identification with them.

We all have this ability to concentrate and exclude thoughts from our consciousness. In fact, we have all experienced it at certain times in our lives. Athletes, for example, must attain one-pointedness in order to excel; even those who engage in sports purely for the sake of enjoyment often attain moments of pure concentration as they pause to putt a golf ball into a hole, or volley a tennis ball back and forth. Artists frequently experience this high level of concentration while writing, painting, or playing a musical instrument, and many of us have experienced states of no-mind and timelessness during sex. When we are completely focused and involved in what we are doing, there is no separation between the act and us, and therefore, no awkward self-consciousness. Suddenly, we are shocked to realize so much time has passed. The same thing occurs when we attain high states of meditation. When the mind is fully concentrated, it is as if time did not exist.

Recently some friends took me two-stepping for the first time, and I joined a beginner's class. As the evening got under way, I kept losing the beat—I suspect from wanting to throw in an extra step due to the influence of Latin rhythm. Besides, I am more accustomed to leading in Latin dancing and was having to adjust to following. At one point, however, while I was dancing with a guy who really knew what he was doing, the DJ played a song with a much faster tempo. Suddenly, I had no time to think about what I was doing, or even mentally count the beat; I had no choice but to follow—and just dance. The effect was one of getting me out of my mind; it was then that I finally got the beat. There was no separation between the beat and me and my partner and me; there was only the dance, and the music, and the two of us dancing in unison, as one—*satori* in a queer country-western bar!

Everything of the mind is temporary and impermanent. In order to attain peace of mind, we must learn to quiet it, to use it so as to go beyond it. By turning its focus inward, we can experience that timeless state of high concentration—a state of meditation.

MANTRA

Mantras are sacred words or sounds which are said to be imbued with spiritual power. A mantra could be a name of God, or a spiritual phrase. A mantra serves to "connect you with the sacred. . . . and provides a boat with which you can float through your thoughts unattached, entering subtler and subtler realms."[18]

Typically, meditation students receive a mantra from a meditation teacher. Examples of mantras are OM (the primordial sound), Ram (Hindu name for God), So-Ham (I Am That), and OM Namah Shivaya (salutations to Shiva). Others opt for more familiar western words such as Jesus Christ, or even "Yes."

The repetition of a mantra is usually coordinated with one's breathing. Most often, the mantra is repeated silently. Experienced meditators report using the mantra as a vehicle to transcend the mind and establish contact with the Divine. At some point in the meditation practice, one may achieve moments of unity with the mantra and may actually experience the mantra taking over and almost having a life of its own. This may result in an ecstatic devotional experience.

DEVOTION

Ram Dass, who aptly fulfills the archetypes of consciousness scout and shaman/priest, refers to the path of devotion as "the way of the heart," adding that it "balances the more impersonal wisdom that comes from all types of meditation. It allows us to cultivate our humanity while we transform our consciousness."[19] Some of its expressions include prayer, sitting in contemplation with an image or icon of a spiritual teacher, or chanting. Great exemplars of the devotional path include the Christian mystic St. Teresa of Avila, poets Kabir and Rumi, and Hindu teacher Paramahansa Yogananda, whose *Autobiography of a Yogi* has served as threshold to Eastern mysticism for countless Westerners.

Also referred to as Bhakti Yoga, the yoga of devotion, this path consists of allowing one's heart to open and consciously flow toward the receiver of devotion. Chanting and Kirtan (the formal singing of a mantra) are examples of this method.

There are many chanting tapes available for purchase, which may be used to learn the process. In my experience, chanting works best when done for a substantial period of time, perhaps one to two hours. Singing ability is not a prerequisite; chanting is about singing from the heart and soul, about allowing our feelings of devotion to surface.

When I first experienced chanting at a retreat some years ago, at first I was self-conscious about my singing ability (or, more accurately, the lack thereof). The retreatants had been divided into groups of four and asked to sign up for two-hour shifts scheduled through the entire night. Getting up to chant from 1 to 3 or 3 to 5 was in itself quite a challenge, and a powerful practice. I will never forget, however, one time when I was chanting a particularly melodic version of Robert Gass's alleluia. About an hour into the process I heard this beautiful voice, when it suddenly dawned on me that it was coming out of *my* throat. The fact that I was singing so beautifully caught me rather off guard, because singing has never been one of my fortes, even alone in the shower. But this was a different experience. It was as if rather than singing, I was "being sung." It is always difficult choosing words to describe what is ultimately beyond verbal description. It felt as if the chant and I were one. The singing was almost involuntary, yet I was an integral part of it and could have stopped it at any point; it was not as if I were taken over by an entity. The experience was amazing, and after some time, actually moved me to tears. As if from above, I saw myself lying prostrate on the carpet, literally sobbing in ecstatic and humble gratitude and devotion, filled with love for Spirit and for the utter miracle of existence.

Although I personally have never achieved that level of transcendent experience in mantra meditation, others report comparable types of ecstatic experiences which they describe in similar ways: that the mantra is "doing" them, or that there is no separation between them and the mantra. Besides being filled with a spiritual presence, or with an ecstatic, quasi-orgasmic love, it is also possible to be overwhelmed with almost heart-breaking feelings of compassion for humanity, or torn by the pain of the awareness of separation from the Godhead.

MINDFULNESS

From the perspective of mindfulness meditation proponents, even such exalted experiences are to be simply observed, and not attached any particular significance.

According to Thynn Thynn, a Burmese doctor, artist, and author of *Living Meditation, Living Insight,* "concentration is only part of meditation. The essence of meditation is to reach a higher form of understanding, panna, to stretch the mind beyond the boundaries of the intellect into the realm of the intuitive, of insight-wisdom. . . . Concentration is pure and simple collectedness of the mind, whereas meditation is the collected mind moving further toward the development of insight-wisdom, or vipassana. In meditation, the awareness of the mind automatically shifts onto the mind itself and of its own accord focuses on its workings and processes, ultimately leading to true self-knowledge."[20] Or as Maia Dhyan would say, "We use the mind to transcend the mind."

That is the essence of mindfulness: staying conscious of everything that is taking place in our body, mind, and emotions in order to discover that which lies beyond their impermanence: our true nature. Jack Kornfield, author of *A Path with Heart* and founder of the Insight Meditation Society in Massachusetts and Spirit Rock Meditation Center in Northern California, points out that the meaning of the word Buddha is "to awaken," and that meditation can be thought of as "the art of awakening."[21]

Vipassana, or Insight Meditation, is also referred to as "penetrative seeing."[22] Its goal is facing reality straight-on; seeing it as it really is underneath the "scales of semi-sleep, subjectivity, projection and fantasy," which normally shield our eyes and cloud our vision.[23] Unfortunately, most of us have little interest in "just being with reality."

We have just forgotten who we really are. To wake up from that dream-like state of forgetfulness, exiled Vietnamese monk Thich Nhat Hahn explains that "mindfulness is the key . . . the base of all Buddhist practice . . . the energy that sheds light on all things and all activities, producing the power for concentration, bringing forth deep insight and awakening." Rather than living like "a dead person," he suggests that we return to life and develop a deep awareness of everything we do.[24]

Conceptually, at least, the process of mindfulness is very simple. In a sitting meditation (*zazen,* in Zen) for example, we simply observe everything that is happening both in and around us, noticing the thoughts that arise without becoming attached to them or giving them any importance. The same detached attitude is applied to emotions, physical sensations, sounds in the room or outside the window, etc. When initially trying this for even a couple of minutes, however, it soon becomes clear that it is much easier said than done. Suddenly we may catch ourselves and realize that we have been thinking about a business discussion we had with a colleague, or planning the perfect retort to the sarcastic remark our lover jabbed us with during a quarrel the night before. The practice, then, is to bring our attention back to the breath, noticing the inhale, and the exhale . . . inhale . . . exhale . . . inhale . . . exhale . . . until we again become aware that again we've been fantasizing about an upcoming exam, or making a grocery shopping list, or planning our next interview, seduction, or vacation. Each time, we simply notice our mental, emotional, and physical patterns, perhaps labeling them with phrases like "There I go again . . . strategizing, or having a sexual fantasy, or problem solving, or tripping down memory lane, or noticing a pain in my leg, or freaking out about finances, or feeling anger at my mother." In this way, we begin to develop awareness of our internal processes rather than existing totally at their whim. Again and again, we consciously return our focus to the breath.

Some teachers suggest that during times of excessive mind activity, it helps to count as we breathe. So, for instance, we may count from one to ten on the inhale, and one to ten on the exhale. This, or other methods of counting, is used for a short time only, and then we go back to observing our breath and anything else that comes up.

Joseph Goldstein asserts that when we first begin to practice mindfulness "a great effort is required. It's the effort to pay attention, to bring the mind into each moment. . . . Mindfulness is that quality of attention which notices without choosing, without preference; it is a choiceless awareness that, like the sun, shines on all things equally."[25] Because our attention is scattered all over creation, it takes conscious, directed work to rein in and focus our minds. At times it might even feel like a hopeless struggle.

The intent, according to Goldstein, is to "weaken the fundamental attachment we have to the sense of 'I,' of 'self,' of 'me,' of 'mine,' those concepts around which our whole lives have revolved. We see that this 'I' is an illusion, a concept that we've created, and we start the journey of integrating the possibility of greater freedom in our lives."[26]

Part of the difficulty stems precisely from trying to go beyond our limited and separate identity, our sense of "I-ness." In a sense, our incessant mind chattering serves to reassure us that we are still present and alive. Therefore, when the mind quiets, we fear for our survival, and suspect that we might disappear, or lose control.

The prospect of relinquishing their queer identity can present a conflict for many gay or lesbian people, who have often struggled against all odds to develop a sense of self. On the other hand, because meditation is so much about self-examination and uncovering our true selves, it ought to have particular appeal or feel quite natural for many queer people, who have already spent years pondering our "true natures" and grappling to figure out our sexuality, why we are different, what makes us tick, and what purpose we serve.

Arinna Weisman leads Vipassana Meditation retreats for the gay and lesbian community. Some are for lesbians only while others, usually co-facilitated with Eric Kolvig, are for both men and women. Although she lives in Massachusetts, where she is in the process of developing a meditation center, and he in New Mexico, they frequently offer one-day and longer retreats through Spirit Rock Center in Northern California. Weisman struggled with her meditation practice for years. During one particular retreat with renowned teacher Ruth Denison, she felt as if she was "stuck in the hell realms; I hated everyone and my body was burning with an inner fire; I thought I was a terrible person." Deciding to give it one last try, she persisted, and eventually experienced a "profound opening. It was as if I had been blind and suddenly was able to see. I saw that there is a different way to be, that the amazing thing about our lives is that they are not predetermined. I felt a great love, and an ease of being. I suddenly felt deeply at home." Weisman earnestly reassures prospective meditators that "it's really worth the effort. In the beginning it does take effort; it's like taking a big leap. As you deepen in practice, it's not so hard. Whatever path you end up on that awakens the heart and the mind is worth it. You can't lose; you just can't lose."

WALKING/EATING MINDFULNESS MEDITATION

Ultimately, the goal of mindfulness is to be able to transfer the practice onto all areas of our lives, not just our sitting meditation. So as we are eating, walking, washing the dishes, or driving, we bring mindfulness and awareness into everything we do.

For example, most of us pay little attention to the process of eating; in fact, we tend to eat rather unconsciously, either watching television, reading, or carrying on a conversation. My sister had a friend in high school who was quite adept at eating breakfast while driving to school, with her food in the one hand that steered, while simultaneously applying makeup with the other. She could even anticipate when bumps in the road were approaching and would simply stop mid-process so that she wouldn't spill food or smear makeup all over her face.

Many of us are so disconnected from our bodies when we eat, it is no wonder that we eat past the point of satiation, or ingest stuff our bodies will later let us know they were not thrilled about receiving. As a result, we too often end up with indigestion, overeating, and overweight.

Imagine once in a while approaching eating as a meditation, applying mindfulness and self-observation to the experience. We might begin in a conscious, quiet environment, as opposed to sharing our table with newspapers, magazines, and piles of mail to be read, or with the television as background accompaniment. In silence, we would bring our awareness to our thoughts, feelings, and physical sensations, including hunger, taste, smell, and texture. Throughout the ensuing process we might bring our attention to each individual act, perhaps making silent mental notes along the way: "Taking fork in my left hand . . . taking knife in the right . . . cutting a bite of food . . . placing knife down . . . taking fork in right hand . . . piercing food with fork . . . raising arm towards mouth . . . opening mouth . . . feeling lower jaw drop and facial muscles contract and expand . . . placing food into mouth . . . noticing taste . . . noticing temperature . . . noticing texture . . . chewing . . . chewing . . . swallowing."

The same type of awareness is brought to a walking meditation, which may be done either indoors or outdoors. Some teachers recommend that if you are doing it outside, you should find a quiet, secluded, and safe area, perhaps a twenty- to thirty-foot stretch on which you can walk back and forth. The pace of a walking meditation can vary, but generally it is slower and more intentional than when we walk with a purpose or destination. The mental notes might sound something like this: "Lifting right foot . . . feeling thigh muscles contract . . . lowering right foot . . . making contact with floor . . .

feeling foot descend into carpet . . . thinking about project at work . . . Oops! Back to walking . . . lifting left foot . . . hearing birds chirping outside . . . hearing car alarm down the block . . . feeling frustrated . . . having sexual fantasy about tonight's date . . . Oops! Back to walking . . . turning around . . . heading in opposite direction . . . feeling tired . . . Hmm, wonder what I'll wear tonight? . . . Oops! Back to walking . . . etc."

As Buddhist teacher Henepola Gunaratana points out, the purpose of meditation is nothing less than "personal transformation." When we learn to incorporate mindfulness into all aspects of our lives, "things begin to fall into place" and our lives become "a glide instead of a struggle."[27]

Movement Practices

Among the several spiritual practices which involve movement are yoga, Qi Gong, and sacred dancing. Because of the degree of concentration required, they can also be approached as meditative techniques.

YOGA

The word yoga stems from a Sanskrit root meaning to join, or unite. Its meaning is therefore reminiscent of the Latin origins of religion (*religare*), meaning, as we have already seen, to rejoin or rebind. Yoga has been interpreted by some to refer to the union between body, mind, and spirit. However, the more traditional interpretation is union between individual consciousness (Jivatman) and the Universal Consciousness (Paramatman).

The path of yoga thus involves different methods or disciplines to assist seekers in attaining union with the divine. Within yoga, there are six major avenues to that union: 1) Raja Yoga—the royal yoga, or the path of stillness; 2) Karma Yoga—the path of service or work; 3) Bhakti Yoga—the path of devotion; 4) Jnana Yoga—the path of wisdom; 5) Tantra Yoga—the path of direct experience (in the West exclusively associated with sexuality); and 6) Hatha Yoga—the path of the body. For our present purposes, we will focus on Hatha Yoga, which includes *asanas,* or postures, and *pranayama* (breathing).

The benefits of Hatha Yoga are manifold. Physiologically, its practice leads to stronger, more flexible bodies and an overall calmer disposition. Hatha Yoga is considered one of the most complete exercise methods available, one which affects all of the body's processes. Because of its inherent adaptability, the system can be customized for a wide variety of body types and physical conditions, from athletes to people with impaired mobility. Yoga also impacts the practitioner on the mental and spiritual levels. Many report an increased ability to concentrate and develop a heightened sense of themselves.

Laura Cornell came to yoga after being a Quaker for many years. She finds the two very compatible; the Quaker practice of sitting in silent contemplation was a great preparation for going within. Cornell, a lesbian, now teaches yoga at the Berkeley YMCA and the Berkeley Yoga Center, where she strives to make it accessible to all types of bodies, including round bodies and those with disabilities. She finds that she often has her deepest meditations after teaching a class: "If one is stressed out or in turmoil, yoga has a calming effect, and it does help to clear the mind. It has brought a deep transformation to me; it's almost as if that calm state of mind I experience when practicing or teaching yoga transfers to other life situations. I have also had numinous experiences while doing certain postures."

For Matt Stern, yoga is definitely a way of going within. In fact, he says, "It was one of the first things that took me there. It was a way to start paying attention to my body, to begin to notice it without identifying with it, without judging it; in short, a way of developing 'witness consciousness,' which is also the heart of meditation." Stern believes that yoga can actually be a quicker process for many because it deals with the coarser elements of the body, rather than elusive mental states. Thus, it can be easier and more powerful for someone starting out on a path of mindfulness to identify the many sensations our bodies are filled with, and then bring the attention back to "what's going on now."

While acknowledging that for many yoga is just a physical practice, not an awareness technique, he adds that "for me, awareness is the heart of yoga. The real benefits of yoga happen through that process rather than by doing a posture perfectly or getting it right. That in itself—recognizing that our postures may be less than perfect—is a spiritual practice: accepting what is true now. In that sense, we are using yoga as a way of being in the present moment exactly as our body is, with the postures as we are able to do them today. This is the beginning of developing concentration, awareness, and mindfulness."

Yoga is also important because it fosters the exploration of body consciousness, prompting such questions as "What is my body?" "Where am I?" "Where am I in my body?" This often leads to the conclusion that we are not separate; that there is no separation between us (our bodies) and the universe. In Stern's case, the result was a certain sense of expansion, "a sense that the space around me is beyond the limits of my physical body. For me, yoga is a way to access the energy body, or prana body. It helps me to recognize that I'm not just a physical body—to develop the awareness that it's not me that's in my body, but my body that's in me." Laughing, he adds that "this is yoga as mindfuck, in the sense that it helps to shatter and expand the limited perceptions of the small mind."

QI GONG

Qi Gong (pronounced "chee gong") means "cultivating energy or vitality." Based on Taoist principles and Chinese medicine, it is a system for developing internal energy (chi). Instead of yoga's stretching movements and *asanas,* Qi Gong teaches practitioners how to sense and consciously move energy in the body.

Qi Gong exercises generally consist of slow, graceful, and flowing movements intended to produce and sustain energy. The process engenders a meditative state and an inward focus. Because of this calming and stress-reducing effect, its practice is thought to strengthen the immune system and promote natural healing, assisting in the treatment and prevention of health disorders. More recently, it is being touted as a way of enhancing sexual potential, particularly in connection with the aging process.

Qi Gong movements are easy to learn and are usually coordinated with certain breathing practices. Almost anyone can benefit from its balancing and strengthening effects. It can be practiced just about anywhere, and a session could take as little as fifteen to twenty minutes.

A life-long student of world-renowned Master Kai Ying Tung, Emilio Gonzalez has been practicing Tai Chi and Qi Gong for over twenty-five years. He has been teaching in the Bay Area since 1976; his drop-in classes are attended by many people living with HIV or suffering from chronic illnesses. Himself HIV-positive since 1986, Gonzalez has never experienced AIDS-related symptoms; he is convinced of the beneficial effects of Qi Gong on his own health. He also believes that it has increased the survival rate and improved the quality of life of many of his students—physically, mentally, and emotionally. Gonzalez says that "in China there is no Freud. If you have severe emotional problems you simply get put away. For minor ones, you do Qi Gong or Tai Chi. Qi Gong changes your emotions without talking about it—through your body—but it definitely ends up correcting things like depression." In addition, many of his students report increased energy levels, a sense of rejuvenation, cleared minds, improved sleep, and enhanced overall health. Gonzalez emphasizes the importance of breathing correctly, asserting that "that in itself raises your spirit. You'll notice that at the end of every class everyone is in high spirits, happy. Qi Gong raises your spirits."

The practice of Qi Gong is experiencing tremendous growth in the United States. Gonzalez refers to the fact that many HMOs and hospitals all over the country are now offering medical Qi Gong—the form he teaches—

as a method of prevention. In addition, PBS aired a special of the bestselling video he co-produced with George Wedemeyer, "Qi Gong for Health," which features original music by San Francisco Symphony musicians. All proceeds from the sale of the video are used to provide health care for people with HIV/AIDS at the Immune Enhancement Project, a nonprofit acupuncture center in San Francisco.

Rich Brown, who is also gay, teaches both Qi Gong and Tai Chi. A student of Taoist philosophy, he considers Taoism to be largely about attaining balance, accepting ourselves, and reaching our greatest potential; as such, it is "very real, and extremely practical." He pursues many of the spiritual aspects of Qi Gong, including various forms of internal meditation and visualization.

As far as the movement aspect of Qi Gong is concerned, Brown says that the bottom line is mindfulness: "The goal is to be in the moment while you're moving—just to be in motion." For the majority of his students who are accustomed to the fast pace of modern life, the first step is slowing down.

According to Brown, the purpose of the exercises is to move the chi through the meridian system, thereby flushing out any stagnant chi, which can cause disease. The system is believed to keep the organs vital and alive; by increasing longevity, he says, it "increases the likelihood of being one with the Tao."

An athlete who enjoys running, cycling, and the martial arts, Brown reports increased stamina from his practice, which he says also helps clear out energetic toxins. In fact, he believes that the practice refines the body's energy to such a point that the system will eventually prevent the taking in of toxins; in his own case, for example, Brown naturally became increasingly sensitive about his diet the more he practiced.

As a spiritual approach, Brown finds that Qi Gong "does not intimidate people, and, in fact, is very congruent with people's beliefs and concerns. As you get closer to the fundamental principles of Taoism, Qi Gong makes you more conscious, more aware, while improving all dimensions of health—even those beyond the physical. Its refined energy makes you more conscious, you have less mind clutter, and are a more unified whole system." Brown reports that Qi Gong enhances his daily meditation practice and it led him to become involved in the study of Taoist texts. "To me everything is balance, and Qi Gong revealed in me a desire to stay in a state of balance." Like Gonzalez, Stern, Cornell, and countless other queer instructors of various spiritual modalities, Brown is fulfilling the role of teacher/healer/caregiver.

TAI CHI

Tai Chi Chuan literally means the "Supreme Ultimate Force." Like Qi Gong, its movements or "forms" are performed slowly, gently, and gracefully; some are influenced by the martial arts, while others mirror the natural movements of birds and other animals. Drawing on such Taoist principles as yielding, balance, softness, centeredness, and a reverence for nature, Tai Chi movements are performed with conscious intent, in a relaxed, circular motion with slow and seamless transitions. Their focused and deliberate rendition has a meditative, calming, and re-energizing effect on both mind and body, and yields an awareness of subtle energy movement and a deep sense of balance and centeredness. One of the many forms of Qi Gong, Tai Chi facilitates the movement of chi within the body, thereby enhancing practitioners' health and vitality.

DingHao Ma, a gay man born in China but raised in Thailand, has been practicing Tai Chi for ten years. He first got into it after a painful and difficult breakup with a lover, after which he tried "everything to distract myself; I took dance classes, ballet, yoga; I even signed up for a country-western square dancing class and wore a cowboy hat!" DingHao also looked into the martial arts but did not find a teacher with a spiritual philosophy; he was interested in them as an art form, not a weapon for combat. "I was seeking answers, fulfillment," he adds, "and had enough sense to realize that I had to learn to be content by myself, instead of always looking for another person to complete me. Finally I came to Tai Chi, and after only a few months my life had changed. Now I practice an hour a day, seven days a week."

To DingHao, Tai Chi has important benefits for mental, physical, and spiritual health. "We get sucked into our lives and forget what is really important and what we really need. By practicing every day I am calmer, more centered and alert." Tai Chi also helps his meditation. "I was always in the fast lane, always practiced fast sports, and used to be a runner. After doing Tai Chi for three years, I tried meditation and was surprised I could even sit still for forty-five minutes." Although he has also studied Qi Gong, he prefers the gracious movements of Tai Chi, which he describes as more elaborate than those of Qi Gong. "The movements take you in," he says. "I love Tai Chi; it is very gracious and reminds me of dance." He finds the movements of Qi Gong much simpler, but, paradoxically, more difficult because they require more concentration.

RITUAL DANCE

Various forms of dance are used as meditative practices. The best example of this is Sufi whirling, used for hundreds of years as a way to achieve ecstatic states. We have already established the prevalence of ecstatic dancing and music among many homoerotically inclined and transgendered spiritual functionaries throughout history and across different cultures, from the *hijras* of India to the *galli* of the goddess Cybele. Indigenous cultures in general use music and dance to achieve altered states and as a vehicle to the Divine. In the West, African dance is increasingly being used in a similar way, and the incidence of drumming circles—inspired by Native American and African rhythms—is on the rise.

Muiz Brinkerhoff was formally initiated into Sufism within the Sufi Islamia Ruhaniat Society; he is a certified Dance Leader within the tradition and is also recognized as a Sheikh (teacher). His Sufi work is informed and deepened by a wide variety of interests and talents from other areas of his life, including his most recent certification as a MotherWave Awakening Practitioner—a new personal transformational technology combining breathwork, movement, and belief system modification techniques—as well as by what he refers to as a "zany and irreverent sense of humor." As the first openly gay Sheikh, he enacts both archetypes of consciousness scout, or "going first," and that of spiritual teacher, or sacred functionary. By incorporating humor and irreverence in his work, he also personifies the role of sacred clown.

The Dances of Universal Peace, he explains, were "brought through by Sam Lewis, an American Sufi master. Although the traditional orders do not use them, it was Lewis's teacher, Inayat Khan, who brought Sufism to the West in 1910." Khan's innovations and distillations of traditional learning from India evolved into American Sufism. Brinkerhoff asserts that the dances are an "expansion of meditation; they come from that same place of stillness, and translate it into movement. They are designed to help people open up to Spirit, by opening up inside first. Originally each one of the dances was centered on sacred phrases or divine names from different traditions. In that sense they were mantric. The movement comes from within as a response to the experience of a sacred phrase."

The Dances of Universal Peace are different from the whirling or turning practiced by another Sufi order, the Mevlevi order founded by Rumi. The name stems from the word *mevlavan*, which means "our lord, our master." The turning is used as a meditative practice to reach high, ecstatic states, although, Brinkerhoff says, "critics, such as renowned Sufi scholar Idries Shah, believe that the Whirling Dervishes are imitating the effects of Rumi's state, rather than what actually led to it."

In any case, the practice takes anywhere from twenty to forty-five minutes, and, from my personal experience, even watching it done can be a transcendent, highly meditative, and intoxicating experience. If you have never had the opportunity to see the Whirling Dervishes, the film *Baraka* includes some excellent footage.

To Gabrielle Roth, recording artist and author of *Sweat Your Prayers,* ecstatic dance is a spiritual practice—"a way to bring the lover, the God, the artist within us to everyday existence, as a celebration of life." In a recent conversation, Roth spoke of her belief that many religions have "made the body the enemy. Spirit has been divorced from flesh through our religious upbringing. Yet, since the body is where life happens, there is no way to have a spiritual experience without it. Where would you have it?" She describes ecstasy as a timeless, egoless state of being that "requires a willingness to completely let go of concepts and constructs and to enter into the mystery itself and be danced, to give it all up to the dance and let the dance rearrange us. That's my spiritual practice. It's a practice designed for artists, lovers, and other wild-hearted persons who wish to directly connect with God—to plug in to the 'Master Vibe.'"

Because her work is so inclusive and nonjudgmental, Roth finds that gay people are drawn to it and "take to it like a duck to water. It's such a permissive body of work which welcomes young and old, gay and straight, men and women, people from all walks of life. This is part of my dream—that we all dance together and celebrate our differences. I don't get it when people think they know more than life. Man makes stupid errors, but God doesn't. How can a mistake come from the source of life? How could being gay be wrong? The sickness is on the other side."

Tim Foskett has trained with Roth and runs a weekly dance group for gay men in London called Mendance. The son of a progressive Protestant minister, Foskett grew up as an atheist, because he "couldn't bear organized religion." After many years of being involved in therapy work, he discovered dance. "Dance is an enormous complement to therapy; it's about embodying all those ideas. To try and figure out who I am while ignoring my body is mad. Gabrielle's work is first of all about learning to listen to our bodies, which carry a great deal of our stories. Dance is excellent for that. After a couple of years I found that I was not so stiff, more relaxed, more loosened up. Now, dance informs almost everything in my life—including my sexuality. In that area it has given me permission to do just what I feel like doing, rather than what I should be doing. I am much more aware of my body, and that reflects on how I am sexually."

"Life is a dance. Life is movement," says Roth. "For me, God—that mysterious force which keeps us going—is a dance. When I surrender to that energy, I get as close to God as I am able to. When I enter into ecstatic dance, it's an attitude shift; I enter into it like a prayer. I offer myself into the dance, saying 'take me, use me.'"

Stephen Gendin is executive vice president of *POZ* magazine. In an unpublished essay titled "A Night of Ecstasy," he describes his experience at New York's Black Party, which is part of the "circuit":

> I felt the magic soon after my friends and I arrived at the club and landed on a floor packed with exquisite men. I felt it in the way I danced, how my usually tight body became fluid, and gracefulness just bloomed in every step I took. My face transformed into a smile and that smile was mirrored back everywhere I looked. Gentleness was all around: the passing caress of someone sliding by, the water offered by an unknown nearby reveler. Soon we were all massaging each others' neck and backs, my usually insensitive fingers probing deeply into sore muscles while other hands worked my back, somehow effortlessly zeroing in on my knots and kinks. I melted. All the dreams that I am usually too scared to let emerge began pouring out, filling my heart and soul with the image of a transfigured me, a Stephen bold and sensitive enough to change the world. My consciousness splintered: I was planning a glorious future while also reveling in the warm glow spreading through my body.

There is obviously a connection—perhaps even an archetypal one—between queer people, tribal music, and ecstatic dancing. The work of Gabrielle Roth and others offers the possibility of attaining those same ecstatic, healing, and transformative states naturally, without uncomfortable and debilitating hangovers and without potentially compromising our health.

THE LABYRINTH

One last meditative practice involving movement is walking the labyrinth. Developed during medieval times, this practice is experiencing a renaissance largely due to the efforts of Lauren Artress, an openly lesbian Episcopalian priest and author of *Walking a Sacred Path: Rediscovering the Labyrinth as a Spiritual Tool.* In addition to her work as a psychotherapist, Artress lectures nationally and internationally and leads pilgrimages to Europe. At an event cosponsored by Q-Spirit and GAYLING (Gays and Lesbians in Grace, San Francisco's cathedral where Artress serves as priest), she explained that the labyrinth is a metaphor for going within. As we wind around and around finding our way into the center, the path becomes a metaphor for our spiritual journey. "The Labyrinth is an archetype, a divine imprint, found in all religious traditions in various forms throughout the world. By walking a replica of the Chartres Labyrinth, laid in the floor of Chartres Cathedral around 1220, we are rediscovering a long-forgotten mystical tradition that is insisting to be reborn."

Considered by many San Francisco's spiritual heart, Grace Cathedral has two labyrinths which are open to the public; one is outside and always accessible; the other is inside and subject to cathedral hours. On two occasions, Grace Cathedral has opened its doors to Q-Spirit. In addition to the event with GAYLING, Anthony Turney, openly gay Director of Development at Grace, previously hosted an evening featuring live organ music while participants walked the labyrinth, explored the altar and choir areas, or sat in quiet meditation in any one of the cathedral's chapels, including the Keith Haring Memorial Chapel with its beautiful altarpiece. For many who had not stepped inside a church for years, it was a profoundly moving and solemn experience to have the cathedral completely to ourselves.

Through Veriditas, the nonprofit organization Artress founded to promote the practice of walking the labyrinth, groups or organizations can invest in portable canvas labyrinths. One of the organization's goals is to establish communities all over the world of people who come together to use the labyrinth for meditation, prayer, group ritual, and transformation. Training sessions are provided periodically in different locations throughout the country for those who feel called to become trained facilitators.

CONTEMPLATION

Different forms of contemplation include praying, reading sacred scriptures, and communing with nature.

Ruth Baetz, lesbian author of *Wild Communion,* defines communing as an "intimate fellowship or rapport." To her, it's about experiencing an intimate relationship with nature with every aspect of ourselves, which could manifest as an "ecstatic experience of oneness with the whole universe, or a calm sense of kinship with the tree beside us." In spiritual terms, she adds, "communing places us in the middle of miracles and mysteries, in the middle of something much larger than ourselves. Here we can ask the big questions about life and death—and we can feel the presence of a higher power."

Interestingly, Baetz feels that queer people have a greater need for nature than heterosexuals:

At some point in our lives we are likely to go through significant trauma without support. Where do we get a deep, enduring sense of belonging, of being nurtured, a sense of kinship? Where do we find a relationship we've had as long as we've had a relationship with our family? Where do we go to reconnect with the holy, with a higher power? Where do we go to feel sacred and accepted and okay again? Where do we go to weep, to collapse, to feel held, to heal? We can go to nature for these things and more.

Which Path to Choose?

In choosing a meditative path, it is important to acknowledge that some techniques will be more effective for some people than for others. Your job is to find one, or a combination, that works for you, one that will increase the likelihood that you will follow through and stick with your chosen discipline. For example, you might consider starting out with a formal concentration method as a step toward practicing mindfulness meditation. In determining which path is best for you, it is important to consider your innate inclinations and temperament. If you have attention deficit disorder, or a high-strung, athletic predisposition, for example, sitting immobile for a half hour might prove frustrating and counterproductive, at least initially. Rather than setting yourself up for a potentially disheartening or upsetting failure, one of the various movement meditations, such as yoga or Qi Gong, may be more compatible. If you are deeply in touch with your emotions and function comfortably at the emotional level, you might be naturally inclined to Bhakti Yoga, and one of the more devotional methods, such as chanting, might be more suitable for you. If you thrive on reading and learning, the path of Jnana Yoga might be the one for you; in that case, you might combine the study of sacred scriptures with mindfulness meditation.

As much as possible, try to approach your practice without expectations. Even when you do not experience the much-touted effects of meditation—a silent, peaceful mind, insight, or ecstatic states—that does not mean you are "doing it wrong." Again, the phenomenal experiences or flashes of insight are not the goal of meditation; the important thing is to persevere in fidelity to your practice, even through those days when you think nothing is happening, or that you are "just not cut out for this." From my personal experience, the results can be subtle and may even sneak up on you. For months, even years, I unsuccessfully attempted mantra meditation and thought I was a miserable failure: My mind always remained active and I never attained a "quiet mind" or the experience of "being one with the mantra" (although I frequently enjoyed inspired ideas and great moments of intuition). One day it dawned on me that even though my mind was doing its thing, just thinking away, my body was actually in a deeply relaxed, quiet, meditative state. The experience is somewhat difficult to describe, but I knew my body was perfectly still, in spite of the mind's activity. The feeling was different, and very pleasant.

That realization actually had a quieting effect on my mind. Ever since then, meditating has become easier. Almost as soon as I sit now, I frequently feel my body moving into that subtly pleasant state. In my case, it was important to stop judging myself and feeling like a failure. I eventually switched to a mindfulness approach, which has worked better for me, although—truth be told—my mind most often remains chirpily active. I have also learned that the goal is not to suppress or stop the thinking process but rather to observe or witness our thoughts as they come and go without attaching to them. When I go for even a few days without meditating, I feel the difference: a slight and nondescript sense of disconnectedness. The point is that meditation works, even when we don't feel its effects consciously or immediately. Choose one method and commit to giving it your best for six months. It will be worth your efforts.

Getting Started

Once we have made the choice to meditate and committed to the process, we need to get clear about how we will make it happen. In the case of sitting meditation, for instance, this means creating a twenty- to thirty-minute space in our day that works for us. Whenever possible, committing to the same time each day is ideal. As we well know, we are creatures of habit. The up side to that is that we can consciously create positive habits by reinforcing our own actions. In the case of meditation, its many benefits are inherently self-rewarding, but we do need to stick to it in order to fully reap them.

The next step is creating an appropriate physical space. Privacy is important, as well as comfort. You may want to sit on a straight-backed chair initially, or, if your body is flexible enough, you may want to invest in a *safu,* or meditation pillow, although any firm pillow will do. The important thing is to ensure that your body is comfortable and your back straight. You may also decide to "spiritualize" your meditation chair, room, or area. Some people even create altars with favorite icons and images, fresh flowers, or natural objects such as shells, stones, or pieces of driftwood. This does not have to be expensive or elaborate; a simple cardboard box turned upside down, perhaps with a piece of wood placed on top to provide a stable surface, and covered with a nice cloth, makes a fine altar. Some people also choose special comfortable clothing that they wear exclusively to meditate. Candles and incense also help to set the mood and ritualize the experience. This is all optional, however; the important thing is sitting our butts down and doing it.

Many people also find it useful to prepare the body before meditating by doing stretching exercises or yoga *asanas* to ensure that the body feels comfortable and relaxed. Others further believe it is best if the body feels fresh and clean and suggest taking a shower or washing your face, hands, and feet before sitting. Unless you live in the country or have a quiet living space, you might consider earplugs to minimize distractions. If you are near a phone, make sure the ringer is turned off. I usually place a timer next to me so that I know when to stop.

Once you have completed the preparations and are seated comfortably with your spine straight, gently close your eyes and focus on your breath. Bring your attention to your breath as you inhale through the nose slowly, softly, and deeply. Keeping the body as still as possible, continue breathing naturally, and consciously begin to relax. One way to do this is to do a brief inventory from the top of your head to your toes, focusing on the different muscle groups, and contracting each for a few seconds as you move down, then releasing. Combined with your steady, easy breathing, this should cause your body to relax more and more deeply. There are several things you can do with your hands. You can simply rest them on top of your legs; or you can press your thumb and forefinger together and place your hands, palms facing up, on your knees; or you can gently cup one hand inside the other, and place them on your lap with the palms facing up and your thumbs touching each other at the tips.

Still breathing easily, and with your eyes closed (assuming, of course, that you are not practicing Zen, or other open-eyed techniques), bring your attention to the point between and behind your eyebrows, almost as if you were looking up into the center of your head. Although at first this may feel uncomfortable and your eyes may tire or even strain, at some point it will become very natural; in fact, you may even find that your eyes just fall into place automatically. When you notice your eyes are down, then simply and gently direct them up again. This is the place where meditation takes place. It is hard to describe, but sometimes it feels like you just fall into it. If you are experiencing discomfort or difficulty with this, do not get caught up in it or let it become a deterrent to your practice. Just do the best that you can, letting the experience be as natural, pleasant, and easy as possible; there is considerable value in simply sitting alone in the silence.

If you decide to try a mantra, one of my favorites is *So-ham,* which means "I AM That." Silently repeat *ham* with your inhale, and *so* as you exhale. At first you may find that it takes effort to continue repeating the mantra without getting distracted. You may suddenly notice that minutes have passed and you just caught yourself in some mental trip, perhaps planning how you will handle a particular conversation with your boss when you get to work. When that happens, simply notice your thoughts and gently bring yourself back to the mantra. Rather than getting upset at yourself or feeling like a failure after this happens repeatedly, remind yourself that it is part of the process; bring in your observer or witness consciousness; recall your attention from the distracting thought or emotion; and return to your mantra.

If you prefer not to use a mantra, simply focus on your breath, remaining aware of your thoughts, emotions, or physical sensations. You can choose to focus your breath on a certain point, such as the nostrils, or the back of your throat, or deep in your belly.

Although it is possible to learn how to meditate from a book, meditation instruction from a qualified and experienced teacher can be essential. Meditation teachers, groups, or centers can be found in most metropolitan areas. The additional benefit of taking a class offers the opportunity to meditate in a group setting. Many people report that meditating in a group generates a synergistic effect, a result of the collective focus and intention. There are a wide variety of meditation types and as many approaches to teaching. Some instructors emphasize stress reduction and health benefits, while others are centered around a spiritual context. What is important is to find one with whom you feel safe and comfortable, someone who displays credibility and integrity; don't be afraid to shop around, or ask for referrals. As always, trust your heart.

Breathwork

For hundreds of years, people in the East have been consciously using their breath for health, purification, and as a means of accessing expanded states of consciousness. That is the basis of the yogic practice of *pranayama*, a Sanskrit word which means "a pause (*ayama*) of the breath (*prana*)." Pranayama encompasses various yogic breathing techniques. Other techniques incorporating conscious breathing include Kundalini Yoga, Kriya Yoga, and Tantric practices; Sufi, Buddhist, and Taoist meditations also utilize the breath as a spiritual practice.

In the West, it was not until the 1970s that breath was really discovered as a psychospiritual healing technique. During that decade, breathwork therapies suddenly proliferated in the United States. The two major approaches that unfolded were Rebirthing and Holotropic Breathwork. Because my training and experience are in the former, we will focus first on that branch.

According to lore, Leonard Orr was sitting in a hot tub (in San Francisco, of course) when he began experimenting with his breath, creating circular breathing patterns by pulling his inhale and connecting it with his exhale. After doing this for some time, he suddenly and unexpectedly experienced an expanded state of awareness, and was forever changed. He enrolled some of his friends in investigating this practice, which they eventually termed "Rebirthing" because many of them were actually reliving past experiences, and in particular, the process of their birth. The other reason it received that name is that practitioners often emerge from a session with a deep sense of starting life anew with freshness, vigor, and a renewed sense of hope.

Although Orr is considered the "father of Rebirthing," his techniques were refined in collaboration with Sondra Ray, a former nurse and author who widely popularized the practice all over the world. Rebirthing is also referred to as "conscious breathing," and occasionally as "Vivation" (from the Latin root for "life").

A simple yogic breathing technique, Rebirthing has a cleansing and healing effect on all levels: physical, emotional, and mental. It often generates a profound sense of centering, focusing, and spiritual reconnection. Deeply relaxing, its results are cumulative—and permanent. It is considered by many experts to be one of the most effective ways to clear past traumas, negative and emotionally confrontational experiences which are usually repressed or suppressed, but which still have an influence on our present behavior.

Rebirthing causes a deeply relaxed state and creates an opening through which we may actually experience our spiritual essence. The process can be intensely pleasurable, even ecstatic. It is an excellent tool for self-discovery, often resulting in a deeper sense of self, as well as increased compassion toward self and others. In the words of Sondra Ray, "Rebirthing is sacred. Once I thought it was a scientific process. Once I thought it was a therapy just to heal my birth trauma. I didn't understand it then . . . Rebirthing is like a sacrament . . . (It is) making love to God. It is God making love to you. . . . It is the Ultimate Cosmic Bath."[28]

Rebirthing is a great adjunct to therapy, and many therapists recommend the practice to their clients because of its effectiveness in triggering, uncovering, and integrating past psychological trauma. The process is quick and extremely effective, often cutting right to the core of the problem and dissolving its root causes, sometimes even bypassing the need to talk about the issue.

Ideally, however, it is recommended that it be done in the presence of a professional, someone who can help create a safe space as well as a context for interpreting and integrating any memories, insights, or revelations. Rebirthing can take place in either individual or group sessions.

The other major school of breathwork, which emerged in the '70s from California's Esalen community, was Holotropic Breathwork, sometimes informally called "Grof-work," in reference to its developers, psychiatrist Stanislav Grof, M.D., and his wife, Christina Grof. The name "Holotropic" stems from the Greek *holos* (whole) and *trepein* (moving in the direction of something), and thus means "moving toward wholeness."

Holotropic Breathwork blends the wisdom of anthropology, transpersonal psychology, Eastern spiritual practices, and some of the world's mystical traditions with modern consciousness research, some of it derived from Grof's years of research with LSD in Europe and later in the United States. The result is a simple and profound technique for healing, self-exploration, and attaining "non-ordinary states of consciousness." Usually conducted in group settings, the process incorporates quickened breathing techniques with evocative music, focused energy release work, and later, artistic expression. Lying on a mat with their eyes closed, practitioners breathe to the rhythm and energy of highly evocative music which takes them into a non-ordinary state.

Lin Erhardt, a self-proclaimed "bi-dyke" who lives in Boulder, has been involved with breathwork for eleven years. Having traveled extensively and facilitated groups with Grof himself, she sees breathwork both as a means for psychological healing and as a spiritual process.

When Grof conducted his studies with LSD in Czechoslovakia, he began to notice that there was an "organic healing process to the psyche. He noticed that the psyche exhibited a self-healing mechanism when it accessed non-ordinary states of consciousness." Erhardt further explains that through the insights made possible by the expansion and opening brought about with hallucinogens, Grof found that people were healing emotionally. For years he observed those aspects—such as music and the breath—of the experience which particularly stimulated his clients' process, and carried these forth in the development of Holotropic Breathwork.

Erhardt notes that Holotropic Breathwork tends to "create a certain synergy which intensifies the experience." Unlike a Rebirthing cycle, which normally lasts about one hour, in this type of work the time frame is left open, with sessions usually lasting about two and a half to three hours. The use of music also differs: Whereas Rebirthing tends to use soft, nonintrusive music only in the beginning and end of the cycle, Holotropic uses it throughout the process in a much more evocative and intentional way: "early on the music is loud, strong, and potent, usually starting out with lower chakra music, perhaps with a tribal beat, then moving to heart-oriented music, and ending with higher chakra, transcendent music."

For Erhardt, breathwork is an intrinsic aspect of her spiritual process. She is a strong believer that "we're here to do some work; we have a purpose here. It is the soul's nature to have different themes, and we tend to recreate repeated but similar experiences in working those themes out. The psyche knows how to direct this; it keeps recreating just what we have to see, whatever we're still in denial about." Part of our work as psychospiritual beings, Erhardt believes, is to "reclaim or integrate all of our shadow aspects into ourselves. It is more than just making the subconscious conscious: It's creating a space where those feelings and experiences can be completed and integrated. We need to ask, 'Where do I have a blind spot?' After becoming aware, we can then do the work to complete the experience. That is where breathwork comes in."

A teacher of music and music theory at Diablo Valley College in the Bay Area, Bruce Cook is also a Holotropic Breathwork practitioner. In fact, he fulfills several of the spiritual archetypes we explored earlier. A creator, keeper, and promoter of beauty through his artistic expression, he is also "going first," expanding boundaries, mediating between groups, as well as facilitating healing and spiritual unfoldment through his involvement with the rave community. Rather unexpectedly, Cook became connected with a group of about fifty people who had been deeply involved in raves, using chemicals (Ecstasy), music, and trance dancing to attain transpersonal experiences and feelings of community. However, they eventually discovered that not everyone was feeling safe or having unifying experiences, but instead felt isolated, abandoned, or alone. After meeting Cook, they gave up the use of Ecstasy and replaced it with Holotropic Breathwork. Their weekend raves are now focused on providing opportunities for healing and personal growth. Whereas the old raves lacked a "safety container or net, they now feel that the breathwork provides that," reports Cook. The drug-free weekend raves are held outdoors in the wilderness. Part of the experience includes a day of breathwork, in which participants are divided into dyads and take turns watching each other as one lies down to breathe. That process, too, has created great opportunities for growth, says Cook. "Being a 'sitter' involves learning how to stay with our partner's process, remaining attentive and responsive to their needs without intruding with our own emotional needs or projections. It's about learning how to hold the space without controlling the space."

Cook also holds breathwork in a spiritual context: "The deeper you dive into the inner space the vaster you become; the vaster the experiences which are available. We are like an iceberg. Our itty-bitty consciousness is like the tip of the iceberg. The main benefit of breathwork is realizing that there is no separation, that we are not alone but part and parcel of this vast consciousness; the practice can create a great sense of unity."

Since the '70s, other derivations and offshoots of breathwork have evolved, including Integrative Breathwork, Radiance Breathwork, Breatherapy, Mother-Wave, TransformBreathing, Primal Breathing, Ecstasy Breathing, and others which incorporate allied techniques such as bodywork.

For example, Jacquelyn Small's Integrative Breathwork is similar to Holotropic Breathwork; also taking place in groups, it has specialized as a transpersonal approach to dealing with addictions. Radiance Breathwork was developed by Gay Hendricks, Ph.D., author of *Conscious Breathing,* and dance therapist Kathlyn Hendricks, Ph.D. Like other forms of breathwork, Radiance claims to help release unresolved emotions held in the musculature and tissues of the body, and clear the effects of birth and other trauma.

Identifying as bisexual, Satiyam Harold is a graduate of Breatherapy Training. He explains that through breathwork we release stress, tension, and negative emotions, which then leaves the body in a lighter and freer state; the result is increased energy and mental acuity, expanded awareness, and a sense of joy. According to Satiyam, Breatherapy uses focused breathing, evocative music, and therapeutic touch to release any kind of blocks, whether physical, mental, or emotional. Breatherapy incorporates ancient breathing techniques founder Tom Lodge was exposed to while living in India. While sharing some parallels with both Holotropic Breathwork and Rebirthing, Breatherapy also claims to be a unique approach to breathwork.

Most breathwork techniques share other elements as well, such as an emphasis on circular, continuous breathing—a seamless connecting of inhale and exhale—and a belief that breathing is not only essential to life but also that how we do it affects the quality of our life. Maia Dhyan, who trained in Rebirthing with Sondra Ray and with whom I apprenticed, asserts that our ability to take in breath is directly proportional to our ability to take in life. These various breathwork systems also conceive of the mind, body, and emotions as interconnected, not separate, entities, and believe that suppressed trauma and emotions are stored in the body. Thus, besides directly impacting our health, breathing is considered vital to mental balance and emotional healing.

As a spiritual practice, breathwork is important in helping expand our perceptions and facilitating altered states of consciousness. The etymological connections between breath and spirit are manifold. The Hebrew word *ruach,* for instance, refers to both "breath" and "spirit." And to *inspire* means both "to draw in (air) by inhaling" and "to affect, guide, or arouse by divine influence."[29]

Breathe!

It is best to approach breathwork with an open attitude, no expectations, and a willingness to surrender, to let go to your own breath and to the experience. Feeling safe with your Rebirther or practitioner is important; again, trust your gut.

I cannot recommend breathwork highly enough. As far as I am concerned, the whole world should be engaging in the process regularly. I can personally attest—both from personal experience and from having witnessed it in others—that breathwork truly changes our lives. It is a powerful and catalytic process, one for which I will always be grateful. Gabrielle Roth refers to the breath as "Supercat," the great catalyst. I could not agree with her more. One of the things which really jumped out at me while researching for this chapter was that, no matter what the technique or tradition, the one constant was the universal importance placed on the breath. Even now, having facilitated hundreds of experiences, I am still profoundly moved each time I lead a group. I frequently find myself overcome with feelings of humility and gratitude that I get to play a role in making that experience available to others.

In my work with Rebirthing, I have seen people's lives change in every possible way. I have witnessed physical, mental, and emotional healings. I have personally experienced some of the most profound spiritual moments of my life and have heard countless testimonies from others to that effect.

"Scott" attended one of my groups and afterwards reported he had heard and felt a snapping in his left ear, which had always had slightly impaired hearing. Ever since then, his hearing improved significantly. "Greg" had always had difficulty and pain in one of his knees; during a Rebirth he remembered being very young and running through a glass door, and that one of his legs—the one with the problem—actually had gotten stuck in the glass. Since the session, his knee condition also improved considerably.

Someone else experienced significant healing from sexual abuse. Having been molested when he was ten, as a teenager he acted out sexually and became very promiscuous. He also developed the habit of compulsive masturbation, often indulging several times a day. Totally guilt-ridden as a teenager due to his religious upbringing, during his twenties he was involved in a series of relationships, which were quite active and fulfilling sexually. However, he still found occasion to masturbate regularly. And even though at this point he felt free of the religion-induced guilt, and was clear that his habit was not adversely affecting his relationships, at some level in the back of his mind he knew that the element of choice was missing. Then he discovered Rebirthing, and during one of his first sessions, he experienced something. It wasn't quite a catharsis, nor a recovered memory, since he had never suppressed the molestation, but something happened which he knew to be related to the incident. Since that time, he reports, he was free. If he wanted to jerk off he did, but could also go for weeks without it if he so desired. "What was missing, what I got back, was the ability to choose," he confides.

When I facilitate a group I feel like a privileged observer of the human drama. I am frequently moved by the entire spectrum of the human experience—a single session often reveals both the pain-filled tragedy and the utter majesty of being human.

Remember to be vigilant about fear. It is normal to feel fear or resistance when approaching breathwork; subconsciously, it signifies change to the ego, whose function is maintaining the status quo—even if that is at best comfortable and, at worst, miserable, and even if the change is in a positive direction. Do whatever it takes to move yourself through the resistance; you will not regret it. One helpful thing to realize is that because of the mind's masterful abilities to suppress information, there is no need to worry—only what you are ready to face will be allowed to surface. If you are not ready to deal with something, it will not come up.

If you choose to embark on this exciting adventure of the inner realms, your life will surely begin to change in ways you cannot imagine. Don't freak out, though; the change does not necessarily have to unfold dramatically. It can actually happen quite gracefully.

Whatever else you do, find a breathwork practitioner, and breathe!

Bodywork

In its widest scope, the term bodywork encompasses a variety of techniques characterized by the manipulation or touching of the body. The major approaches to bodywork include: 1) massage therapy; 2) body-centered psychotherapy; and 3) touch therapy, also referred to as energy work or "hands-on healing."

As such, these practices target different aspects of the body. For example, chiropractors and osteopaths work with the structure of the body, whereas body-centered psychotherapists, such as Reichian practitioners, work with what they refer to as the "body armor." Techniques such as acupressure, acupuncture, Reiki, and Therapeutic Touch focus on the body's "subtle" or energy body, and work with its *chi* or "vital energy." The goal of different massage therapies (e.g., Traeger, Swedish, or deep tissue) is the relaxation of the musculature and the consequent release of tension and repressed emotions held in our tissues. Generally, however, the word "bodyworkers" refers to practitioners of any form of massage therapy, excluding related practices such as chiropractic, body-centered psychotherapy, touch therapy, or acupuncture.

Giovanni Alfieri agrees that bodywork is a tool for "tuning in and developing awareness about what's going on inside, a way to connect what's going on in our lives (like stress at work) with what happens in the body." He believes that bodywork also helps us to realize that we have the ability to transcend and move beyond the circumstances of our lives. Mindfulness and self-awareness are important, he adds, because "the most important thing on the spiritual path is understanding yourself and sharing that with the world."

"I hold bodywork in a very sacred way," he says, "and approach each session by taking time to go within, calling in all my guides and angels, and asking for assistance so that the healing may be the highest." Alfieri specializes in deep tissue work because he believes that is the best way to access and release energies that we hold really deep in the body; having studied Reiki, he also combines energy work in his sessions. He acknowledges that what he does is a very intuitive process, one in which he does not put a great deal of conscious thought.

Entheogens

A discussion of paths for inner exploration would not be complete without mention of entheogens, a relatively new term to the English language referring to "plants and chemical substances which awaken or generate mystical experience."[30] Sharing the same roots as "enthusiasm," the word "entheogen" refers to bringing God within. The use of entheogens has been documented among the religious and mystical practices of many cultures throughout the world. While their impact on a person's psyche is very powerful and often difficult to describe, these substances are considered by some "among the biologically safest drugs known."[31]

Based in Southern California, "John" is an openly gay man who facilitates guided journeys with entheogens for both individuals and groups. "We are talking essentially about plants which have a long history of use in a shamanic sense, over centuries, all over the world. One would first have to accept the idea that there is an ordinary reality, and alternate realities. How does one access or experience these alternate realities? There are several ways: yoga, meditation, fasting, monastic life. This is one more way to get to those alternate realities. It is different because it is very direct—an immediate route. Other ways may be equally effective, but they are a slower process. It is very important, however, that these substances be used properly. For them to produce results, they need to be used in a ritual or sacred context, not just casually. They are not for everybody."

Many gay people use chemical substances like Ecstasy because of the feelings of belonging it generates, as well as a general sense of lovingness, unconditional acceptance of self and others, removal of interpersonal and intrapersonal boundaries, and elimination of self-consciousness. Ecstasy has been used in psychotherapeutic contexts for those same effects—it seems to be effective as a means to temporarily remove the ego, making it possible for participants to really come from their heart. With the ego's innate defensiveness and its denial and avoidance mechanisms out of the way, the use of Ecstasy can facilitate profound personal insights as well as support deep, meaningful communication between people.

"John" says that "if you're climbing a mountain or a building, from the top you have a better view, more of a perspective. Through this practice you abandon unnecessary beliefs, attitudes, and ways of behavior—you stop doing them. Life gets tremendously enriched, and you see the universe from a varied and enhanced perspective, one more colorful and filled with mystery. Often you get a sense of connection, of unity with the universe; isolation, separation, and alienation diminish or disappear. You also begin to see the world as energy, an ever-changing energy, and begin to see how it works. You develop a much deeper perception, sensitivity, and intuition; you are able to see behind appearances, behind the obvious; you acquire a sense of depth through which to see life."

As enticing as his description may sound, it is important to remember that there are other ways to transcend fear, personal limitations, and discomfort, other ways to develop self-confidence and learn communication, other ways to have direct and transcendent experiences, that are not so radical and taxing on the body. Ultimately, it comes down to making a conscious, informed, personal choice. You need to weigh the potential benefits of the experience against the effects these substances may have on your body. You need to ask yourself: What does using this substance do for you? Does it make you a better person? Does it expand your awareness, help you see yourself and reality more clearly? Or does it numb you out, deaden you, tire you out, diminish you, alienate you? As always, we need to honor and respect the body as a temple of the Divine. One other potential trap presented by entheogens, but also applicable to other practices like meditation or breathwork, is getting stuck in the phenomenal experience. Many teachers warn that transformation is not about attaining altered states, no matter how spectacular they may be, but about the slow, sometimes painstaking, dissolution of the ego construct which keeps us separate from our true spiritual essence.

In Part 3 we will explore one final path for going within, exploring consciousness, and reaching the Divine: sexuality. Because this is such a huge and highly charged subject, one which is a cause of much confusion and controversy, I felt it required separate treatment. At the end of that chapter, we will take a brief look at relationships used as a spiritual path.

The Faces of Passion

3

Introduction: Sexual Civil Wars

Our society in general is "obsexed"—we are obsessed with sex. Sexuality is up for us to look at. It can no longer be contained or suppressed. Sexuality is at the heart of some of the most divisive issues in this country. We can't seem to get enough sex, or enough about sex. Those who are not obsessing about how to get it are scheming about how to suppress it. The problem stems from the accumulation of hundreds of years of misguided efforts to contain natural human sexual impulses and behavior, unhealthy, harmful, and ultimately doomed attempts at dissecting flesh from spirit. The dam has broken. It seems that the more we try to repress sexuality, the more it oozes out and finds expression.

The sexual revolution of the 1960s was an uprising against society's rigid and repressive rules restricting sex to the confines of marriage. As a result, sex was finally freed from functionality, from its inevitable association with reproduction. Perhaps for the first time in many hundreds of years, Westerners gave themselves collective permission to enjoy sex for the sake of sex, to purely revel in the joy of sex. The '60s and '70s triggered an era of unbridled sexual exploration by many, one made possible not only by a confluence of social factors, but also by the widespread advent of the pill.

Not surprisingly, the exploration and rebellion against sexual oppression reached its apogee in the gay community. We were doing what we so often do: enacting the archetype of "consciousness scouts"—going first to investigate for the rest of the tribe what lay ahead—as well as testing limits and expanding boundaries. The stories of what are, to some, the "good old days" of virtually unrestrained sexual activity in the baths, backrooms, and alleys of New York and San Francisco, are now often idealized and have reached almost epic proportions. To younger queers born in the Age of AIDS, these extremes will likely remain fantasy—the stuff of legends.

Although understandable and necessary in terms of the proverbial pendulum effect, was unabashed promiscuity really the cutting edge of sexuality? Was the sexual frontier ever in the mind-boggling number of nameless or quasi-anonymous encounters some of us can attest to? Is more necessarily better? Is quantity a substitute for quality? What defines the cutting edge in these sexually cautionary days? These are all important—and difficult—questions.

Ironically, however, despite our society's obsession with sex, confusion and ignorance regarding sexuality reign. Misinformation still runs rampant in most circles, including the gay population. Dan Savage, who writes a nationally syndicated column about sexuality called "Savage Love" and hosts a weekly call-in radio show in Seattle, is appalled and disturbed by the number and types of questions revealing the extent of our ignorance about sexual matters. He believes that more than AIDS education, what we really need is sex education. "AIDS education has compartmentalized all other issues pertaining to sexuality, and created a kind of blissful ignorance," he said at a National Gay and Lesbian Task Force forum. What he—and other experts—advocate is a broader discussion about sexuality in general.

The sexual revolution created a state of flux in which old beliefs were being discarded and new ways of being sexual explored and redefined; confusion was to be expected. Then, in the early '80s, the HIV pandemic began confusing matters even more and causing chaos in the gay community.

At first it was as if we had had the wind knocked out of us. Once it became clear that this perplexing illness was caused by a sexually transmitted, relentless killer whose casualties quickly began to add up, and we realized that the medical establishment was either stumped or in denial, we went into a collective vital shock—one from which we still have not fully emerged. Fear was widespread, and still is in many ways. There are still men who have not had sex for much of the fifteen years of the AIDS War. We did the best we could, and many a valiant and heroic effort has been made to halt the onslaught, and tend to our wounded.

In the late '90s, however, a backlash against the years of fear and restraint occurred. Fueled by anger, impatience, frustration, and a sense of fatalism and helplessness, as well as by optimism over the promise of protease inhibitors, many gay men began discarding safer sex guidelines, choosing to take their chances. The ensuing "barebacking" (anal sex without a condom) controversy resulted in a dramatic polarization in our community between those advocating a radical sexual libertarianism—the right to have sex with whomever, wherever, whenever, and however they choose—and those advocating further restraint. The lines between sexual freedom and responsibility were drawn in 1997 with the release of Gabriel Rotello's *Sexual Ecology: AIDS and the Destiny of Gay Men,* which attempted to describe the crisis in terms of ecology, from the point of view of the virus, using epidemiological research to ascertain why the virus took hold in the gay male population, and did not, as had been expected, spread on the same scale in comparable heterosexual populations in developed countries. His findings point to the failure of what has been termed the "condom code" as a means of prevention. Among his controversial conclusions, Rotello advocates the need for gay men to reassess our sexual practices and behavior, limiting the number of our sexual partners, and exploring options such as monogamy and serial monogamy.

That same year, Michelangelo Signorile released *Life Outside: The Signorile Report on Gay Men: Sex, Drugs, Muscles, and the Passages of Life.* A chapter titled "The Evangelical Church of the Circuit" critiques gay men's circuit party culture as narcissistic, hedonistic, and characterized by obsessive body worship, pervasive drug use, and indiscriminate sex. "Thus the drug-fueled parties of the circuit, weekend-long events attended by men who make pilgrimages from places far and wide, are spiritual retreats for the most devoted. . . . Some of the circuit's devotees even espouse what can only be called a *church theology,* often describing the circuit as a sort of religious institution—one that draws upon ancient traditions of faith, and one that requires its adherents to conform to shared behavior and thought."[1] Signorile's book, like Rotello's, caused a great deal of controversy and consternation. In it he depicts life in the "gay ghettos" as centered around a "cult of masculinity" and describes the history of our obsession with idealized physical beauty from the onset of the sexual revolution, to the clones of the '70s, and culminating with the present day "hypermasculine" ideal which is ubiquitously sought and deified in our gyms, bars, circuit parties, neighborhoods, publications, web sites, and personal ads. Signorile exhorts readers to venture beyond the confines of the "gay scene" and encounter a more "rewarding, fuller, and richer life, outside."

Not surprisingly, both Rotello and Signorile, along with Andrew Sullivan, former editor of *The New Republic* and author of *Same-Sex Marriage,*

Larry Kramer, vocal activist and author of *Faggots,* and *New York Post* columnist Jonathan Capehart, caused quite a furor and were met with irate accusations of being "sex-negative," "neo-conservatives," and "Neo-Puritans" for their criticisms of gay men's public sex subcultures. They were also referred to as "the backlash boys," and "turdz" by their detractors, who blamed them for originating a "sex panic" by publicly criticizing gay male promiscuity and advocating the closure of gay baths and sex clubs.

Respected gay historian Allan Bérubé, author of *Coming Out Under Fire,* defines a sex panic as a "moral purity crusade that leads to crackdowns on sexual outsiders. . . . [They are] engineered crises that thrive on the fear of sexual monsters. They are the justifications and the machinery that legislative bodies use to enact new anti-sex laws which police then enforce by enacting sexual crackdowns, which themselves eventually become part of the ebb and flow of routine law enforcement—the everyday policing of people's sex lives."

According to Bérubé, this particular sex panic singles out and "demonizes" gay men's multi-partner sex in public spaces. What makes this one different, he and others claim, is that it is being fueled by a coterie of gay journalists who are using their positions within the mainstream media to influence public attitudes against promiscuous gay sexual behavior. Pointing to phrases used to describe the gay bath scene, like "the killing fields of AIDS," and "bustling hives of contagion" where he witnessed "sex murder/suicides," used by Rotello in his *Newsday* column, and "factories of destruction," used by Capehart, sex-panic proponents hold these writers responsible for the "crackdown" against gays, including the closure of bars, baths, and sex clubs in New York City. They further accuse the "neo-Puritans" of perpetuating the image of the "immature, sex-crazed, unclean homosexual who is both suicidally and homicidally addicted to diseased orgies in public places."

Coming Together

For a population that defines itself based on sexual behavior, there is still a great deal of confusion, lack of information, and unhealed behavior going on in the queer community. This is not surprising, given that it has only been thirty years since we have been dealing with issues of sex openly, and attempting to redefine and reverse hundreds of years of sex negativity and repression. How should we be with each other? What is appropriate? When? Does anything go? Anytime? Anywhere?

The discussion within these pages is not about moralizing—or imposing external rules to determine what is right or wrong based on ancient dogma, inherited traditions, and unexamined belief systems. It's about going inside and finding what is right for us, both as individuals and as a community, consciously and responsibly.

Going inside in general is not an easy process; the sexual element adds an extra charge to the effort. How do we find balance between individual rights and public safety? Let's take, for instance, the case of security in airports. In order to ensure safety, we agree to submit ourselves to a process whereby our property is X-rayed and sometimes manually inspected, our bodies scanned with metal detectors. If we happen to be wearing a metal belt buckle, for example, we are pulled aside and subjected to a somewhat demeaning and invasive process. Like common criminals, we are told to stand with legs and arms spread while the guard invades our personal space with a manual metal-detecting probe, sometimes even frisking us. Nevertheless, we unquestioningly cooperate with this invasion of privacy because we know that it is being done to ensure our safety, with our best interest in mind, and to increase the chances that we reach our final destination safely and without complications.

Perhaps it would help if we switched our thinking concerning sexual behavior a bit along these lines. The gay male community is under siege by a powerful external threat, the most dangerous virus humanity has yet encountered. Rather than pointing fingers and calling each other names like "body fascists," or "neo-conservatives," we need to come together and face this threat. In the process, we may have to make some tough decisions in order to ensure our survival—both personally and communally.

The truth is we all want the same freedom and the right to be ourselves, to love as we choose and openly express our sexuality without fear of discrimination or violence. Democrat or Republican, monogamist or sexual radical, assimilationist or liberationist, we are all queer. The truth is that simply by virtue of being gay we are all sex radicals residing at the cutting edge, particularly when compared to the mass of humanity.

To those who already are HIV positive I say: Don't give up; a cure is always possible, and recent medical developments are certainly hope-inspiring. In the meantime, faced with mortality, you have a powerful and potentially life-changing opportunity to grow and evolve. Take advantage of that. At the same time, please think of the ones who follow, and the legacy they have inherited—in the words of twenty-six-year-old Derek Marshall, a world in which "sex was always dangerous."

It is possible for us to lick this virus, but it may entail continued changes in our behavior. We must at least give serious consideration to Rotello's arguments. We can't write off whole ways of thinking because they don't fit with our desires, our particular sexual practices, or our political agendas.

The issue is bigger than my personal right to get my dick sucked whenever, wherever, and by whomever I want. If Rotello and the epidemiologists on whose research he has based his conclusions are right, the problem is extremely serious and is not about to go away. The implications are multi-layered, potentially impacting other areas such as treatment and prevention funding, and threatening the continued support of our natural allies, including our lesbian sisters and the straight liberals and libertarians who have supported us and fought on our behalf. We have to at least entertain the possibility that a change in behavior is advisable. In times of crisis, nothing less than heroism is called for. Our ability—and willingness—to re-evaluate and, if necessary, consciously put aside some of our personal preferences and individual rights for some time is nothing less than heroic. It is important that we do this for the greater good of all.

Sexual Ecology reveals a great deal of understanding, compassion, and sensitivity to the political and social implications of its conclusions. The author seems well aware that the information could be appropriated by conservative hate-mongers to fuel pre-existing homophobic tendencies in society. Having spent considerable time carefully reading Sex Panic! literature and studying the case they present, I still find Rotello's analysis well thought out, level-headed, and his conclusions compelling. Contrary to what has been said about him, I find the tone of the book to be dispassionately matter-of-fact, and lacking in judgment, accusations, or blame. In a letter to participants at the first national Sex Panic! forum in 1997, Rotello writes that "the 'us' we're talking about includes me. I went to sex clubs and baths. I sucked and fucked my way through the golden age of promiscuity. This is not about blame. It is about biology, and viruses, and how epidemics work, and why we are in one."

Both he and Signorile vehemently reject the label of neo-conservative, and have independently listed their stands on a variety of issues so as to provide evidence to the contrary. We need to remember that their intentions are good, and their controversial stands, courageous. I do not believe that they are out to "fight sex, not AIDS." By the same token, it is perfectly understandable that Sex Panic! activists feel enraged, hurt, and betrayed, their worlds threatened and intruded upon. And they bring up some valid concerns which also require careful consideration.

Is it possible that all the parties involved could take a collective deep breath, and cut each other some slack? We are all still in the same boat. We must try to focus on our common ground—those shared dreams and goals toward which we all strive. Ultimately, we all want respect and acknowledgment of who we are. We want to be treated with justice, fairness, and equality. We all wish AIDS was gone; we are all deeply grievous of the toll AIDS has taken on our community; and none of us wants to lose any more of our precious friends, relatives, or lovers to HIV. Remember our common purpose, the many goals we share. We may not agree on the best way to get there, but that's where discussion and communication and strategizing and compromise and conflict resolution come into play. We are strongest together.

I have always thought that if humanity experienced an external threat, such as an alien invasion or collision with a comet, we would quickly become unified, and artificial boundaries based on differences in languages, skin color, place of birth, or political or religious beliefs, would rapidly dissipate. The truth is that our community *is* experiencing an alien threat—in the form of a virus which finds itself quite at home and is thriving in our midst. Rather than calling each other names or allowing ourselves to splinter into separate factions, we need to come together—now more than ever. If there was ever a time to put differences aside, this is it. We have enough enemies, besides HIV, as it is. Furthermore, if Sex Panic! is right, we need to brace ourselves for an oncoming assault from a reactionary right wing whose tactics can often be as virulent and insidious as HIV itself. We need to come together like we never have before. Some fatalists hypothesize that HIV will always be around, and we just need to accept that there will always be a percentage of us who will eventually fall prey to its voracious appetite, no matter what prevention strategies are implemented. I cannot resign myself to a scenario in which 50 percent of all gay men are inevitably doomed to become infected. I believe that we must come together if we are to eradicate its presence amongst us.

A Healthy Sexuality

Regardless of where they fall on the broad spectrum of sexual values, beliefs, and behaviors, one common theme heard over and over again from individuals I interviewed, or whose words I studied while researching this chapter, was the prevailing belief that our culture has not yet developed a healthy attitude about sexuality, and that most of us—gay or straight—are in dire need of sex education and open discussion about such issues.

Sexuality is an intrinsic part of the human experience. It can serve to boost us towards the fulfillment of our potential, or—when its energy gets derailed—it can interfere with our growth and happiness. Although rooted in our biology, sexuality encompasses or imbues all other aspects of being human; it is an integral component of who we are, and how we express ourselves in the world.

If society at large is "obsexed," a perfunctory glance through one of the gay publications in any major metropolitan area might lead an outside observer to the conclusion that gay men are "adickted." Most likely, they would find ad after ad depicting pecs and abs galore; page after page of masseurs and escorts, many of them photographed in various degrees of undress, and personal ads revealing fetishes that often stretch the imagination.

Let me be very clear. I am not saying that I find this objectionable or immoral. I love being in my body and connecting with other human beings through theirs. However, I think we need to take a closer look at our behavior. It's a matter of our survival, and a communal responsibility. It's about preventing the senseless loss of more talented, intelligent, beauty-filled, gay men. It's about the future, and the shape in which we leave the world for future generations.

It should be no secret that there is a great deal of unwholesome sex taking place in the gay community, but, for that matter, the rest of humanity is far from an ideal model of healthy sexuality. In the hope that they might provide assistance and insight for some in determining the difference between a healthy or unhealthy sexuality, the following paragraph contains a few questions from Sexual Compulsives Anonymous (SCA), a twelve-step program which began in New York in 1982. Based on the principles of Sexaholics Anonymous (SA), SCA's gay founders felt there was a need for a more gay-sensitive organization. They also distanced themselves from SA with their decision that members would define sexual sobriety and design their own recovery plan for themselves. Although exclusively gay in the beginning, SCA is now open to all sexual orientations; their goal is to support anyone who seeks to "recover from sexual compulsion." Organization literature specifies that their goal is not to "repress our God-given sexuality, but to learn how to express it in ways that will not make unreasonable demands on our time and energy, place us in legal jeopardy, or endanger our mental, physical or spiritual health."

Some of the signs which may indicate sexual compulsion include the compartmentalization of sex, as opposed to its integration into our lives; the use of sex as a drug, to escape from feelings of anxiety, loneliness, anger, self-hatred, or even joy; the use of sex as a means to feel validated and complete because of low self-esteem. Among the questions, which, if answered positively, may indicate a problem are:

- Do you feel your sexual drive and activity are getting out of control?
- Have you repeatedly tried to stop or reduce certain sexual behaviors, but inevitably you could not?

- Have you neglected your family, friends, spouse, or relationship because of the time you spend in sexual activity?
- Do your sexual pursuits interfere with your work or professional development?
- Has your sexual activity prevented you from developing a close, loving relationship with a partner?
- Has the money you spent on pornography, videos, phone sex, or hustlers/prostitutes strained your financial resources?[2]

The question of whether a certain sexual behavior or pattern of behaviors is an addiction is a complex one. Just because you answered yes to some of the questions may not necessarily indicate you have a problem, but it may be worth your time to explore that possibility with either a professional or an anonymous support group.

I agree with Bob Barzan, author of a booklet titled *Sacred Sex: How to Live an Erotic Life,* that in the ultimate analysis, the question to ask is: Is a given behavior making you a better, happier, more fulfilled, and more compassionate human being? A similar question to gauge one's behavior is posed by Joseph Kramer: "Energetically, do you feel fragmented afterwards, or do you feel whole?"

Archetypal Sex

All our lives we have been bombarded by images in film, television, advertising, literature, and songs, as well as by implicit and explicit messages from parents, family members, teachers, and religious leaders, that a romantic, one-on-one, exclusive relationship that would last the rest of our lives was the goal we should be striving for. Anything else falls short of that ideal.

But for many people, that path is simply not appealing. Freed from the societal expectations that restrict the behavior of heterosexuals (at the same time that they support their interpersonal and family structures), gay men in particular have opted for or been forced to practice "anonymous sex," "casual sex," or "multi-partner" sex.

In his characterization of the sex panic, Allan Bérubé argues that it "demonizes gay men . . . for stealing moments of sexual semi-privacy with other men in places such as public parks; public toilets in subways, bus and train stations, libraries and department stores; movie theater balconies; military bases; public baths, gyms, YMCAs and hotel rooms; backstreets and alleys;

trucks, docks, ships and piers; booths in porn shops; gay bars, sex clubs and bathhouses; S/M dungeons and other sex play spaces, and, recently, cyberspace." Bérubé asserts that "it is absolutely essential that my peers and I find a language much richer and truer than lifeless words like 'public sex' or 'multiple partners'—a better language to describe, honor, defend, and critique this remarkable thing we have been creating together against impossible odds for such a long, long time."

Clint Seiter, a San Franciscan gay Buddhist environmentalist who does extensive volunteer work with the homeless, has attempted this richer naming. In his essay "Applying Buddhist Dharma to Casual Sex," published in *Queer Dharma,* Seiter differentiates between Intimate Sex—the kind idealized and sought after by most members of our society—and Archetypal Sex. This latter form of "sexual motivation," he writes, "draws strength primarily from fantasy, where the partner is actually a vessel for something bigger, the ideal of The Male (in gay sex)."

Seiter claims that because of the primacy and idealization of Intimate Sex in our culture, Archetypal Sex has been relegated either to the realm of sin or of illness. For this reason, assessing Archetypal Sex objectively and without prejudice presents an inordinate challenge, and those who are drawn to it are most often forced to suppress their desire, sublimate it, or express it surreptitiously.

In this type of sex the partner is actually enacting a role—an archetype—such as The Daddy, The Beautiful Youth, or The Rough Trade, among others. As described by Seiter, the success of this type of sexual interaction corresponds directly to the degree to which the partner is able to fulfill the particular archetype. Therefore, "personal disclosure is lethal to Archetypal Sex." The more you know about the partner's personality, the less he will be able to convincingly play out a given archetype. Hence the need for limited communication.[3]

In its unadulterated state, Seiter asserts, Archetypal Sex is not only a valid expression of sexuality, but one that can also assume the qualities of a religious experience:

Archetypal Sex seeks to *transcend,* to connect and identify with a concept greater than our personal selves. The partner loses his own personality and identity and becomes an ideal of The Male. In successful Archetypal Sex, the egos of both partners can dissolve into the act of sex itself. Archetypal Sex is a form of worship to a principle of beauty momentarily incorporated within the body of a partner.[4]

"David" is in his late thirties and, by most standards, would be considered a serious spiritual seeker, having spent several years in an ashram, and continuing to attend *satsangs* with his teacher regularly. After several years of celibacy, he re-entered the gay world with a vengeance. Hearing him share his experience, though, it becomes clear that he is approaching his sexual life consciously, not just as an instinctive and blind reaction to the previous lean years.

When I go to sex clubs I am constantly self-reflecting, checking in with myself. I actually experience a type of high in which "I" no longer exist. I check out of my mind, and don't know where it goes. I allow myself to just follow that energy, that wave. It's an incredible high for me; I can really plug into people's erogenous zones. I can actually feel their energy, their ecstasy; it's a constant chance to completely surrender, to just let go of ego control. I consciously do not engage in familiar behavior, or sex by rote, and instead allow spontaneity to have its way. I definitely find Spirit in these experiences: my mind switches off, and I feel a sense of expansion, a sweetness, a lack of identification with the small self, just a sense of spaciousness where nothing else is needed or wanted. I feel very happy, sweet, like I'm making love to the Divine. I can honestly say I have had spiritual experiences in sex clubs.

"David" brings up a valid point about the safety available in sex clubs, which, he contends, "makes it possible to reach these timeless states; you don't have to worry about getting busted, as you might in a park or tea room. In those places you can't afford to go there because you're on the lookout, in constant danger—which, of course, is part of the thrill for some people."

Former porn star and artist Annie Sprinkle, who identifies as "metamorphosexual"—an allusion to her belief that our sexuality, like all else in life, is in a constant state of change—agrees that spirituality can be experienced in environments where public sex occurs. She remembers the early days in New York City, when she was one of only a handful of women who frequented bars like the Mine Shaft. "A lot was happening spiritually there those days," she says, "with trance-inducing music, tons of sex and bodies and breathing and movement. What would happen to me was a sense of timeless ecstasy, bliss deep within, connections with people, emotional revelations, weightlessness, light, a sense of being in the body, but not—in short—actual physical sensations which you only heard talked about in church or spiritual circles. It was very extreme and intense, an extreme orgy. You'd be fistfucking some guy, and it was like he was having a baby." According to Sprinkle, in the beginning, the unspoken intention was one of exploration and self-discovery.

Then things changed, and the scene became "sleazy, slimy, greedy, abusive, squirmy—it was about 'what can I get for myself?'" Whereas at first it was "a spontaneous combustion of energy and enthusiasm," once the experience changed "people latched on to its residue." To Sprinkle, who embodies several queer archetypes, including artist, healer, and consciousness scout, a lot depends on the intention: "I've also been to lightweight, silly orgies, and agree that calling that sacred sex can sometimes be an excuse. What I'm talking about was life on the edge."

In his essay, Seiter likewise notes that because of societal condemnation of Archetypal Sex, negative attitudes toward it are internalized and can be evidenced in the "lack of respect towards one's partners, contempt, rudeness, [and] emotional coldness," sometimes experienced in anonymous encounters. Archetypal Sex gets compartmentalized and banished to a separate, hidden closet in the person's life, "not *incorporated* into the rest of our personality, or imbued with our humanity and compassion. What results is a type of schizophrenia."

Regardless of what we call it, Archetypal Sex alone cannot meet a human being's need for intimacy and love. As we strive for balance and fulfillment in our lives, it is important that we do not allow fear of intimacy to limit our sexual expression. If a person is stuck in having *only* anonymous sex, that is probably symptomatic of arrested emotional development and an imbalance in other areas of his or her life, often resulting in loneliness and depression. Learning to integrate sexuality with intimacy and affection is a crucial, and satisfying, part of the human experience.

Sacred Sex

In her book *The Art of Sexual Ecstasy,* Margo Anand writes that "our culture has lost the understanding that sexual energy is a physical expression of spiritual power." Anand and others have suggested that a human being's hunger for sexual union is ultimately an expression of a subconscious spiritual drive for wholeness and completion, a desire to transcend our universal sense of separation and alienation. It is a soul-level longing to re-experience the sense of union we felt in the womb, and, even more, a yearning to recapture a sense of oneness with creation. Feeling trapped, abandoned, and lonely in our small, separate, and isolated cells, we long to feel the freedom, expansion, and unlimitedness of union with All-That-Is.

Seeking that transcendent experience of union in ordinary sex (or drug-enhanced states, for that matter) is doomed to be unsatisfactory, because of those experiences' transitory and impermanent nature. Although we can and do have occasional glimpses of freedom during lovemaking, at the moment of orgasm, or during chemically induced states, they are not lasting, and inevitably leave us feeling separate and lonely again. So we go back for more, hoping against all odds that one more sexual encounter, or hit, or line, or pint of vodka or ice cream will do it.

Human sexuality is a complex phenomenon involving all aspects of our humanity—including the physical, mental, emotional, and spiritual realms. Sexuality and spirituality are inseparable. In fact, many Eastern sages point out that the Kundalini energy—which resides at the base of the spine in the root chakra, and which, when triggered, rises up the spine and is integral to the process of enlightenment—*is* the sexual energy. As Westerners we have been trained to view the world in terms of dualism and hierarchies, but many of the world's mystical traditions reveal a holistic nexus between body, mind, and spirit. Rather than arbitrary dichotomies between body and mind, or spirit and flesh, they teach that the body-mind-spirit are one. This approach heals the long-established fixation among many religious traditions of denigrating the physical realm in favor of a "higher" spiritual reality. Obviously, as part of the physical realm, the body—and in particular, sexuality—has long been relegated to this "lower" reality.

Because Western Judeo-Christian-Islamic beliefs and values spread throughout the world by means of colonization and aggressive programs of conversion and evangelization, many Eastern and Indigenous cultures that previously honored the body and celebrated the erotic now exhibit what some refer to as "erotophobia"—fear of the erotic. Sex became functional, and reproduction its sole purpose. This notion was (and still is) indivisible from the oppression of women as reproductive machines which, like houses, cattle, or other property, belonged to their husbands. When sexuality was split from the sacred, the missionary position between man and woman became the only acceptable form of sex, and any behavior that deviated from that was deemed a "waste of the seed," shameful, and morally reprehensible.

Erotic energy is powerful, sacred, and universal. It is creative and transformative. It is the same as the universal forces of creation, which cause flowers to bloom in sensual displays of color, texture, and scent; which cause volcanoes to erupt and generate new land masses; and which give birth to new, unimaginable star systems. We live in a sexual universe.

When we are able to discard the perceived (and false) dichotomy that separates humanity from the rest of the universe, when we can identify and feel as part of the natural world, then we can acknowledge at a deeper level that we, too, are sexual, and that our sexuality is to be celebrated. Whatever "moral" beliefs and negative judgments now exist about sexuality have been added on by misguided humans. The truth is that when we develop, or remember, a sense of cosmology—of our place in and as part of the cosmos—we realize that all forms of sexuality (and not just its reproductive aspects) are sacred.

Sexuality devoid of its sacred element is limited in scope and is often relegated to the realm of "animalistic" instinctual drives. When sex is not regarded with reverence, it can deteriorate into a weapon of power, control, and dominance, and some of the consequences of that are sexual abuse, rape, and other violent or disrespectful expressions. When we acknowledge its sacred dimension, sexuality makes possible a deepened sense of connection with all of life, and becomes a catalyst for healthy relationships (of all kinds, not just sexual ones).

According to Anand, "'having' sex, as one 'has' other things, seems to be self-limiting. Using sex for relief, entertainment, or reassurance that one is attractive appeals to needs generated by the ego but diverts attention from our real sex potential. We need to bring the Spirit—the inspiration to manifest our highest potential—back into sex."[5]

To the mystics of any religion, the goal of life is nothing less than the direct experience of God. Professing beliefs, attending services, performing particular acts, rituals, or practices, and following dogma is not enough. Many mystical traditions and ancient mystery schools taught sexuality as a direct path to the divine, a means to develop love and compassion, expand consciousness, deepen wisdom, and connect with Spirit.

Explaining that there are really three kinds of food: junk food, health food, and gourmet food, Annie Sprinkle uses food as a metaphor. She describes junk food as "not particularly nourishing or satisfying, but it gets you by." In America, the average sexual experience is equivalent to junk food. She says, "We are a junk sex country." When it comes to health food, according to her theory, "not everyone has a taste for it, and you need a certain skill to prepare it." This is the level of "sex for health: for emotional healing, for curing a headache, for anal or vaginal health, as therapy, or even as aerobic exercise." Finally there is gourmet food, which is "an art. You put a lot more into making it, and it can be a spiritual experience. It is sensuous, deeply satisfying, takes more time, and can make life a magnificent experience. It requires skill and knowledge, but instead of everyday reality, we end up with paradise." That is the level of sacred sexuality.

TANTRA

Tracing its roots back seven thousand years to what we today call India, Tantra is an "ancient Eastern science of spiritual enlightenment . . . which included sexuality as a doorway to ecstasy and enlightenment."[6] The word Tantra means "weaving," a reference to its goal of integrating the different aspects of the self into one unified and coherent whole. It also connotes the consequent "expansion" which then occurs. Evolving originally as a reaction to the rigid asceticism of the Brahmin caste, Tantra grew in popularity, eventually impacting both Taoism and Buddhism.

In *The Eastern Way of Love,* Kamala Devi offers the following description of Tantra:

> Tantra is a cult of ecstasy, a personal religion based on the mystical experience of joy rather than established dogma. Sex is holy to a Tantric. It is worship; it is energizing and life-giving. Tantric art, writings, and religious rituals glorify sex. Tantrics are anti-ascetic; they affirm life. They teach the discovery of the divine through the exaltation of the total human. They use all of the senses, the mind and the Spirit to reach mystic peaks.[7]

Tantra teaches that it is possible to experience a divine connection with the ultimate creative source when the sacredness of the sexual union is consciously acknowledged and cultivated. "This connection lifts your consciousness beyond the physical plane into a field of power and energy much greater than your own. Then you feel linked, through your partner, to everything that lives and loves. You feel that you are a part of the great dance of existence; you feel one with it."[8] Through these practices we can learn to perceive and honor the essential divine nature in our partners—and in that mirror, recognize and accept our own.

The Tantric approach teaches that every experience is an opportunity for spiritual growth, for developing a deeper awareness of who we are and why we act in certain ways, for shedding light on modes of behavior and personality aspects which are often repressed and hidden from view. Because of its inherent inclusiveness, writes Anand, "the Tantra vision *accepts everything.* There is nothing forbidden in Tantra. . . . Tantra places no moral judgment on your sexual preferences. In Tantra, the focus is not so much on with whom you do it but rather on how you do it. Hence, Tantra can be practiced by anyone."[9]

Armin-Christoph Heining, a former Benedictine monk and graduate of Anand's SkyDancing Tantra Institute, confirms that the main goal of Sky-Dancing Tantra is to reach the divine through sex. One of the practices they teach at the Gay Tantric Institute which he founded in Germany is called the "wave of bliss," and its purpose is "to bring people together in the traditional Tibetan position of the *yab yum*—the union of bliss and emptiness—in which, through a combination of sitting position, breathing, and visualization, the partners are able to go higher and higher in energy exchange." At the end, partners fall into a deep sense of blissful silence, similar to high states of meditation. Breathing is the basis for many of the practices, and practitioners are taught how to open up the body through massage, how to express feelings, and how to move energy through the body. Heining states that a "direct experience of the Divine is available through Tantra. It's about a much different level of sexual exchange—honoring the Divine in each other. It's about the God in you making love to the God in me."

Within this discussion of Tantra, it is important to further clarify its meaning. Brother William Schindler is the founder of Ashram West, a gay spiritual community in West Hollywood. With degrees in Sanskrit and Psychology, Schindler has lived and studied in India, where he joined the Ramakrishna Order as a monk for some time. Ramakrishna was a nineteenth-century Bengali mystic regarded by many as an avatar, or incarnation of God. According to Schindler, some of Ramakrishna's teachings were kept secret until recently; among them are "practices and visions, recorded in detailed written conversations with him, that are clearly homoerotic in content, material that has been omitted from the available English translations."

Ashram West offers weekly gatherings that include a social hour, chanting, meditation, pot luck dinner, and discussion, as well as individual instruction and other spiritual events. The teachings are based on the life and "spiritual technologies" of Ramakrishna, who, according to Schindler, is the "only incarnation of God in the recorded history of mysticism who so clearly reveals the ultimate meaning and fulfillment of what it means to be gay."

According to Schindler, the exclusive association of Tantra with sexuality is a recent development and a misconception. In Tantra, every aspect of life is holy and sacred, he says, and that includes sexuality, but "sexuality is no more or less important than anything else." Schindler asserts that the appropriation of the word to refer solely to sexual practices is "simply wrong, and has nothing to do with traditional Tantra." He further explains that Tantric teachings have always been esoteric and taught very secretly. Because of their subtle nature, they often need to be taught individually. "Just calling sex Tantra, or having an intention that it be sacred, does not make it Tantra," he concludes.

Schindler suggests that it is important not to dumb down or romanticize the ecstatic approach to spirituality. In contrast to asceticism, in which sensual experience is renounced in order to strive for a "one-pointed state of mind or a transformative insight," the ecstatic approach embraces sensory experience as a way to experience the Divine in the world. According to Schindler, "encountering the Divine through the erotic is one of the best-known and yet least-understood aspects of the Tantra. Compared with monastic celibacy,

Tantric sexuality may seem the patently more appealing option. Enjoying an exciting sex partner would seem preferable to abstaining from sex entirely. Unless, of course, the goal is God realization, an experience of the divine Self." Schindler emphasizes that the ecstatic approach requires discipline no less than the ascetic approach, and in many ways it is more difficult. That is why ascetic practices are taught publicly, while ecstatic practices are often reserved for qualified initiates. Furthermore, he observes that "unrestricted, unconscious sense enjoyment . . . typically obscures the divine presence, keeping the mind unfocused, restless, and uncontrollably oscillating between poles of pleasure and pain, happiness and misery, hope and despair. Erotic sense enjoyment is the most intense and powerful of all; engaged unconsciously, the erotic conceals the divine most profoundly. . . . Engaged consciously, the erotic is the most direct path to God."

While acknowledging that sexuality is only one of the many actual practices used in Tantra to reach union, others insist that it *is* its primary symbol. Schindler's observations notwithstanding, for the purposes of this discussion we will continue to refer to Tantra in the nontraditional sense of indicating the path of sacred sexuality.

THE TAO OF SEX

In Taoism, sexuality, like everything else, is part of the Tao and therefore considered sacred. We have already seen that Qi Gong teaches how to identify and consciously direct the divine energy or life force that courses through our bodies. Like Tantra, Taoist sexual techniques recognize that above all, sex is about energy.

B. J. Santerre was born in France and now lives in South Miami Beach. An openly gay certified Healing Tao instructor, he explains that according to Taoist belief, the body is covered with meridians, or channels, through which the life energy, or Chi, flows. "In acupuncture we undo blockages in meridians by using needles. Through Taoist practices, such as breathing, Qi Gong, or Tai Chi, we do our own therapy without the needles; we stimulate the meridians and cleanse the system." Santerre adds that by practicing releasing techniques through breathing "you can transform negative emotions, allowing more room for love to grow. It's like composting. All these negative emotions are transformed when they are given back to the earth, so that the rose can bloom."

One of the main goals of Taoist sexual practices is postponing the orgasm in order to attain progressively higher levels of pleasure and consciousness. For men, this means learning how to separate ejaculation from the orgasm.

In *The Multi-Orgasmic Man,* Taoist master Mantak Chia writes that "male sexuality in the West remains incorrectly focused on the inevitably disappointing goal of ejaculation ('getting off') instead of the orgasmic process of lovemaking." His book promotes the benefits—in terms of physical health and longevity, enhanced sexual pleasure, and spiritual development—of learning how to "transform the momentary release of ejaculation into countless peaks of whole-body orgasm." Chia reminds us that it has only been forty years since women were told about multiple orgasms. Since that time, the number of women reporting the experience of multiple orgasms has increased from 14 to over 50 percent, and the main reason for that dramatic increase is simply "that they were told that it was possible."[10]

A chapter titled "Yang and Yang" specifically addresses the concerns of gay men. Interestingly, the authors point out that what makes sex between two men different is the fact that each of their yang energy "charges the other, increasing rather than diminishing their sexual desire." Perhaps this helps explain some gay men's high sexual drives. Interviewed in *Multi-Orgasmic Man*, Santerre says that "most straight men are going to do it once or twice in an evening. For gay men it's really common that they need more than that in a night. With this practice you are going to be able to fully satisfy this desire whether you have a partner or not."[11]

Developing the ability to contain sexual energy is crucial for gay men because of the "expansiveness" and highly charged nature of yang energy. The only way we know to balance that energy is by ejaculating, which brings us to a quieter, calmer, yin-like state. However, according to Taoists beliefs, these constant cycles of ejaculation actually deplete the body and the immune system of life energy. That is the reason why it is crucial that men learn how to cultivate our sexual energy and then circulate it throughout the entire body.

"Learning to circulate sexual energy through practices like the Big Draw," says Santerre, "enables us to have full-body orgasms." The practice consists of learning how to move the sexual energy from the genital area through the spine and up into the crown chakra at the top of the head, then down the front line of the body to the navel and back again to the perineum, located between the anus and the scrotum.

Santerre reassuringly asserts that "orgasm without ejaculation is actually better. When you get it, you never want to go back." In order to really learn how to do it, though, he recommends working with a coach, because "the process can take time and it's hard to get it from a book," pointing out that because there is no one to give feedback, answer questions, or provide adjustments, it is easy to get discouraged or frustrated. Additionally, Santerre recommends taking one's time. He works with clients at more basic levels for a while before even introducing practices involving sexual energies. "These are very strong energies," he says, "and if you have a rusty old wire, and give it too much voltage, it will burst. It's the same thing here; you are playing with high energies, and if you are not used to circulating these powerful energies, it could lead to problems." In some ways, he prefers working with people with terminal diseases, because, in general, he finds them to be more committed. "This work takes commitment," he says, adding that "I can demonstrate a movement or teach the philosophy of Tao, but the person must practice for there to be real progress. This is not magic. People need to want to help themselves."

With its emphasis on health—not morality—when addressing sexuality, Taoism does not teach that there is anything wrong with multiple partners (assuming that one is practicing safer sex). However, the authors observe that Taoist sexual practices require "a profound connection of body, heart, mind, and spirit, which is difficult to achieve with even one partner, let alone many. According to the Tao, one profound sexual union, gay or straight, is better than countless superficial ones."[12]

Cultivating sexual energy may be particularly beneficial for those living with HIV or AIDS. It is not uncommon for people with life-threatening illnesses to lose their sexual drive at a time when they could really benefit from their sexual energy. Guilt and fear can also confound the experience of sexuality for people with HIV, who often feel conflicting attitudes towards sex because they "got it through sex" or "don't want to get others sick."[13]

Santerre, a longtime AIDS survivor who has had two illness-related near-death experiences, is convinced that his Taoist practices are making a difference. For over a year now his viral load has been undetectable, even though he is not on "the cocktail." Besides his regimen of homeopathy, acupuncture, and Taoist self-practice, he "tries to lead a pretty healthy lifestyle, which does include alcohol, meat, and even cigarettes, but only occasionally."

TRIBAL TANTRA

Former Catholic monk and best-selling author Thomas Moore comments in his book, *The Soul of Sex,* that the "very point of sexual experimentation may be to sense together, in mutual generosity and complicity, the joy of transcending rules and expectations. In this spirit, communities have often celebrated important religious festivals with orgies and other kinds of sexual license, breaking into the realm of the spirit by means of sexual overstepping."[14]

As part of her studies of queer and feminist sacred sexuality, Loraine Hutchins, co-author of *Bi Any Other Name,* has been researching sacred sex forums all over the U.S. Although she has found groups scattered across the country, she finds that, for the most part, they are still fringe—"people are still put off by erotic ritual." Hutchins observes that while Tantra is making significant inroads into mainstream America, the emphasis is really on practices such as incorporating intimacy and sexual pleasure, moving orgasm beyond the genitals, and eroticizing other parts of the body. This increasingly popular movement is acceptable, she says, as long as it involves couples—"anything beyond that becomes divisive and controversial." Hutchins, who is involved with the fledgling Polyamory Movement—which is trying to expand and redefine traditional concepts of family and relationships—hopes to create community by convening spiritually based safer sex parties in the D.C. area.

Traditionally, says Joseph Kramer, the men's movement has said very little about sex: "Iron John has no genitals. Although now that's changing, because sex sells." After founding the Body Electric School in Oakland in 1984 (named after one of Walt Whitman's poems), Kramer helped open other Body Electric schools in Berlin, Hamburg, Zurich, and Amsterdam. He sold the Oakland center in 1992, and founded the EroSpirit Research Institute, a "think tank for queer ecstatics," a place where "sexual healers and teachers, erotic choreographers and bodyworkers, theologians and AIDS educators" could convene to produce and distribute erotic information.

Kramer's signature work is his two-day, hands-on workshop, Celebrating the Body Erotic, which he once described as a place where men could "relearn sex as sacred, playful, non-addictive, non-compulsive, and non-stop."[15] Although he has not taught it himself in several years, the course is offered (for men and, increasingly, for women) by Body Electric schools all over the world. Influenced by Taoist, Tantric, and Native American rituals, the workshop combines shamanic drumming and conscious breathing with several processes, which help foster intimacy through eye contact, create an energetic connection between the heart and the genitals, and cultivate erotic energy through group erotic massage without ejaculation.

To Kramer, the techniques he created and synthesized are about "disengaging the normal control system." The image he conjures up is one of Gulliver tied down by a bunch of little threads—in this case, unexamined behavior habits and societal conditioning which keep us from freedom, happiness, and fulfillment. "What I've created is a social context in which men can have an erotic experience outside of their normal pattern that they have learned—with people that may not even be their type. Normally, eroticism stays within the same river bank, the same rut, from the time of puberty. What I give them is a safe, playful, different approach to sex, a different way of running energy in their bodies, an opportunity to have a new experience, something different. Even though they may not know it, people really want to experience things differently; letting go of our desire to control everything is really refreshing."

An erotic massage à la Kramer—whether an individual session or in a group setting—normally ends in a process whose name, the Big Draw, was borrowed from Mantak Chia. After experiencing continuous conscious breathing (Rebirthing style) with simultaneous massage and genital stimulation for an extended period of time, the person receiving the massage is instructed to tense up all his muscles while at the same time taking a deep breath, holding it for thirty seconds, and then releasing it. The effect, according to Kramer, can be quite dramatic: "Half the people enter into a trance state, and some have profound mystical experiences, including visitations from ancestors, colors, songs, time distortion, understanding what death is ('If this is what death is I'm totally comfortable with it'), feeling one with everything, losing all sense of boundaries, sensing the void. Often, they will have images of God, whether it's a triangle with an eye in it, Buddha, or Jesus." Still visibly moved by the memory, Kramer shares a story of a time when, after a workshop, he was approached by a gay man who was dying with AIDS. Breaking down and crying, the man said to him, "I couldn't say this in a group of gay men right after we had our cocks jerked off, but after the Big Draw I looked up and saw the heart of Jesus, and the heart of Jesus invited me to come up into it. Here I am in what I thought was a sex workshop, and all of a sudden I'm in the heart of Jesus!"

Kramer thinks that this type of initiatory experience presented by his work would be specially supportive for young people who are in the process of coming out. In providing a safe and sacred context for their sexuality, he asks, "What if they were initiated into this level first, and within this erotic playground found someone they wished to go further with?"

Concerning the question of AIDS prevention and sexual behavior in the gay *population* (which, he is quick to point out, is not *really* a community), Kramer does not believe that the problem is one of promiscuity. "I don't think that a promiscuous lifestyle is the problem, because Tribal Tantra [what he calls his group sex work] is promiscuous in the sense that it's being erotic with many people," he notes. "But it's no-risk sex," he adds, "it's erotic touch, erotic play."

EVOLUTIONARY MASTURBATION

The new focus of Kramer's work is "erotic mentoring," his term for masturbation coaching. Asserting that the foundation of a powerful sexuality with others lies in self-sexuality, Kramer states that "you can tell everything about a person's spirituality by how they masturbate," adding that the good news is that "you can quickly change your spirituality by changing how you masturbate." He suggests that the major change we can implement is incorporating conscious, rhythmic breathing techniques. In a sex-negative culture, one in which we never receive any substantive education about sex, masturbation is a learned behavior, one which usually involves "constriction of the body." In fact, Kramer says, it is the constriction of the muscles and the holding of breath that contribute to an expelling of sperm, tension, and energy during ejaculation. He believes that, to a great degree, ejaculation is shame-based, because we are not taught or prepared to handle pleasure. "The ego does not want mystical experiences, and that's what sex is; that's what Tantra is—a fast track. If you could really stay right on the path, it would dissolve the ego fast." He continues:

> In a sense, ejaculation is actually about getting rid of a feeling, getting rid of pleasure in a quick way. We are almost embarrassed to be carrying this pleasure around; it's related to shame and body image, and the resulting masturbatory experience is far from being sensuous. It's also about the heart and genitals never coming together; release-oriented masturbation is not connected to the heart. There is a Cherokee teacher who refers to masturbation as "heart-pleasuring." I call it "heart-warming."

While discussing these techniques and, specifically, non-ejaculatory orgasm (with or without the Big Draw), Kramer reports that over his years of teaching, at least one hundred times people have voiced, even shouted out, "Oh, my God! If this is what's possible, then I'm never going to come again!" Once we learn that we have different options, he adds, we realize that there is more pleasure because we are not stuck in a certain pattern: "We can go on and on, we can melt, or we can be separate and spark off of each other." Kramer believes that besides the increased pleasure resulting from learning to control ejaculation, the clenching and toning of the anus muscles necessary for the process are essential to the flow of energy through the body and to feeling good, healthy, and not constricted. "It's in every sex book, but don't take my word or anybody else's for it," he says. "Try it for yourself; give yourself options and try them; at least try it for one month." Besides the archetypes of healer and caregiver, Kramer personifies a modern version of the ancient role of sacred prostitute—or Sacred Intimate, the term he occasionally uses.

LEATHERSEX

Many people are repelled by or afraid of the S/M scene; others are just not attracted to it. Still others, however, feel that inherent in that type of extreme experience is the opportunity for self-transcendence. There is always the potential for transcendence and transformation in the act of surrendering, whether it's to a guru, a leather master, one's concept of God, or even a rock, for that matter. And there is the potential for selfless, sensitive, and transformative service from the perspective of a top, if they are doing it consciously with that intention.

Increasingly, there are some within the leather community—a frontier within a frontier—who are speaking out and describing their experiences in terms of spirituality. Bobby Gray writes in *White Crane Journal* that "it is time for Leatherfolk to 'come out' of the spiritual 'closet,' time to declare that there is more to Leathersex than 'play,' time to express our 'spiritual dimension' and joyously celebrate our transcendent experiences, time to look at ourselves in a different way, as spiritual seekers—not just thrill seekers. If there is to be reality in the concept of 'brotherhood' among Leatherfolk, it may well be from the spiritual dimension that it grows."[16]

Gray speaks in terms of a "Leather Soul"—a drive to experience that "which is beyond the common and the ordinary, to step out on the edge and find . . . What? Some Leatherfolk describe it as 'going out there.' Somewhere beyond pain, beyond simple pleasure, beyond simple sensory output. This is an experience which may include pleasure and pain but which transcends both, an experience often so powerful, it is as life changing as religious conversion. . . . Seeking this 'out there' experience is what I and my friends call spirituality."[17]

The word "ecstasy" originates from the ancient Greek *ek stasis,* which may be translated as "standing apart." In this sense ecstasy refers not so much to the blissful feeling with which we have come to associate the word, but rather, to a state of being where the "Witness Consciousness" or the "Experiencer" is "standing apart from anything that it is experiencing. At this level, there is no judgment of good or bad, right or wrong, pleasant or unpleasant. . . . There is also no time."[18] This particular way of looking at the concept of ecstasy, found in one of my Rebirthing texts, provides a possible explanation for what occurs in Leathersex activities, and may help us understand some of the experiences of consciousness expansion people are obviously having in those settings.

"S/M is a spiritual discipline," says Elias Farajajé-Jones, while explaining that humiliation and denigration are part of the initiatory path. "The old person has to be completely dismembered before they can be reconstructed." In his book *Gay Body*, Mark Thompson also alludes to this while describing his experiences in the world of sadomasochism. "By submitting at the feet of a masterful guide, I was, in effect, signing a contract wherein my ego-driven self could be temporarily annihilated, loosed from its mooring."[19] In order to grow spiritually, Thompson suggests, it is imperative to expose one's limits, and "submit to fiery tests." To him, an initiation "must necessarily involve ritual death—that is, transcendence of ego—before a deeper awareness of life can be reached."[20]

While we may not all have personally desired or experienced S/M practices, we can understand how the border between pleasure and pain is not always clearly demarcated. I do believe that for some people, S/M can be a path to enlightenment, an effective way to achieve ego dissolution and the resulting expansion which could undoubtedly be classified as a spiritual experience. For some, myself included, it's hard to grasp how some S/M activities could not remain denigrating. How does one reinstate the inherent worth of a human being after he or she has licked the soles of your boots, or been on the receiving end of golden showers? Others warn that S/M can too easily lend itself to a misuse of power and feel that we need to get beyond dominance and submission roles, which are both exploitative. Perhaps due to ignorance or naïveté, some believe that aspects of the S/M scene still seem to be antithetical to what I consider to be our ultimate goals: to help each other realize our inherent value as humans, to transcend the limitations of our social conditioning, and to become more than we have ever been before.

LESBIAN SEXUALITY

This discussion of sexuality has been particularly focused on gay male sexuality. Although I have included the voices of several (mostly) queer women in the chapter, overall its balance is clearly weighted toward men's issues. There are two basic reasons for that: 1) I am not a lesbian; I am obviously much more in tune with male sexuality; and I am unqualified to take on the complexities of lesbian sexuality, and 2) I felt compelled by the current "sex wars" in the men's community to try to bring the discussion of sexuality to the next level of dialogue, framed within a higher context. To me, it's a matter of life and death. Of course, most of what was discussed about sacred sexuality applies to anyone, regardless of gender or sexual orientation.

I believe that perhaps one of the ways in which lesbians can advance the overall evolution of the species may be in the area of sexuality. I think it is pretty evident that women are innately—physiologically—more in tune with the natural rhythms of the earth. Also, in terms of evolution, it seems that sex is a bigger deal for the female of any species. In the natural world, it is generally advantageous for the males of the species to spread their genes among as many female receptacles as possible, thus increasing the chances that one of their genes, and not one belonging to another competitor, will be the one to impregnate the female and thus ensure its survival. This is one of the reasons why men in general—regardless of sexual orientation—tend to be more promiscuous than females.

In contrast, scientific research generally indicates that for the female it pays to be selective, waiting for the candidate with the strongest and best genes, and the one most likely to help rear the offspring. Even from a physiological perspective, it makes sense that women have evolved a higher propensity for caution about sexuality, since they are actually taking something into their bodies. While it could be argued that so do many gay men who engage in anally or orally receptive behavior, we are referring to adaptive behavior patterns that may have developed for each of the sexes over thousands of years. In contrast, it is easier for men to just "stick it in anything that moves"; and there is, one would think, less physical and psychological risk involved in that than in the act of being penetrated.

Jalaja Bonheim, author of *Aphrodite's Daughters: Women's Sexual Stories and the Journey of the Soul,* notes that if you look at the experience of women in general, up until the very recent past there was no effective means of birth control, and untold numbers of women died in childbirth. "Subconsciously," she observes, "for women it's been ingrained at a very deep level that sex is a big deal," one fraught with the constant danger of pregnancy and death. For women, "the connection between sex and death was always real, while for gay men, that awareness was missing up until recently, when, in some strange way, nature forced them to face that through AIDS. Sex is not a lightweight thing."

Because of their intrinsic sensitivity to natural cycles and their evolved respect for sexuality, one could claim, then, that women in general are more in tune with the deeper expressions of sexuality. For the most part, women also tend to be more in tune with their emotions than men, who are far too often conditioned to suppress them. Even physiologically, the process of sexual arousal takes longer for women; therefore, factors such as intimacy, love, affection, the right setting, and the right "mood" generally acquire more significance.

Could we not conclude, then, that women in general have an advantage at this point in our evolution in terms of how equipped they are to travel the cutting edge of sexuality, and particularly, sexuality as a spiritual path? In the case of women loving other women, it could be argued that those advantages are heightened by the elimination of the potential interference of inter-gender competition, and by the reduction of the traditional patriarchal associations of dominance, control, and possession with which sex is imbued (although, admittedly, these power dynamics have been internalized by many women as well). Furthermore, because most lesbians and gay men are freed from the possibility of procreation (which we pursue only intentionally, and usually very consciously), we are naturally predisposed to learn about the intricacies of sexuality for its own sake. As outsiders, lesbians are also less bound than heterosexual women by societal rules and conditioning. Thus, the case could be made that lesbians are ideally suited for sexual exploration, to enact the role of scouts, pathfinders, and trailblazers in the arena of sexuality for the entire species, and to lead the way in discovering how far we can take it, what planes of consciousness and new ways of being can be attained.

Of course, in no way is this theorizing meant to restrict lesbian sexual expression, nor imply that either heterosexuals (or gay men) cannot serve this function. In fact, we know that many have; that's what the ancient Tantric traditions—most of which clearly emphasized heterosexual love—are all about. I simply suggest that lesbians are in a unique place to do this, that they may have a built-in advantage to assume this function.

In her book, *Lesbian Sacred Sexuality,* Diane Mariechild observes that "in lesbian relationships there is the strong desire to merge and reclaim lost parts of ourselves. This desire to merge, the heart's longing for union/reunion, holds the possibility for a powerful transformation."[21] Although Jalaja Bonheim is heterosexual, she works with many lesbian and gay couples in her psychotherapy practice. She has found that the merging that can occur among lesbians has a shadow aspect, and can manifest as a diminished sexual life after a couple of years—in other words, "lesbian bed death." Bonheim explains that this "hooks into the sexual repression of women in general. Women are trained not to own sexual desire, not to initiate sex. What is occurring, in the case of some lesbian couples, is that their sexual life and energy is not being fueled or nourished; it's like having a fire and letting it go out because you don't feed it. Lesbians need to tend that sacred fire and not let it go out. They need to keep sex alive. Most couples I've worked with really grieve that loss of sex."

Selah Martha is the Director of the Women's Program at Body Electric Oakland. Based on her own experience of being both with men and women, and identifying as bisexual, she feels that she has gained insight into what she refers to as the "dynamic between security and passion. With women, it's almost as if a meltdown, or a merging, occurs. Then it's harder to create a charge—which means more risk taking, more hunger for the other, for mystery. There needs to be some separation in order for a charge to occur. If you merge there's no one to relate to." Martha points out that we all, even men, have a tendency to merge; with women, it becomes more intense because women are "more complex emotionally, or perhaps just more aware of their emotional complexity." When asked to describe her personal experience of merging, she explains that in previous relationships with women, she had "an unreasonable expectation that they would take care of me, that they would understand everything I was thinking and feeling without my having to even say it. And that they would never do anything to hurt or frighten me. I felt that in such deep intimacy I should be able to do anything I want and they should understand. I now realize that was immature and regressive thinking. I was seeking merging, and that just doesn't go with adult sexuality, because, for adults, that level of merging can only be felt in union with divine presence. I was seeking unconditional love, and I learned to go to God for that, not to my partners. In a relationship, there needs to be a combination of trust, intimacy, and separateness—we need to feel our own separateness so that we can truly reach out for another."

Judy Grahn describes her experience of sacred sexuality with charming honesty and humor. She explains that it wasn't until her forties that she learned how to do it, and that the main instruction she received from the woman who taught her was to "hold still and trust." Grahn says that both lovers have to agree that this is what they're going to do, and trust that they will come through for each other. The partners take turns giving and receiving sexual stimulation. The one doing the stimulating is "containing the space" for the experience, which can also be described as "spotting," such as would occur in weight training, diving, or a trampoline. (Leave it to a lesbian to come up with a sports metaphor for describing sacred sex!) In any case, the "spotter" agrees that she will continue even if her partner is "passed out, in la-la land." The one receiving can then "go out as far as she wants."

Describing the experience, which she also calls "psychic sex," Grahn says that it is important to understand "the sex center as a place of phenomenal energy that can connect us to each other and other creatures in very powerful ways, but we need to do it from a place of heart." It is important to "set a sacred space about it," she adds, "to set a sacred intention." When Grahn and her partner began to experiment with sacred sex, they had no one with whom they could speak about it. So they kept a notebook, and, after a period of ecstasy which could have "gone on for hours," one would elbow the other to indicate it was her turn to write down the experience; they took copious notes of their "exquisite visions," so that they would not forget them and could later compare them. They began to realize that there was a great deal of similarity in their visions—that, in Grahn's words, "we were in the same mind." Eventually, they learned to visualize the energy, and where in the body it was originating from. They tried to devise ways to try to chart this energy, and even invented a new vocabulary to describe their experiences—words like "volt-o-meter, to gauge the voltage change." The shared aspect of the experience never ceased to amaze them, and is the "psychic element" Grahn refers to.

Conscious Relationships

Regardless of where we fall on the spectrum of human sexual behavior, few things seem to occupy our attention and capture our energy as fully as our love relationships—or the absence thereof.

Most of us have experienced the intense rapture of "being in love," with the ensuing dissolution of personal ego boundaries and the collapse of interpersonal walls, which keep us in the illusion of separateness. In that ecstatic state, we feel invincible, like nothing can go wrong. It's no wonder that we spend so much time preparing our bodies, reading self-help books and romance novels, attending seminars, and fantasizing about meeting that "special one."

The sad thing is that our relationships, like that indescribable and unpredictable period of "being in love," most often turn out to be only temporary, stopgap respites to our sense of loneliness. For in reality, at some point after the honeymoon ends and the walls of individual will and personal preferences begin to rise up again, we realize that we are still—and ultimately—alone. Too often, our genuine and heartfelt attempts at having successful relationships fail because of our own unrealistic expectations that one person should fill the gaping hole in our guts. It is imperative for us to realize that no one human being can fill that void. Well, perhaps only one: ourselves.

In *The Road Less Traveled,* one of the bestselling books of all time, psychiatrist Scott Peck defines love as "the will to extend one's self for the purpose of nurturing one's own or another's spiritual growth."[22] I highly recommend that anyone interested in developing a conscious relationship read the entire section dedicated to love in Peck's book. Before we can have relationships that work, we must assume responsibility for cultivating our own gardens—for discovering who we are; what values we hold; what makes us tick; what turns us on as human beings, and what doesn't; and for identifying those areas in ourselves which are less than whole.

We are much more likely to experience success when, having done our inner work, we are able to approach relationships without grasping and neediness. Our attempts will yield better results when, having identified in ourselves those areas of strength and those in need of healing, we look for another to complement us, to learn and grow with, to partner with us in life, whether for a short while or for the rest of our lives. Obviously, an important step is clearing our own obstacles to relationships, including negative beliefs and misconceptions or myths we may have about relationships. As *A Course in Miracles* says: "Your task is not to seek for love, but merely to seek and find all of the barriers within yourself that you have built against it."[23]

There are many models of relationship, and it is important to find one that works for you, one that you feel comfortable with. Here we will only touch superficially on what is obviously a much broader topic. The issue of monogamy has already been alluded to several times in this chapter on sexuality. During the first decades of gay liberation, monogamy was typically rejected and scorned by many gay people as a patriarchal, heterosexist construct, something no self-respecting queer would ever engage in. However, in recent times advocates for monogamy seem to be coming out of the closet in droves.

Monogamy is certainly a viable path, but not one for everyone. "Maria," who has been in a committed relationship with another woman for over twenty-one years, believes that monogamy is indeed "an intense spiritual journey, one in which you get to work with another person through all barriers to intimacy." She observes, however, that our society does put a premium on longterm monogamous relationships, and different people have different needs. "Just because it works for me doesn't mean that others should pursue it."

Both Tom Moon, a psychotherapist whose column "The Examined Life" appears regularly in *San Francisco Frontiers,* and Kurt Wagner, founder of Manifest, a Bay Area organization that specializes in the spiritual and emotional "re-awakening" of gay men, work with individuals and couples striving to make sense of their relationships. Interestingly, they report that the majority of their clients who have open relationships find them to be very difficult. Wagner reports that most of his clients actually *hated* the experience. This, of course, does not imply that everyone has a similar experience. In those cases where an open arrangement seems to work, both partners are in genuine agreement about the type of relationship they want, and its boundaries and rules are clearly demarcated and consistently honored by both parties.

Regardless of the particular form a relationship takes, the context in which we hold it is important. Ram Dass teaches that there are two basic approaches to relationships. On the first level, which he refers to as "psychological symbiosis," two separate individuals merely come together unconsciously and out of needfulness, to fulfill each other's needs.

On the second level, relationships are approached consciously as a spiritual path. Within this context, Ram Dass suggests three ways to view them. First, relationships are a means to fulfill our basic human needs for sex, love, and intimacy so that we can stop obsessing about them and focus on our spiritual practices and growth. Here a relationship serves more as a support system and has little to do directly with our spiritual work. Second, relationships can also serve as catalysts for our spiritual evolution by challenging us to grow; to stretch; to become more accepting, less judgmental, and more compassionate; and by flushing out personality areas in need of attention and improvement. Here we are intentionally using the relationship *as* spiritual process. Ram Dass calls this "relationship as yoga, as a vehicle for the two coming into the One." Finally, and I suspect most of us don't need to overly concern ourselves about this one yet, there are relationships where both parties enjoy the full realization that they are a manifestation of the Divine and simply revel in reflecting that for one another. The relationship becomes an expression of "the dance of the One playing as two." We are "resting in the One," *and* we also happen to be in relationship. The rest of this brief discussion will focus on relationships as a path to spiritual evolution.

When approached with intention, relationships present an invaluable opportunity for spiritual growth. Essentially, we are creating a safe space where all our "stuff"—our insecurities, jealousies, control issues, and other unhealed dynamics—will be triggered and allowed to surface so that we can look at them and then make the necessary or desired changes. In this context, relationships can be extremely challenging. However, the payoff is quick growth, since it is generally difficult to grow or make progress in a vacuum. Manifest's Kurt Wagner agrees that we need the mirror that relationships provide, and that they are, indeed, one of the fastest ways through which we can discover who we are.

In this sense, relationships are a laboratory for self-awareness and self-discovery. Undoubtedly, it takes great courage to persistently confront ourselves or our partners when we are committed to living truthfully and being fully ourselves in a relationship. Needless to say, facing our unhealed behavior patterns and having our "buttons" constantly pressed is not fun. However, the truth is that those buttons are getting pushed even if we are not aware of it, and, whether we know it or not, we are constantly reacting from unhealed areas and unresolved past relationships. It is preferable then, to submit ourselves to the occasionally harrowing process of self-examination, one which at least holds the promise of eventual healing and freedom from the subconscious patterns which have been the source of unhappiness in our previous relationships.

A conscious relationship requires constant work and attention. It is an ongoing struggle to make sure we are coming from a place of truth and not one of reactivity, a continuing process of self-analysis and checking in with oneself to determine: Am I just "being right" in this situation? Am I projecting my stuff onto my partner? Is there a legitimate concern here, or is the problem being caused by my judgments or my expectations that my partner be or behave in a certain way? Am I trying to change him or re-create her in my own image? Am I really committed to being who I say I am, or are these just nice words I am using to feel good about myself?

There are many benefits. One is the level of trust, loyalty, and commitment that is engendered. We begin to view our lovers as partners in life, as fellow voyagers with whom we share all of life's moments—both good and bad, exciting and mundane. It is a wonderful privilege to be able to witness each other's growth. What we strive to create is a safe and supportive environment where each partner *actively* supports the other in their individual evolutionary journey, where each is committed to their own growth and to the growth of the other—above all else.

For "Maria," all relationships are an "opportunity to practice my intentions in life, whether that intention is to be a loving mate, an intimate friend, or a contributor to my community." Being a loving mate means "being willing to tell the truth when I'm in the wrong, to ask what it is that will bring the other pleasure and fulfillment, to refrain from fixing them, to support them in whatever their goals and dreams are, even if they don't include me. It is more important that they be fulfilled than they be with me." One of Maria's practices is constantly asking herself: "How can I demonstrate *right now* what it is to be a loving mate?"—a challenging, powerful, and transformative spiritual discipline by any standard.

Relationships are also a place to test our limits; they are about our prodding each other to be more than we have even imagined we could be. They are about our calling each other forth to our magnificence. Although that includes calling each other on our shortcomings as well, the practice is to do so from a place of understanding and compassion, not one of self-righteousness. The challenge is not to come from a place of fixing or teaching one another; it is about remaining vigilant for any signs of neediness or controlling tendencies in ourselves. It is about approaching the relationship as equal and evolving individuals who are freely coming together to love each other, enjoy each other, and travel together on life's journey. For how long, no one ever knows. Because of that, we try to treasure each opportunity and strive to stay in the present. Life goes by fast enough.

Our lover is not only someone we do things with, share a home with, and have sex with, but a partner in evolution. We come together not just to fill a hole (literally and figuratively, but particularly the latter). We come together in order to become better human beings, and support each other to grow—to become more compassionate, less judgmental, more flexible, more patient, more understanding; to discover new ways of being, sexually and otherwise. To me, relationships involve a (perhaps unconscious) soul-level agreement to push each other along individual paths of healing and spiritual evolution. They are a place to discover: What are my limits? When does my heart close and I stop loving? When do I move into being right, and allow the flow of love and communication to be stopped by that? When do I move into thinking I'm better or know more? At what point does that become more important than being in a space of love, acceptance, and harmony? How far am I willing to go? How much am I willing to give?

Of course, there will be times when we just want to chuck the whole thing. "This is too much work," we'll think, perhaps (if we are monogamous) resenting the fact that our single friends are going out, having fun, and getting laid every weekend. This is the grass-is-always-greener syndrome. The truth is that many of those same friends wish they had what we have. It can get very lonely out there, even when one is surrounded by hundreds of hot bodies.

During the rough times, it is important that you give the relationship time and room to breathe. Try not to act simply in response to hormonal impulses. If and when you consciously choose to leave the relationship, there will be plenty of opportunities for sexual interactions; for most of us, these are readily available. Perhaps at some time you will need to renegotiate the rules of the relationship and try an open relationship of some type. It is also important not to react from anger but instead come from that place of truth which resides beneath the anger, the hurt, and the sadness. Whatever happens, honor the relationship, this childlike third entity that you have created together. Think of it as something sacred, a holy laboratory for evolution. Even if it is not "forever," even if it is conflict-ridden, it is an opportunity to get clearer about who we are, what we stand for, what we're about; an opportunity to learn to love at deeper levels. It is an opportunity for selfless giving—to give more just when we thought there was nothing more left to give. That is the point where growth occurs, in that expansion of personal boundaries and previous limitations. When we keep stretching these out, and expanding our zones of comfort, we widen our definition of who we are. Our self-concept gets pushed out to include new behaviors, new ways of being, new growth. Often, the resulting experience is one of: "Wow! I never thought I could do that!" That's how growth happens.

In this discussion of selflessness, it is important to clarify that what is being suggested here is not an unhealthy codependence, or being somebody's doormat. It is also not about using the relationship to play small or concealing "our light under a bushel." It is not about hiding from ourselves, from the world, from our life mission. On the contrary, it is about fully becoming who we are—in all our shining majesty.

Sometimes we do outgrow relationships, and that's okay. This need not be a sign of failure, and it does not have to be an occasion for interpersonal strife. To whatever degree is possible at the time, it is helpful to remember to be thankful that the relationship has taken us this far, and cannot take us any further on our path. The truth is that more than likely, both partners have served each other well, even if that is not evident at the time of separation. Wouldn't it be great if we could simply recognize that, thank each other, bow to each other, and wish each other well on our journeys? Wouldn't life be easier if we were able to let go of our attachment to drama, and remember that ultimately, we are all doing our best—even if, frequently, our best is not that great?

As a final note, one good measure of any relationship, not just intimate loving ones, is whether it is supporting our growth and evolution as human beings in every sense of the word: physically, emotionally, mentally, and spiritually. I always gauge a relationship by whether it's helping me become a better human being, one who is stronger, clearer, more loving, more compassionate—a brighter light in the world.

The Sexual Frontier

We have explored several significant aspects of sex and relationships—the different faces of passion. We have seen how, particularly in the latter half of the twentieth century, humanity has been testing the limits of the sexual frontier. And, not surprisingly, how queer people—pioneers that we are, after all—have been and remain at the forefront of that movement.

Gay men in particular seem to have taken to an extreme the exploration of unrestrained sexuality—some would say, with dire consequences. Personally, I find nothing intrinsically wrong, morally or psychologically, with the practice of anonymous and multi-partner sex. As the section on Archetypal Sex indicates, it is obviously possible for people to find sexual, emotional, and even spiritual fulfillment through this form of sexual expression. However, I suspect that for many others, it is not meeting their fundamental needs for human warmth, affection, and intimacy. My guess is that the majority of people are not approaching sexuality with a very clear or conscious intention and consequently are missing out on a vital means of self-discovery, personal fulfillment, and spiritual evolution. My hope is that this discussion will at least inspire some of us to approach it a bit more consciously, to bring our experience to the next level, to expand our sexual repertoire.

What does sexual liberation ultimately mean? If one is compulsively having sex with ten different men per night several times a week—risking one's health, perpetuating the prevalence of the virus in our community, putting others at risk—that doesn't feel very enlightening or liberating. Even removing the element of personal or public health from the equation, to me, that's still no liberation. Sexual compulsion is only a different form of enslavement.

In some ways, the path of anonymous sex seems like a dead-end road. Hasn't that frontier already been crossed? And, if not, what will it take to reach it? Will another one hundred, five hundred, or a thousand anonymous encounters do it? Will we then find happiness, or fulfillment, or meaning, or satisfaction? I doubt it. I suspect that at that level, the desire for ever more sex becomes insatiable. To me, the untested frontier is in the realm of conscious, sacred sexuality, discovering how far and how high we can take that experience with a partner or partners. Ironically, the cutting edge of sex may just be in the type of sexual experiences which are likelier to occur in safe spaces, incorporating elements of intimacy, trust, and love.

How different might our sexual expression be if only we realized that we are the eyes and ears and mouth and hands and feet and, yes, even the sexual organs of Spirit in this material plane. That through us—*as* us—It can experience this realm and know Itself. What a humbling and sobering and freeing and revolutionary thought that is! If we could only remember and live from that realization for just twenty minutes a week, our lives would change drastically. No longer would we place ourselves in situations less than honoring of our bodies, which ignore the majesty that human beings are. No longer would we approach the gift of our sexuality casually and unconsciously, but instead we might recognize it as an indescribable miracle and potential source of radical ecstasy and transformation. No longer would we experience ourselves as lacking or unworthy and act out in ways that reflect that. No longer would we feel separate, alienated, and lonely, and feel compelled to find human contact in cold, dark, dangerous places and unfulfilling situations. No longer would we feel driven to act in ways that were less than affirming of who we are. No longer would we forget that our bodies *are* temples—in the sense of something that contains within it a divine presence—and neglect to respect them accordingly.

Sex with love is my trip. I'm into making love. To me that means literally bringing the exquisite, ecstatic energy of love into the world. It means being a clear, pure channel for the erotic. It is possible to make love with a complete stranger; I've had that experience. But usually making love occurs within the context of loving and trusting relationships. By reclaiming the sacred aspects of sexuality, and introducing some of the concepts and techniques discussed earlier, we can continually revitalize our relationships. Monogamous sex does not have to be boring or deteriorate into routine, repetitive ruts. As someone said, monogamy does not have to mean monotony. We have seen that with the right intention and know-how, even solo sex—redefined by Joseph Kramer as "heart-pleasuring" and "heart-warming"—can be a vehicle for healing and opening our hearts.

According to one of our wisest elders, poet and artist James Broughton:

The Holy Male is potential in every one of us. Men should be shown how to reach and to cherish the Divine in one another. A quest for the ecstatic goes beyond cruising for a congenial sex object. It is not enough to get it up, get it on, and get it over with. In the urgency of our present situation we should look toward connecting imaginatively with the souls of our brothers. How else will we become soul brothers? This does not mean denying sexuality. On the contrary, sexualized feelings as a creative force is the great drive for the flourishing of the Spirit. We need lovingness in all our relationships. Love can take sexual drive on a glory drive to the soaring heavens.[24]

Of course, the same applies to the Holy Female. In the words of Diane Mariechild:

Sexuality and spirituality are facilitated by a deep intimacy with one's inner nature, with the physical body, and intimacy with the natural world. This intimacy brings a quality of loving connection and sensitivity to life. It is energetic, spontaneous, and joyful. Sexual or creative energy radiates though all life. Erotic, creative, divine, Goddess energy. Fertile, rich, passionate, abundant energy. There is nothing—that is no thing—that exists outside of or is untouched by this energy. It is life itself and as such is sacred. The sexual act is but one expression of this energy. We make our sex sacred, in the same way we make any life experience sacred, through our intention.[25]

Sexuality can be much more than the "frantic moment and shy good-bye" Evita sings about. It does not have to be a "hurried and tense affair, fraught with the dangers of disease (transmitted by partners who do not take the time for thorough preparation), but a safe and healthy exchange between partners who respect and know each other intellectually, emotionally, and sensually before they enter into sexual union." Margo Anand says that "what is urgently needed today [is] a playful, loving, and comprehensive perspective on sex that makes it safe and ecstatic at the same time. A modern resurrection of Tantra can offer these alternatives, reducing the carelessness that contributes to sexually transmitted diseases."[26]

As we have seen, healthy, conscious sexuality is about learning to love ourselves. You don't need to take drugs to experience expanded states in sex. There are techniques that will create states of being that will blow your socks off. There are people and resources out there that will turn you on to practices that will blow your minds away—safely, with no chemical repercussions. We want you alive. Play, but please, play safely.

When we really break the chains of fear, guilt, and shame which have bound our sexuality not only will we set ourselves free but we will set society free. We have been gifted with a delicious and awe-inspiring sexuality. When we learn to reunite sex and Spirit in our lives, we will experience change and healing beyond our wildest dreams. As we heal, our relationships will be healed. And we will then "begin to heal the planet itself—for according to the Tao, we are as much a part of nature as nature is part of us."[27]

4 Coming Out

Introduction: Coming Out

What are some of the actions you will take to advance your spiritual process, your own process of evolution? What is next for you in that process? What are you willing to do to make a difference in our community, and in the world? These are some of the questions we will explore in this final chapter. The answers will surely come from within, as we explore together possible courses of action and hear from other queer folk actively making a difference in the world.

Coming out is a crucial step in terms of our spiritual development. There are many books available on coming out, which, as most of us know, is a multi-level and continuous process extending throughout our lives—because every time we meet a new person, begin a new job, or move to a new neighborhood or city, we face that choice all over again.

The Rev. Deborah Johnson, an African-American lesbian, has been involved in social and political movements for a long time. In college, she majored in political science with a minor in religion. She received her first spiritual "calling" when she was only sixteen: "At first, it blew me away; I thought it meant I had to become straight." Reminding us that "the personal is political—something we learned from the feminist movement"—Johnson says that "even the least politically involved gay or lesbian couples who just go out and have a baby are changing the world in ways that are probably more lasting than any piece of legislation we could come up with. That act is profoundly political—and profoundly spiritual—because they are redefining the family, and recreating society."

Christina Hutchins, a United Church of Christ (UCC) minister, observes that "to believe is to care and to care is to do. Faith belongs in the world; it's not just about personal faith. It's about moving, changing the world toward increased vitality for all people. Faith is about doing, rather than just about being." Hutchins and her lover, who is also an ordained minister, walked together in a Pride Day celebration; her description of that event helps illustrate the symbolic power of coming out. "We walked hand in hand the entire length of the parade wearing signs on our backs reading 'Rev. Sally' and 'Rev. Christina,' holding hands and raising our arms. Our bodies were telling a story. It was the story of our love, but it was also the story of the community's love, the love of God. To me, those are all connected, and I need those connections. They nourish me as well as challenge me."

As a further illustration of the power of becoming visible, I offer my experience with Paulina, a fifteen-year-old Mexican-American youth delegate from Los Angeles, whom I met at the 1997 URI Conference. On the first day we were paired off together and asked to do an "appreciative inquiry" process, which involved interviewing each other with a series of questions designed for getting to know more about the other person: what they did, why they were there. Paulina and I hit it off, and she became my little sister for the week. A couple of days later she expressed interest in an afternoon field trip from the Stanford campus to San Francisco, which she had never visited. Figuring that the average teenager does not have a lot of financial resources, I arranged to pay for her twenty-dollar fare. Although I had mentioned to her what I did for a living, apparently my being gay did not register. Paulina was stunned when I read my statement. She avoided me the rest of that day, but on Friday, as we were getting ready to go home, she approached me with a hand-made thank-you card. Moved to tears as we embraced and bid each other good-bye, she confessed that because of her family and cultural conditioning, she had always believed gay men only wore stuff like pink hot pants.

The following year Linda Maxwell, her youth group facilitator, told me that Paulina had been forever changed by our interactions. Maxwell offers Buddhist-based peace programs which emphasize diversity training through a program called We Care for Youth. Since our meeting, Paulina had increased her involvement and leadership in the group, and, inevitably, whenever it was her turn to speak, she shared the story about me and the URI, usually ending up in tears. Furthermore, whenever Paulina was shut down and did not want to participate, Maxwell would simply look her in the eyes, say my name: "Christian," and Paulina would immediately soften. The point is we just never know what the ripple effect of our actions might be, particularly when they are motivated by truth, compassion, generosity, and conviction.

Needless to say, it is important to use common sense when coming out. If coming out at work means we'll be out of a job, it may be best to postpone that decision until we have something else lined up. And screaming "I'm gay" while riding a bus filled with skinheads may not be in our highest good. Nevertheless, coming out is something we will have to do sooner or later if our goal is to be fully human, and fully ourselves.

For those needing assistance or support with coming out, I recommend two books among the many available. These are the ones I have found most effective and with whose authors I have connected personally. The first is by Roy Eichberg, founder of the Experience. His book, *Coming Out: An Act of Love,* was instrumental in my coming out to my parents. While I had been out to myself for years and later to siblings and friends, I delayed coming out to my parents for as long as I could. I would tell myself that I was protecting them from unnecessary pain, that they had already experienced far too much trauma in their lives. In the end, though my parents were upset (and I'm sure still wish things were different), their love for me proved steadfast and unquestionable.

The other book I recommend to those contemplating or struggling with coming out is Torie Osborn's *Coming Home to America.* Written with much understanding, compassion, perspective, and hopefulness, the book includes many insightful and poignant anecdotes—both personal and from the many people Osborn has met over the thirty years she has been an activist. Without naming it so, Osborn raises the act to the archetypal level when she writes that coming out means "you become a revolutionary in America's newest social movement, whether you choose it or not."[1]

Coming Out Spiritually

For yoga teacher Matt Stern, coming out spiritually was an integral part of coming out. "I see it as a continuity," he says. "What happened for me in college was that I thought that by simply saying to the world, 'I am gay,' everything would be taken care of. *Then* I could be all that I could be. *Then* I would be OK. But I found that it was superficial. I still had no idea of who I was, and remained pretty shut down—shut off. This was probably part of being 'the other' sexually. When I began using the words 'I'm gay,' it led to other inner questions such as 'What else am I?' 'Who am I as a person?' 'What makes me unique?'" Stern felt compelled to dig deep inside and find his own essence; this led to his first spiritual awakening. "I see my life as a coming out process: a process of discovering what is true about me, the world, the universe—a continuing process of discernment. I feel incredibly grateful for being gay, because I didn't have the rigid, crystallized structures through which to look at the world."

For many others, coming out of the queer closet was easier than coming out of the spiritual one. Tim Phillips finds it ironic that it is much easier for him to be open about being a gay man than a Baptist minister. "Gay people in the Midwest, where I used to live, were very suspicious of me; they saw me as complicit in a history of oppression. I find this unfair. It is doing to one another the same oppressing and labeling that has been done to us."

Through her private business, the Motivational Institute, Deborah Johnson travels all over the country consulting for nonprofit groups and major corporations on organizational development issues, with a particular focus on diversity training. Like Phillips, she often finds it easier to come out as a lesbian than as a minister. "Too many people—including my mother—think it's a contradiction in terms for me to be a lesbian and a minister. It's still not 'fashionable' to be a queer person of faith." Johnson reports having felt apprehensive of the Christian Right when she decided to step out as a queer spiritual leader. But much more so, she feared "being considered a traitor by the very community I loved the most. For many of us, it's still our secret that we believe in something. It's still our secret that we practice and that we go to church. We're apologetic about it. We're just as afraid to come out as spiritual people among queer folk as we are to come out as queer among straight folk. The good thing is that once you learn how to come out, the skill is applicable. What I'm finding is that the more people that stand up and be counted, the better—the same way it works with sexuality."

In a sense, coming out means freeing ourselves from the hang-ups and neuroses inherited from our families and culture. It means releasing and rejecting unhealthy patterns of behavior that no longer serve us, and which prevent our peace of mind and fulfillment as human beings. It means emerging as who we are—who we *really* are. Viewed in this context, coming out is a universal imperative, not just an exclusively queer experience. For the truth is that most humans are still covered with layers of gunk which prevent our inner light, innate beauty, innocence, and majesty from shining through.

That is why coming out first entails coming in—plunging into the depths of ourselves to discover who we are and what lies beneath the murky waters of our conditioning. It requires that we do our homework and cultivate our own gardens, whether that means going to therapy, or developing some other method of self-awareness and self-observation for confronting our own inner (or outer) demons. In this ultimate sense, coming out—from whichever closet—is about healing ourselves. It means shedding the skins of our old identities of woundedness and victimization, and emerging transformed as the beings that we really are: empowered, compassionate, loving, ready to make a difference in the world, and fully able to embrace the totality of life. Coming out—and coming out spiritually—requires courage. In the words of Nancy Nangeroni, the transgendered host of Gender Talk, a radio show airing in Boston and on the Internet, courage is "honesty backed by integrity, the honesty to recognize the truth and the integrity to act on it."

Moving Through Fear

Facing ourselves can be a daunting and terrifying process. So can coming out. It calls for releasing our fearful and tenuous hold on the status quo of our lives. In the moment of letting go, we free ourselves from fear, transcend our limitations, and discover who we are. Letting go is all it takes.

There is only one way to overcome fear, and that is by moving through it—in the words of psychologist Susan Jeffers, to "feel the fear and do it anyway," also the title of her bestselling book. Every time we consciously move through our fear, we expand our comfort zone, in effect establishing our life spheres—the circles in which we move and function—at a broader, higher, more spacious level. Expanding our comfort zones is simple, though not necessarily easy.

Here is how it works: We place ourselves in situations that are progressively a bit more of a stretch for us but not so uncomfortable that we flip out and slink back into our caves, tails between our legs, never to be seen or heard from again. We take steps of appropriate size. It is also important to be gentle and compassionate with ourselves, while not letting ourselves off the hook. We take ourselves as far as we can, and as gradually as we want, to the edge—to our limit. This means stretching, rising above previous limitations. It means taking risks and moving beyond our zones of safety and comfort, which, of course, will be different for each one of us. Only we know where that line is. It is important to push it out, and to do so regularly. It will be worth any temporary discomfort, which is the sacrifice we make as we commit to excel, to grow, to overcome our pasts, and liberate ourselves from our own fear, limitations, and self-made prisons.

All we have to lose is self-consciousness, and the fear that has held us back up to now. Why not let them go? Here is an example of how this might work. Say that we are shy, yet long for intimacy, friends, and a loving relationship. Those things cannot come about in a vacuum. We need to cooperate with the divine choreography by placing ourselves in situations where we will meet new people. So we might commit to meeting a new person every week, starting off with easy tasks, perhaps by introducing ourselves to someone while waiting in line, or striking up a conversation with a stranger on the bus. It does not matter who the person is; we are doing this as a practice. We then take it to the next level, whatever that may be: perhaps going to a lecture, spiritual service, or other social situation, or telling someone we have engaged in conversation that we have really enjoyed meeting them and would like to continue the conversation sometime, then asking for their phone number. Remember that even if the person says no, we still come out ahead. For every time we take another step we are stretching out our boundaries, our comfort zone. By the mere act of asking, we are stretching, and therefore winning. Don't take "no" as a personal rejection, and remember that this is not about them but about us—about becoming more than we have been before.

This is the method I instinctively employed to overcome my morbid shyness and fear of speaking in groups. For too long I had let myself be limited by fear and had suffered for it; by my early twenties I decided I'd had enough. I knew that if I wanted to excel, fully develop my potential, and make a real contribution, I needed to come out of my shell. So little by little, I pecked and scratched myself out of my egg. For that is what I was unwittingly doing: embarking on a journey of giving birth to myself. So I took a job in computer sales that forced me to make cold calls both by phone and in person—something I absolutely dreaded and despised. When I later signed up for a Dale Carnegie public speaking course, each week I thrust myself in front of groups—a terrifying endeavor. However, the more cold calls I made, and each time I stood up in front of a group, the easier it became. Each week I pushed through my fear and pushed out my comfort zone, without really knowing what I was doing. The beauty of it is that once we expand our boundaries, they do not shrink back. We become established at new levels of being and behaving.

One of my favorite modern-day parables is told by Richard Bach in *Illusions: The Adventures of a Reluctant Messiah*. He tells of a race of little creatures living at the bottom of a river. Always subject to the river's relentless current, they survived by grabbing on to stones, twigs, or branches at the river bottom. There they lived, in the mud, at the mercy of the current and passing debris, "for clinging was their way of life and resisting the current what each had learned from birth." Eventually one of the creatures tired of his life and announced that he was going to let go, because if he didn't, he would "die of boredom." Mocking him, but more than likely terrified inside, the others warned him: "Fool! That current you worship will throw you tumbled and smashed across the rocks, and you will die quicker than boredom!" But the creature had had enough of his meaningless existence. He let go. Sure enough, at first he was tossed and tumbled and thrown against stones, but eventually the current lifted him up and steadied him. The creature was liberated from his fearful, clinging existence; easily and gracefully he floated downstream, at one with the current, as if he were flying. Eventually, he drifted over another village of creatures who had never seen one of their kind do anything but hold on for dear life at the river bottom. Looking up in awestruck amazement, they called out "See, a miracle! A creature like ourselves, yet he flies. See the Messiah, come to save us all!" The creature responded, "I am no more Messiah than you. The river delights to lift us free, if only we dare to let go. Our true work is this voyage, this adventure!" And then he was swept away, leaving the others to make up elaborate stories about their savior.[2]

Like the river creatures, the only way we can free ourselves is by stretching, by risking, by letting go. That is how we test our limits and discover who we are, how far we can go, what we are made of. Who wants to be stuck with the bottom-feeders? It is time to let go. Increasing numbers of people, gay and straight, are letting go, allowing the current of life to sweep them along. At first, we roll and we tumble and we slip and we fall and we lose our sense of direction; we get sand in our eyes; we can't see clearly; we get disoriented. But if only we resist the temptation to grab on again, we eventually stabilize and stop tumbling. We actually begin to navigate through life's currents, going with the flow, instead of resisting it; merging with it; learning how to navigate it. It then becomes easier to stay out of pain's way and avoid the obstacles and pitfalls obstructing our course as we learn to swim, float, or fly around them, speeding by ever more skillfully.

Admittedly, in this process of intentional expansion there will be times when we will not want to play, when we would rather stay in bed and pull the covers over our heads or "vege out" in front of the tube. That's to be expected. But no longer will we allow ourselves to get stuck in "lives of quiet desperation"—to borrow Thoreau's expression—in relationships that do not work or that are stunting our growth, or in dead-end jobs that make us miserable and numb our souls. Ultimately, life is about risking. If we don't risk, we don't grow, and we feel stuck, bored, and disillusioned. Overcoming fear is simply a life imperative. Deep down inside, we all long for adventure. We are all explorers at heart yet rarely give expression to that part of ourselves. With this in mind, for queers, in particular, enacting our archetypical pioneering functions becomes even more of a compelling necessity.

It is safe to let go. We might get a bit bruised up, confused, frustrated, angry, or scared. But at some point, we'll catch the Spirit wave and be swept away by it, using its force, riding its power, becoming one with it. What could happen if only, as gay people, we decided to stretch, risk, and let go together in large numbers? How far could we take it, if we decided to really explore what we could do together instead of alone?

Let us now consider some possible practices and paths of action both to support our own evolution and to make a difference in the world. All of the practices for "coming in" covered in Part 2 could also be included here, because one leads to the other—coming in and coming out are two sides of the same coin, the inhale and the exhale. For, as James Allen says in *As We Think,* "You cannot travel *within* and stand still without."[3] We begin with slightly more introspective, somewhat transitional, practices than the more meditative ones mentioned in Part 2. Increasingly, we will move toward the other end of the spectrum, in which we engage with the world more actively.

A Gratitude Attitude

One of the most effective practices I have discovered, one which seldom fails me, is the conscious cultivation of gratitude as a state of being, a gratitude state of mind. Often I will go for a walk in natural settings where I live and, almost always, no matter what is going on or whatever concerns about work or issues in my relationship are demanding attention, I am moved into a state of gratitude, a state of grace. First I begin tuning in to the beauty around me and then begin to feel grateful for living in such a beautiful place as the Bay Area. I begin to notice the different types of trees, then tune in to the roar of the Pacific Ocean as it passionately hurls itself onto the western edge of the American continent. Beyond a certain point, I am able to see the Golden Gate, where the Pacific penetrates the continent, carving out San Francisco Bay. A bit further, I encounter at a distance the dignified and striking burnt-orange bridge—a destination for millions of tourists from all over the world. Walking along rocky cliffs, which drop down several hundred feet at some places, I am surrounded by beautiful vegetation, the occasional metallic sound of a hummingbird, or the soul-inspiring sight of a hawk in suspended flight as it rides the wind currents, hovering. Inevitably, the feeling of awe and gratitude spreads or generalizes to other areas of my life, and soon I find myself in a general state of thankfulness, in which all my problems are again viewed with perspective. I really appreciate the connection in the Spanish language between gratitude and grace. *Gracias,* the word used to say thank you, can also mean the plural of "grace" (although, in that context, the word is not typically used in the plural). What a wonderful way to say "thank you," by wishing grace upon another.

One New Year's Eve, several years ago, I was feeling particularly lonely, conflicted, and trapped by the circumstances of my life. I found myself sitting atop a hill overlooking Golden Gate Park on one side and the Pacific on another, missing my family, friends, and freedom. I opened my notebook, labeled the top of a page "What I hate about my life," and began to furiously write down everything I could think of, beginning with the present and then naturally flowing into my past. When I could think of nothing else, I started a second list, labeled "Things I'm grateful for in my life." The list began pouring forth, and before I knew it, I had filled several pages. What dawned on me, upon completion, was that my inner experience had completely shifted. That simple practice had gotten me out of a major funk. My depression had lifted.

I recommend this as a daily action: every morning, after getting up, take a couple of minutes—for it should not take longer than that—and jot down even a couple of things for which you are grateful. You might even keep them together in a "gratitude journal." This simple practice could have potentially life-changing effects; particularly when done regularly, it can help to shift the perspective through which we view our lives. If writing things down is not your style, get in the habit of mentally listing the things for which you are grateful while in the shower, on the drive to work, or as you prepare for sleep—whenever it works for you. It is best to pick the same time or situation to facilitate the formation of a habit. If you pick up nothing else from this book, cultivating a gratitude attitude will shift your life in radical and favorable ways.

The Liberating Act of Reading

Reading is another effective technique for escaping the confinement of our minds. I frequently start out the day by reading something inspirational that will anchor my consciousness in a positive context and remind me of a larger or global view. This inevitably has the effect of bringing my concerns into perspective; it reminds me that I am not alone, that there are others out there who share a sense of mission, urgency, and understanding about what is going on here on our planet at this time. It helps to refuel my sense of dedication and commitment. Books like *The Universe Is a Green Dragon, Starseed Transmissions,* and *Conversations with God* all lend themselves to casual reading and have supported me at different points in my life. Any book that reminds us of a spiritual reality or an evolutionary context—that there is something going on here which is larger than ourselves and our particular set of life challenges—will be effective. There are also many books of daily meditations, or others, like the Workbook to *A Course in Miracles,* which present a different lesson each day. Although this practice of reading for even ten minutes can be undertaken at any time, I find that it works well to start out the day by filling my mind with positive, high thoughts rather than glum or sensationalistic news. It sets the tone for the day and allows me to see the forest from the trees.

Reading, whether in the form described above, or in general, is another action you could take immediately to support your spiritual unfoldment. So, buy that book you have been meaning to read, or pick up the one you started months ago and finish it! Reading clubs are springing up throughout the country and can serve both as structure and support for reading. Another possible action might be starting your own spirituality reading club. Simply contact a few of your friends, agree to meet once a month, or however often you decide. If you wanted to expand your group's potential membership, you could offer it through a like-minded organization or a local bookstore.

The Call of the Wild

Although I have always enjoyed beautiful sceneries and have been drawn to natural settings—in particular, the ocean—it really wasn't until I left my home in Miami and went off on a spiritual journey that my connection with nature deepened and intensified. The places I have seen and felt in recent years are beautiful beyond description, awe-inspiring, and humbling. Places like Maui's magical Road to Hana, California's breathtakingly rugged Pacific Coast Highway, the crystalline beauty of the Grand Tetons in Wyoming, the otherworldly rock formations of Southern Utah, the majestic grandeur of the Grand Canyon, the palpable enchantment of Santa Fe and Northern New Mexico, and others, have carved indelible images in my mind and soul. More recently, I developed a deep connection with the redwoods of Northern California's Russian River area, where I lived in solitude while writing this book.

There is definite magic—spiritual magic—available when we spend time alone in nature. The Hawaiians have a name for that mystical feeling that is so evident on the islands: *mana*—spiritual essence or divine energy. During my writing retreat, I found my sensitivity and connection to nature intensifying, as well as my awareness of its whispered messages. My body quieted and relaxed as it became more in tune with the natural cycles. Increasingly I found myself moved to humility and gratitude. Prompted by my Indigenous friend Rosalía, I even began to speak to the trees. At first I didn't think they were speaking back, for I was projecting onto them human forms of communication and half expecting to hear inner voices in response. Then one day I had a sudden realization, one of those Aha! moments we have all had, that nature communicates at the feeling level. Rather than a voice, what I "heard" was a feeling/thought, a feeling which translated into thought. It was a deeply moving experience for me.

A Cosmic View

Brian Swimme, mathematical cosmologist and author of *The Universe Story* and *The Universe Is a Green Dragon,* bridges science and spirituality and merges the mystic and the astrophysicist in his writings, while presenting an explanation of the universe in simple, understandable, and eloquent poetic language, which expands the mind and inspires the soul. Citing recent scientific evidence, he writes that in our times "mechanistic . . . science opened out to include a science of mystery: the encounter with the ultimacy of no-thingness that is simultaneously a realm of generative potentiality; the dawning recognition that the universe and the Earth can be considered living entities; the awareness that the human person, rather than a separate unit within the world, is the culminating presence of a billion-year process; and the realization that, rather than having a universe filled with things, we are enveloped by a universe that is a single energetic event, a whole, unified, multiform, and glorious outpouring of being."[4]

What Swimme and others are calling for is the development of a cosmological perspective, a realization of our place within and our connectedness to the universe. Only that will save us from the ecological and social crises in which we find ourselves—all caused by what Swimme calls the "most terrifying pathology in the history of the universe," referring to the estrangement of the human from nature and the rest of the cosmos, the divorce of science from Spirit which has characterized modern Western culture for hundreds of years.

Once we reestablish our rightful place in relationship with nature and the rest of the universe, everything else will fall into place. We will learn to treat the Earth, its resources, and its other inhabitants with respect, responsibility, and a sense of stewardship. Once we begin to see each other as the "culmination of a billion-year process" and realize that we are not different or separate but actually made of the same stuff as the stars, we will learn to truly honor each other—and racism, sexism, homophobia, and other social and economic inequities will naturally fall by the wayside. The only appropriate response to this new understanding of our collective story is one of awe, and a humble, joyful celebration of all creation. What we desperately need is a real experience of awe engendered by a new sense of cosmology. For how can one harm, destroy, neglect, or abuse something, whether it's an ecosystem or another human, of which one is in utter awe?

Developing a sense of cosmology also helps put everything into perspective. It is easy to forget, or deny, that we inhabit this tiny planet—infinitesimal, compared to the rest of the universe—which at this very moment is hurtling at great speeds through a space so vast that our minds cannot even begin to comprehend it, while simultaneously rotating on its axis. And on this planet, the only one of its kind as far as our extremely limited capabilities and perspectives can identify, exists an amazingly complex ecosystem: oceans, mountains, rivers, clouds, volcanoes, and tornadoes; it is teeming with life, from the tiniest microscopic organisms living in the darkest depths of the ocean or inside slowly brewing volcanoes, to the thousands of varieties of plants and flowers, to the huge mammals roaming both plain and sea, to the colorful rainbow of feathered and scaled creatures. If only we could *really* see ourselves from the outside as this tiny, indescribably beautiful living planet, everything would change.

Compassion in Action

Ram Dass's *Compassion in Action: Setting Out on the Path of Service,* is addressed to "those who feel called to reduce the suffering that surrounds us on the planet and who also feel that the deepest responsibility of each of us is to become more fully who we are, to live closer to the truth." The book reveals that both of these aspects are interconnected, occur at the same time, and energize each other. Karma Yoga, or the path of service, "uses as its vehicle for transformation our actions themselves; that is, we gain internal freedom through external action. . . . There is an elegance in the use of our acts of service for our spiritual work. It lies in the fact that the very acts that we perform to relieve the suffering of another being, be they through offering a glass of water, holding a hand, building a road, or protesting against injustice, can also serve as grist for the mill of our own spiritual growth, which, in turn, improves the effectiveness of our caring acts."[5]

How can coming out fully—spiritually—through active engagement, develop your inner being and change your life? In my case, if I had to choose one of the yogic paths by which to categorize myself, it would probably have to be the path of service. I am definitely attracted to and fed by the Jnana path of wisdom, and thrive on learning and understanding. I enjoy Bhakti Yoga or devotional techniques such as chanting, and am frequently moved to spontaneous moments of love and gratitude when I experience innocence in people or beauty in art and nature. I am also drawn to movement and other body-based practices. However, what really drives me more than anything else is the desire to serve. To me, it is more than a desire, a neurotic need, or a compulsion. I feel passionately about the state of humanity and the world, and nothing else motivates me to action like our precarious condition, and my desire to help others and to support the unfolding story of the universe (which could all be translated as serving God). When I am actively engaged in service I feel connected and highly energized—I am "in the flow," and can feel and see the magic at work all around me. Service gives my life a sense of context and meaning.

Swimme speaks beautifully and movingly of "generosity" as one of the cosmic dynamics—universal qualities that are evidenced throughout the cosmos. Planets, stars, solar systems, and life itself came about because of the cosmic generosity of a supernova which, in exploding, brought all of this into existence. Swimme reminds us that humans share that very generosity of being, for, in a real sense, our atoms, our blood, our bones, and our tissues are made of the same star stuff as the supernovas. That may be why we have a deep-seated desire to help, to make a difference, to serve, to give ourselves away like the exploding supernovas. Swimme writes that "the ground of being is *generosity.* The ultimate source of all that is, the support and well of being, is Ultimate Generosity. All being comes forth and shines, glimmers and glistens, because the root reality of the universe is generosity of being. That's *why* the ground of being is empty: every *thing* has been given over to the universe; all existence has been poured forth; all being has gushed forth because Ultimate Generosity retains no thing."[6]

It is time for queer people to tap deeper than we ever have before into that universal quality of generosity, evidenced in our age-old roles as healers, teachers, and caregivers. Even though we have been and continue to be rejected and maligned by many, I believe that it is time for us to shine forth as exemplars of service and compassion. In the process we will discover a source of self-respect and personal fulfillment. The respect of others will follow eventually, although, more than likely, having found respect in ourselves, we will no longer need it from others.

Making It Happen

There are as many ways of serving and making a difference as there are human beings. It helps to first discover or determine what you are passionate about, what causes or situations really concern you and pull your heartstrings. There are books that can help you sort these things out. I recommend beginning with *Compassion in Action,* which encompasses both the spiritual context for service and a practical discussion of issues like how to get started, and the importance of doing our homework before devoting ourselves to an organization. It also provides a practical resource guide. For now, let us gather some ideas and, hopefully, inspiration, from the selfless actions of a few queer individuals who are living out the cosmic dynamic of generosity.

For years, my friend David Charlsen has been "playing uncle" to both his real nephew, Malachi Johnson, and to many others—the children of friends and neighbors whom he has helped raise. Charlsen usually takes one kid at a time (although sometimes they overlap), devoting one day of the week to them. He takes them to the movies, the theater, the park, or the aquarium, depending on the kid's age and predilections. He cooks their favorite foods for them, rents them movies, and basically lets them be kids. He helps build up their self-confidence and self-esteem. A more generous and compassionate person I have seldom encountered. Not surprisingly, given the karmic law that what you give is what you get, what goes around comes around, Charlsen is adored by his kids—the oldest of whom is now in college—and by his friends, who are fiercely loyal to and protective of him. It was Charlsen's cabin in the redwoods I stayed in while writing this book.

Joe Rodriguez undertook a similar approach when he placed an ad in the parenting section of the *San Francisco Bay Times* offering his "services" as a big brother to an interested lesbian couple with a male child. Having felt drawn to mentoring for some time, he had not found a program which offered him exactly what he was looking for. The previous year, Rodriguez, who is thirty-eight, took eight months off from work. He traveled to Thailand, where he attended several retreats, practiced yoga, and spent time in meditation and deep reflection. "It was a time to really go inside. What came out, once I got in touch with my inner voice, was what I wanted my life to be about—the core principles by which I wanted to live. In terms of service, I got clear that for me it would no longer be about what I *should* do, or thought I'd be good at, or what society needed. I decided to approach it from a more 'selfish' place, and got in touch with what I am really passionate about, what I love, which is being around kids. So I decided to become a mentor." Rodriguez says he is "ecstatic" about his big brother relationship with Jason, who was six when they met. As an added benefit, he has noticed that he is no longer dating guys "who need a lot of mentoring—obviously those needs are being met now." He also does volunteer work for San Francisco's Community United Against Violence (CUAV), going into schools and speaking with young people about what it is like to be a gay man. "For me, it's about showing up in the life of young people. There is nothing more beautiful than standing up for who you are, as who you are. And that is what I model for them—authenticity and coming from the heart." Rodriguez realized that when he had done volunteer work in the past out of a sense of duty or responsibility, he ended up burning out, and resenting what he was doing. "It became an obligation, because I was not coming from a deep place of passion. Now, what I do has to be in line with my values, *and* it has to get me excited. My advice is to do what you love to do, and the overflow is what will benefit other people and society as a whole."

DeAnna Martin is co-facilitator of Seattle's "Alternatives to Violence" project, where she works with women in prisons, facilitating discussion on issues like nonviolence and providing instruction on communication and conflict resolution skills. Describing her experience as "totally amazing," Martin admits that she has had to overcome her fear in order to "become a peacemaker," and is grateful that she has been able to witness "miracles and life-transforming realizations" through her work. In the highest sense, Martin translates her volunteer work as helping people "open to the Divine, whatever that means to them." She believes that we are here on Earth to "learn how to love, and we do that through serving others. My service work teaches me how to interact with the Divine, and how to give others an experience of that. Through service I have learned a lot about how to love. The opposite of love is fear; and in order to learn to love we have to confront our fears, and move past them. Our fears are only layers covering the love within us."

Martin is also the volunteer coordinator of the Global Youth Alliance, a loose-knit, international network of young people, ages thirteen to twenty-one, who first came together in San Francisco at the State of the World Forum in 1995. Describing their group as primarily a support network, Martin explains that they felt the need for it because too often they hear from adults things like "idealism is great, but just wait until you get older; it won't be a part of your life any more." After their initial meeting they felt the need to support each other to "grow up together without losing that sense of idealism, hope, optimism, and commitment to the work that we do." Although Martin was not raised religiously and used to think of herself as an atheist, she discovered and evolved her own spirituality through a self-study course as a junior in high school. By then she was already involved in social activism, but spirituality "provided a missing piece. Now when I work toward making the world a better place, I do it in the name of that Greater Being." Her precocious wisdom and degree of involvement in service and social activism are impressive and inspiring.

For Unity lay minister Sherryl Hodgins, "spirituality is not a lot about theory, but about bringing the divinity down to the practical nature." At her church, Hodgins is the Director of the Children's Program, in which she incorporates Rudolf Steiner's principles of spiritual awareness. Regarding her volunteer work with children she observes that "I had always used my sexuality to hold myself back: I can't do that because someone will think this or the next thing. I also used it as an excuse for not getting into any kind of spiritual circle. The big thing about me now is my participation. I know I've made a considerable contribution, and I hadn't done that for quite a while." Hodgins tells a story about a young four-year-old girl who asks her parents to leave her alone with her newborn baby brother. Concerned, the parents asked the family doctor what she thought, and her response was, "Well, you have the remote monitors and can check up on her that way, so let her." What the parents overheard was the girl asking her brother, "Baby, please remind me about God; I'm beginning to forget." The story reminds Hodgins why she works with children. "Working with children brings me closer to what my true essence is. It's a joy and a delight having had that opportunity."

Patricia Nell Warren, lesbian author of the *Front Runner* series, agrees that it is important for the "gay community to listen to our kids, because they are twice handicapped," by being young and queer. Additionally, their perspective "offers a counterbalance to what most everyone else is into—and they are incredibly creative." Warren volunteered for the Eagle Center, the queer school in Los Angeles in which she taught writing for six months; she then served for two years on the Gay and Lesbian Education Commission, which was later disbanded by the L.A. Board of Education. Warren points out that relating to younger people would be beneficial for many gay adults as well, because "a lot of them have never talked to a kid since they were kids." Warren, who has Native American ancestry, talks about "responsible volunteering." "Needless to say, there should be no strings attached to any help offered," she emphasizes. Warren further points out that "our young people have a tremendous hunger for spiritual things, and they find that our community places too much emphasis on sex and disease. They are turned off by the religions of their parents but have a deep aching place inside—a need for prayer and healing. They know something is missing. They loved the spiritual aspects of *Billy's Boy,* the fact that he became the keeper of the flame, and then the keeper of the box of family relics; they related to his questioning of life and death."

In 1994, Matt Garrigan founded the Universal Endowment for Human Empowerment, an umbrella organization for Radiant Light Ministries in San Francisco, which offers weekly Celebrations, and for the Liberty Experience Training, a weekend seminar that has "contributed to thousands of people experiencing breakthroughs in communication, health, relationships, and well-being." Drawing from many different traditions, Garrigan is committed to empowering people. "I started a ministry because I was guided to. It's as simple as that. I really believe that our spirituality is active. We can sit and meditate every day and get in touch with the Divine. However, if we don't actualize that, it just sits dormant within us. It does not become a contribution to the community."

Originally from Edmonton, Canada, Richard Link is working toward a degree in Somatic Psychology and Transformative Arts at John F. Kennedy University in the Bay Area. Link's thesis is on creative expression as a spiritual practice. "As an artist, it's not enough for me to be transformed by playing the piano or writing music. I also have to be taking that energy and working within the larger community—and not just the community of human beings, but one which includes all the plants and animals. It seems to me very crucial that we include the entire world at this time." Besides being the volunteer coordinator for Q-Spirit, Link also donates time to environmental groups such as Headwaters, an organization which teaches kids in schools about environmental issues and how they are directly impacted by them.

If you are not already doing so, I urge you to take time for service on a regular basis. Find an area of life about which you feel concern or passion and do something about it. As I recently heard someone say, "If you see a need, you are probably being called to fill it." Volunteer for a group that is tackling the problem, or do something on your own. You will not regret it.

Spirit at Work

Too often, we allow our spirituality to become compartmentalized and separate from the rest of our lives: it's just something we do once a week or relegate to our twenty-minute daily meditation. Yet, as we strive to become more integrated and complete human beings, it becomes increasingly important that we incorporate our spiritual beliefs into our everyday lives. It is often challenging, for example, to remember our spiritual essence when we are in the midst of a heated argument with our lover, or to call forth spiritual teachings when dealing with an ornery boss, recalcitrant employee, or difficult vendor. For many of us, reconciling our spiritual lives with the need to work and make money to support ourselves presents a real challenge, and, in some cases, a fundamental conflict. The people presented here have all found ways to harmonize these two critical aspects of their lives, and have in the process discovered the path of service through their work.

In 1985, when she was only twenty-two, Tami Simon founded Sounds True as a conference recording company. Based in Boulder, Colorado, the company soon evolved into one of the major producers of original audio material specializing in the areas of spirituality, creativity, and healing. It has published more than three hundred spoken-word audio titles, featuring some of the best-known teachers of our time, including Clarissa Pinkola Estés, Ram Dass, Carolyn Myss, Deepak Chopra, Thomas Moore, Thich Nhat Hanh, Julia Cameron, Jack Kornfield, Alice Walker, and many other respected voices. Sounds True also has a new line of instructional videos, and a sacred world music label. By 1998, it had grown into a multi-million dollar company with sixty-five employees.

Simon says that "people tend to put everything into boxes: love, work, spirituality. To me, it's all braided together. Spirituality means to be sourced by something greater than ourselves. Since that is happening all the time, with every breath that I take, how can I begin to separate it from the rest of my life?" While acknowledging that due to the practicalities of our economic system, we are sometimes asked by our employers to do things that contradict our values, Simon reminds us that "we have a lot of choices about entrepreneurial opportunities, choices as to how to handle a particular situation at work, or the choice to become a 'reformer,' if the work environment can handle that. If it can't, we have the choice to leave."

Besides the importance of being out at work, which is just a "basic part of being authentic," Simon believes that it is important for our work to reflect our values. In her case, she asks, "How could I squeeze my employees in order to produce spiritual tapes? That would be divorcing the product from the process." In line with her belief that "spirituality is about the action we take in our lives," Simon has successfully created a cutting-edge corporate culture, a truly spiritually based workplace. "For me the bottom line is not only about money; I believe that the bottom line for a corporation has to include the happiness of the employees, the harmony of the work environment, and how that environment supports people reaching their individual goals outside of the company. In effect, this involves the redefinition of success."

Among the innovative programs implemented by Sounds True are a meditation room as well as a monthly meditation class offered during company time. A prison program recycles the used tapes customers return and donates them to prison libraries. Customers receive a ten-dollar gift certificate toward their next purchase. Employees can make use of a flex-time program, and are welcome to bring their dogs to work. "We operate from a place of trust and trustworthiness. Our policy is 'Here is what you need to get done; how do *you* want to get it done?' The animals are part of our community, and that tends to humanize the workplace." One of the company's key philosophies is allowing room for feelings in addition to thought. "I hate an office environment filled with gossip and office politics. That saps everybody's energy. What that means to me as a company leader is that I have to make time to listen to my employees and ask about their personal lives: 'How did this new policy or that change in deadline affect you?' Taking time to listen means you have to go a little slower, but the benefit is you don't have a work environment filled with toxicity. And where are we all rushing to, anyway?"

LaShonda Barnett is studying for her Master's at Sarah Lawrence College in Bronxville, New York. She is conducting a study of African-American lesbians in the process of reclaiming their spirituality and says that "for most African-Americans, the church is integral to our culture; I met two of my partners in church." Barnett, who is twenty-four years old, says that the Generation X'ers are having a particularly difficult time reconciling religion and sexuality. She is particularly angry at the black church because of its silence on HIV—the "main killer of African-Americans under forty, whether male or female, gay or straight." The project on which she is working has helped her rediscover her spirituality and her desire to serve. "I have met with amazing Bible scholars and understood the real message that God is love and religion is not supposed to be oppressive." Through her studies she is finding an avenue for spiritual reconnection and service.

Prior to his mayoral appointment as a San Francisco City Supervisor, Mark Leno ran his business of over twenty years, Budget Signs, Inc., and was deeply involved in civic, cultural, and political activities. He was co-chair of the capital campaign for the city's Community Center Project, and before that led the successful local effort to raise $1.5 million nationally from the LGBT community to benefit the U.S. Holocaust Museum in Washington, D.C. What many people do not know, however, is that before his involvement in the worlds of business and politics, Leno completed two years of study in the rabbinic program at New York's Hebrew Union College. He is a man whose integrity and deep-seated spiritual convictions are palpable.

One Saturday each month, Supervisor Leno volunteers as chef for the hot meal program at All Saints Episcopal Church, which forms part of the Haight-Ashbury Community Service Committee. His connection to All Saints stems from his deceased partner Doug Jackson's close ties to that church. In response to my surprised, "I didn't know you could cook!" Leno responded, "I don't. All my friends laugh about it because they know I don't even cook for one. I can make one meal: pasta casserole for one hundred and fifty."

When asked how the worlds of politics and service converge for him, Leno responded that Mahatma Gandhi has been a big influence. "He was remarkable in actually living, exemplifying, what nonviolent confrontation and resistance are about. This was a man who brought the British Empire—at its zenith—to its knees, without firing one shot. He did this by loving his adversary, by truly loving his adversary. One can only do that by being completely fearless."

I spoke with Leno during his election campaign in the fall of 1998, when he was right in the midst of making fund-raising calls. At the time, we also touched bases about the 1998 Q-Spirit lecture series on "Practical Spirituality." Offering panels on sex, money, work, and relationships, the series explored—from a queer perspective—ways in which we can reconcile our spirituality with those key aspects of our lives. Leno was scheduled to participate on the panel on work. Pressed to speak a bit more about how he personally brought his spiritual principles and beliefs to the world of politics, he replied thoughtfully: "The public service I now attend to I see as a direct continuation and augmentation of many years of community service, and the community service I have always felt compelled to do. I have always enjoyed my work and my profession, but I found my passion in community service. But official public service brings with it additional obligations, responsibilities, and challenges—particularly at a time when elected officials are so poorly regarded by the general public, for all too many good reasons. I knew I only wanted to go forward with this aspect of my service if I could do it in its truest form—and if I could give it my very best."

Leno also spoke of a conversation he had with writer Fenton Johnson (*Geography of the Heart*), during which he was telling Johnson something he had discovered about Gandhi in a book he was reading. When informed of Gandhi's three self-imposed vows of poverty, chastity, and obedience, Johnson responded, "Those are the same three vows that the Benedictines take." (Other religious orders take the same vows.) "Johnson pointed out that the flip side of those three vows is money, sex, and power," continued Leno, "which, of course, is what rules Washington, D.C. So, if a public person could approach service with that position—not for money, power, or sex, but for the purpose of service—that person would be uncommon."

An article in the *Dallas Morning News* presents a vivid example of how a business can make a positive social contribution, perhaps even affecting societal attitudes in profound ways. JR's is a successful gay bar in Dallas's predominantly gay Oak Lawn neighborhood, with revenues exceeding four million dollars a year. Only a block away is Sam Houston Elementary, a cash-strapped elementary school home to many economically disadvantaged children. The relationship between these two unlikely partners began to unfold during the pre-Christmas season in 1997, when JR manager Sam Solomon approached the school and asked if he and his employees could "adopt" a couple of kids for the holidays. As he explained to the assistant principal, "Christmas is for children . . . (and) we don't have kids. Some of our families reject us." When the principals responded that they could not arbitrarily pick just a couple of children, Solomon checked with his associates and returned to ask if they could adopt an entire class. After considering the new offer, the principals explained that they could not choose just one class and ignore the other seven. Again, Solomon consulted with his employees, and they unanimously agreed to adopt the *entire* kindergarten class: one hundred and seventy children.

The children's letters to Santa, carefully omitting their last names, were displayed at the bar for customers to read. By the time Christmas arrived, many customers and employees had chipped in, one wealthy patron alone fulfilling the requests of thirty children. The day of the Christmas party, during physical education class, JR employees slipped unnoticed into the school, delivering holiday decorations, party goodies, and the collected gifts. The experience exceeded everyone's expectations; the school president is quoted as saying, "One hundred and seventy kids, and all of them got what they wanted and more. . . . I'm not talking little toys. I'm talking skateboards, Barbies. The teachers were in shock. They told me they'd never seen anything like it. Nobody had ever adopted a whole class before."

Over time the relationship has evolved so that if the school runs out of ice, they send someone to JR's. Because parking is at a premium, the bar has made its lot available for teachers to use during the day. During Easter, bar employees sponsored an egg hunt for the kids, providing eggs filled with candy and a stuffed animal for each child. According to Solomon, not a single employee had to be coerced into volunteering. They found their reward in observing the joy in the children's faces, faces that, as the manager observed, "did not yet reflect hate." Later that year, employees also cleaned up the school's yard, and in collaboration with some of their suppliers, donated brand new playground equipment. Their generosity did not end there. When subsequently approached by the school principal, JR's owner Jack Polachek, who owns three other gay bars, agreed to ask his other businesses if they would consider adopting the three remaining grades in the school. The answer was an unequivocal "Yes!"[7]

The ripple effect of actions like this are hard to gauge. Not only did JR employees help to change the perception of parents, teachers, and others who were directly involved, but because of the media attention it generated, it surely touched the hearts of countless others. And who can guess the effect it will have on the kids as they grow older? How many lives will they, in turn, impact? This is the type of action that will slowly change the way the world views gay people. Through their selflessness and generosity, people like JR employees, the others mentioned here, and countless other queers are creating profound and irreversible change.

Spiritual Activism

Independent minister Deborah Johnson both compares and contrasts the queer movement to the civil rights movement. "The civil rights movement didn't start off as a civil rights movement; the civil rights part of it came afterwards. It started off as a spiritual movement which, in fact, originated in the churches. The issue that was at stake was not just about sitting at lunch counters or having equal access to jobs. It was about a whole world view that changed the position, the relative humanity, of black people in this society. Black people were not equal under the Constitution of the United States; they were two-thirds of a person, which is why they were able to be sold. That notion of being an equal person was a profound shift." Johnson believes that establishing our equality on a spiritual level should be the starting-off point for the queer movement. "It is on that foundation that civil rights can stand, so that we can then say, 'It is immoral *not* to provide them, because in the eyes of God we are all equal, and to not have them goes against nature.' Then it becomes a battle over defining what is natural." For years, Johnson has been trying to tell her gay activist friends that what we are engaged in is not just a battle about civil rights but a holy war, with profound spiritual roots. "Unless we can come to the table as spiritual beings, unless we can claim our original place in the universe, we will not get very far. The notion of being able to step up, unapologetically, and say: 'I am here, and I have a right to be here,' goes to the heart of issues of spirituality—to the crux and the core of the nature of being, the nature of who we are, how the world ought to be, how we should treat each other. These are profound spiritual issues." After years as a Religious Science minister, Johnson founded her own church—the Inner Light Ministries in Santa Cruz, California. With her partner, Valerie Fidmont, as musical director, they regularly draw several hundred congregants to the twice-monthly services. Although they are open about their sexuality and their relationship, their ministry is composed mainly of heterosexuals.

Marc Adams and Todd Tuttle are also spiritual activists, albeit with a completely different mission. They met as students at Jerry Falwell's Liberty University. Born into a fundamentalist Baptist home, Adams is the son of a minister, and author of *Preacher's Son*. His family was so strictly fundamentalist that they considered Falwell a liberal; in fact, Adams attended Liberty as an act of rebellion. Adams and Tuttle worked together in the yearbook office; for the first time in his life, Adams felt he had found someone with whom he could share his struggle with sexuality. "Let's just say that we were developing more than pictures in the darkroom," he confides. During his senior year he began questioning his Christian beliefs due to his budding homosexuality, and embarked on a slow and arduous process of coming out. "At the time I would have died for these beliefs. I had always been promised peace but never found it; I only began to feel peace when I began to come out." He now considers himself a "recovering fundamentalist; even the word spirituality carries a lot of baggage for me."

Tuttle is a former Baptist minister himself. Once his mother figured out what was going on, she pulled Tuttle from school. Out of touch for three years, Tuttle and Adams reunited serendipitously and have now been together for ten years. As a team, they founded HeartStrong, a nonprofit outreach program attempting to reach gay and lesbian students in fundamentalist Christian schools and universities to counterbalance the biased, anti-gay messages with which they are typically indoctrinated. Adams says that there are "about five thousand of these schools, which are very sheltered; the students are hard to reach, because most don't even watch TV." Tuttle and Adams now live in Seattle and lecture throughout the country at university gay groups, P-FLAG (Parents, Families and Friends of Lesbians and Gays) meetings, and queer community centers, churches, and business guilds; they spend a lot of time on the road—about two hundred nights a year. Besides attending these public forums, students find their way to HeartStrong through the Internet. Drawing on their past experience as evangelists, Tuttle and Adams have appropriated one of their former methodologies—the dissemination of brightly colored tracts—and often leave leaflets with GLBT-positive messages at airports, phone booths, and just about everywhere they go. Adams observes that he used to spend "a lot of free time doing everything to recruit people into the fundamentalist Christian lifestyle, especially children and youth. I had been taught, and believed, that if I did not bring the 'lost' over to our side, their blood would be on my hands. For me, what could be more important now than reaching these kids no one else is trying to reach or even knows how to reach? We know because we lived it."

For New Yorker Eva Yaa Asantewaa, a spiritual leader and organizer of Caribbean heritage, "my spirituality is very active and involved with the community. My spiritual path is about direct experience of Spirit. I bring everything I learn into my work with people; I'm always passing on things I find useful, being an instrument or a channel as open-handed and open-hearted as I can possibly be for others as Spirit has been with me." Yaa Asantewaa says that she is primarily a communicator. As a teacher and holistic educator, she is not so interested in "fixing people," although she does consider herself a healer. "I offer people tools and techniques (such as meditation or a shamanic approach to dreams) that they can experiment with in daily life and adapt as necessary." Some years ago, Yaa Asantewaa produced Inside Out, a two-day queer spirituality conference which attracted a substantial crowd and featured speakers from a wide variety of spiritual traditions. Like so many others profiled within these pages, Yaa Asantewaa combines the queer spiritual archetypes or roles of healer/caregiver and social activist. "If anything characterizes how I see spirituality operating in my life it is the Jewish concept of tikkun—of repairing the world and raising the sparks. So, for me spirituality is first about the direct experience of Spirit, and then about direct action."

A self-described "lesbian evangelist," Janie Spahr is a Presbyterian minister whose spiritual activism was catalyzed when her call to assume the role of co-pastor at Rochester's Downtown United Presbyterian Church in 1991 was challenged by a group of churches in the New York–area Presbytery. This would have been the first time that a member congregation of the Presbyterian Church (USA) had chosen an openly lesbian pastor. After several appeals, the church refused to approve Spahr's post. Since that time, Spahr has been traveling across the country under the aegis of a group called That All May Freely Serve, a joint project of the Downtown Presbyterian Church of Rochester and Westminster Presbyterian Church in Tiburon, California. Her educational ministry involves advocating for change in attitudes and policy, and for greater inclusiveness of LGBT people—including the opportunity to serve openly as clergy and elders—within the Presbyterian Church.

Besides those mentioned above, there are numerous other gay people who are serving the role of spiritual activists, heroically standing up for who they are and for queer rights within their own traditions. Still others persist in their roles of spiritual activists outside the realm of individual religions or denominations, advocating for further spiritual awareness within the queer community as well as for greater acceptance and inclusion among spiritual and religious groups in general.

A Circle Closes

I approached the week leading up to the 1998 global summit of the URI with great resistance. The bottom line is that I simply did not want to be there: I was in the midst of a very busy and productive time with my work and felt apprehensive about taking a whole week off. However, I think the resistance ran deeper than that. It was that old familiar feeling that John Irving aptly named the "undertoad" in *The World According to Garp*. Garp and his wife had a coded phrase—the undertow—they would use in front of their children when they felt below-the-surface tension between them, or that nebulous feeling we have all felt when something is wrong, but we can't quite put our finger on it. Once, when one of the children overheard them speaking about the undertow, and asked: "What's the undertoad?" the expression stuck, becoming a private joke.

The previous year I had left the summit in a somewhat elated, if stunned, "high," elicited by the standing ovation and positive response to my statement. This time, I was beginning the process already out to half of the delegates, who, like me, were returning for another round. Very soon I began to notice that some seemed uncomfortable with me or averted their eyes as we crossed paths with each other in the hallways. For the most part, however, I experienced very warm and loving connections with my colleagues.

On Monday, the first work day of the conference, we again broke up into small groups to tackle different issues. While introducing myself during the very first group of which I formed part, I mentioned my work with the gay and lesbian community. Unexpectedly, a middle-aged Iranian Muslim interrupted me, "Excuse me, but what is *gay?*" I responded, "Homosexual." Visibly surprised, he blurted out, "Homosexuals have no religion!" Taken aback, I replied, "It is true that I don't belong to any religion, but there isn't a priest, minister, rabbi, or imam in this world who can question my spirituality, or my connection to the Divine." Before the situation had a chance to escalate, another member of the group intervened, cutting short the interaction. After the session, the Muslim approached me and asked if we could speak. I agreed, and we went for a walk. He began telling me that he was a philosopher and was frequently asked questions by his students; he wondered if he could ask me a question. When I answered "Sure," he proceeded to ask me, "Exactly how do gay men have sex?" Although I found the question a bit strange, thinking that it doesn't take much imagination to figure that out, since the body has a limited number of protuberances and orifices, I thought to myself, "Okay, here's an opportunity to foster understanding." After a few minutes, however, it became evident that the conversation was taking an increasingly personal direction, and that it was becoming imbued with a prurient sexual energy. He also seemed to be particularly fixated on anal sex. I began trying to extricate myself from the conversation. Finally, he said, "Well, I guess I can understand anal sex, but only with young girls or boys up until they are thirteen or fourteen." In that moment I understood the mechanics, as well as the irony, of the situation and excused myself. To me, it was basic Psychology 101—the defense mechanism of projection—making wrong in others what we cannot accept in ourselves. As Robert Goss points out in *Jesus Acted Up*, this type of behavior could also be caused by another defense mechanism: "Their homophobia is a 'reaction conversion' response, masking their own deep-seated same-sex attractions and the need to stamp out their own same-sex feelings by stamping out those feelings in other people."[8] While repulsed by this man, I saw how trapped he was by his life and culture and felt compassion for him.

On Tuesday, Ma Jaya, the Brooklyn-born guru and founder of Kashi Ashram in Central Florida, a tireless advocate for queer people who has long maintained a viable AIDS ministry, spoke up during the general plenary and asked if there would be a place in the URI for her "gay and lesbian children." She was greeted with a deadening silence, and a visibly uncomfortable facilitator who said something to the effect of, "We'll need to consider that later."

By Wednesday, my suspicions had crystallized; the issue of gay and lesbian inclusion had been glossed over, and I knew that, again, I would have to say something. I agonized over what to do, how and when to do it, whether to do it at all. Should I risk throwing a wedge in what I knew to be a delicate religious, political, and cultural process? Should I specifically mention the Muslims, perhaps giving them a reason to leave the table? From a personal perspective, did I really want to place myself out there again? What were the implications for my future involvement with the URI? Was I thereby committing myself to a long and arduous process? Would I feel obligated to go back if I spoke up and requested dialogue about queer issues? Yet, at a deeper level, I knew. In fact, it felt as if I was having a dual experience—part of me felt torn, distressed, and unable to sleep due to the inner confusion, conflict, and fear, while, at the same time, another part hovered above in a somewhat detached state. I felt like an actor playing his inevitable part in some play.

Once again, I could see the divine choreography at work. Four new groups had formed on Wednesday morning, and I was approached by Brahma Das, the man in charge of media relations for Kashi Ashram, who informed me that he was convening a group to explore how the URI should address moral issues. "You need to be there," he added. The meeting took place in the Lambda Room. As the discussion ensued, I pointed out this irony, explaining that lambda was that Greek letter which had been appropriated as a symbol by the gay liberation movement. I also said that although I was certainly not a single-issue person, I felt compelled to use gay inclusion as an example or case study of a conflictive moral issue. After much discussion, the group arrived at certain general suggestions or scenarios as to how resolutions on moral issues might be made. For example, it was suggested that a statement could be signed by the delegates of the 1998 Global Summit, or by a particular regional group, but that no central statement could be made since no actual United Religions organization existed as of yet.

The next morning, time was set aside for the four new groups to report their conclusions. Our group had decided that we would all stand in the center of the hall alongside our appointed spokesperson. I knew that Brahma Das had asked for two minutes at the end of the presentation to convey Ma's regret for having had to leave early due to an impending death in her ashram. I arranged to stand next to Brahma Das, and when he finished speaking, I took the mike from his hand.

The rest happened very quickly. I turned around and addressed my group, "What I have to say is fundamental to this conversation, but it's really my issue, so please feel free to sit down," which they did. At the same time, one of the facilitators attempted to stop me, eventually agreeing to cede the floor as long as we obtained the participants' permission. I turned around and asked if I could have two minutes; when enough people clapped their approval, I began to speak. Again, not trusting my nerves, I chose to read a statement I had prepared throughout the course of the night and early that morning:

Many words have been spoken here over the past few days. I would like to invite us to take a brief moment, close our eyes, and *feel* the Divine—however we think of it—whether it's God, Goddess, the Great Spirit, Allah, Krishna, Jesus, Mary, Yemanja, the Buddha Nature, the Tao, the Universe, the Higher Self.

When you're ready, please bring yourselves back.

To me, it doesn't matter so much what we call the Divine Mystery. But it does matter a great deal that we feel its Presence.

This week has been very difficult for me, and there have been times when I had to fight my impulse to pack it up and go home. You see, I started out on Monday confronted by a member of the great religion of Islam. We were working in a small group, and, in response to something I shared about my work, he blurted "Homosexuals have no religion."

I personally know countless gay and lesbian Christians. In fact, the largest gay and lesbian organization in the world is the Metropolitan Community Church, a Christian denomination. I know homosexual Buddhists. I know women who love women and think of themselves as Taoists. I know men who love men who are Jews, Wiccans, and Sufis. I know gay and lesbian priests, ministers, bishops, monks, nuns, and rabbis. I even know an openly gay Sufi sheikh. Although I personally don't belong to any religion, I can appreciate and have been touched by the beauty and essence of many spiritual traditions.

Let me be very clear. I am a homosexual. I am gay. And there is no priest, minister, rabbi, or imam in this world who can tell me that I am not spiritual, or feel a connection to the Divine. I have felt it in my own body.

I am very blessed to live in San Francisco, one of the most beautiful, open, and tolerant cities in the world. I am spoiled. I work for myself and surround myself with people who are open, loving, and accepting of who I am. And although I am keenly aware of how much homophobia and violence against gays there is still in the world, I can't remember the last time I experienced it in my own life.

I felt it this week, here in this supposedly sacred and safe space we have all helped to create. It happened to be triggered by a Muslim, but we all know it could have come from almost any religion. I have also felt people's discomfort and their judgment, and I have noticed when they averted their eyes or avoided me. To be fair, I have also felt a great deal of love, support, and understanding here; it was that that kept me here, holding on to hope. Who do we think we are, questioning each other's connection to the Divine? Why? Why can't we live together? Why does it matter how I express my love?

Is it because you fear for your children? Let me assure you, most of us are not interested in children in that way. In fact, something like ninety percent of child sexual abuse is committed by heterosexual men, usually on a family member.

Is it because you think it is unnatural? Well, let me tell you, to me it feels *only* natural. And science has identified at least fifty-four other species where homosexuality is found.

Is it because your holy texts say that it is a sin or an abomination? I think we need to get really honest, and acknowledge that many of those texts have been mistranslated, and sometimes adapted to meet some specific agenda, and that we need to consider them within the context of the cultures and times in which they were written. Modern scholarship is questioning some of those texts. For example, many experts and etymologists now think that the sin of Sodom and Gomorrah was not homosexuality but inhospitality to strangers. They are also shedding new light on the Leviticus Holiness Code, where the concept of abomination originates. Besides, why is it that we focus exclusively on some of those biblical prohibitions, while ignoring others, such as the wearing of clothing of mixed fabrics, or eating shellfish?

I, and others here, need to know, will there be a forum at the URI for this kind of dialogue? We need to know: when we throw around words like peace, love, nonviolence, tolerance, unity, and compassion, does that include *everyone?*

I know this is challenging and uncomfortable for many. Believe me, I don't want to be up here any more than you want me to be up here. I have thought long and hard before doing this. I was concerned about bringing up—again—a difficult and divisive topic into what is already a delicate and sensitive process.

I, too, dream of a world without violence, war, hatred, injustice, and inequality. I still have hope that the religions of the world can come together and help create a world where we can *all* live in peace, with respect for each others' needs and differences.

But I also believe that if we are serious about creating such a world, if these aren't just nice words we are throwing around to help us feel good about ourselves and reduce our guilt about the conditions of the world we are leaving to our children, they must apply to *all* of us. We can't hold on to *some* hatred, spouting it out of one side of our mouth while declaring our love for God and humanity from the other. Otherwise, we are no different than those hate- and fear-filled bigots who tried to disrupt our program last night.[9]

I am here to ask that the URI include a forum for dialogue about these issues. I have here a simple petition to that effect and ask that you sign it if you agree with its premise. I will circulate copies now and also leave some in the resource room.

Homophobia is caused by fear and ignorance; studies have shown that it is greatly diminished when we know someone gay. I would like to invite those who are either gay or lesbian, or who have a homosexual family member or friend, to please stand.

I did not foresee the response. A woman stood from behind and headed towards me, embracing me. Later, I found out that she was a Sufi, and had been rebuked by other Muslims for her instinctive act of support. From another direction Mae Beata, a sixty-seven-year-old Candomblé priestess from Brazil, came rushing toward me, tears streaming down her ebony face as she called out in Portuguese, "My son, my son! Bless you!" Suddenly, I found myself enveloped in a womb-like cocoon of fifteen to twenty people, mostly women; we all huddled and held each other, weeping. By someone's estimate, in response to my request, 80 to 90 of those present stood in support. At one point, once the emotion began to dissipate, Rosalía Gutierrez, my friend from the Kolla tribe in Argentina who was also a veteran of the previous summit, faced the audience and spoke passionately in Spanish, through a translator: "No more discrimination! We, too, have been discriminated against during the past five hundred years. It must stop now!"

Finally, I took the mike once more and said something like, "I was asked not to do this, but I can't *not* do it. I found out that last night the youth contingency stayed up until 11:30 creating a prayer, only to be bumped from this morning's schedule. To me, that is not all right. We've flown these young people here from all over the world, and are now sending them the message that they are of secondary importance. Given the condition in which we are leaving this world for them, the least we could do is give them three minutes of our time to hear their prayer."

After some initial awkwardness, the youth contingent stood, as I made my way to the back of the room, where I was greeted by another stream of people thanking me, embracing me, crying with me. The youth prayer turned out to be the most powerful, Spirit-filled prayer of the week. After the excess of words and headiness we had all experienced, they managed to capture the essence of what the URI is attempting—working together, as one, toward world peace—and conveyed it brilliantly by using a coordinated series of movements, without uttering a single word. What a lesson they gave us all, underscoring the importance of listening to their voice and including them in our programs, organizations, and endeavors.

The rest of the day I was approached by many who expressed their support and gratitude for my having had the courage to "open the space" and bring in reality and truth. A Muslim woman approached me and spoke of how sorry she was that it was a Muslim who had told me gays have no religion, assuring me that not all Muslims feel that way.

Others were not so pleased. One European reported that while he sympathized with my pain, he resented my methods and felt like he had been "hijacked." Another European felt that while he respected my feelings and opinions, such issues were best discussed in private, not in a public forum. I was told that still others had expressed their disapproval at my bringing a "political agenda" into the process.

I also heard that the Muslim delegation and the Asian regional group had experienced a great deal of discomfort and upset and strongly disapproved of my methods and message. I was later informed that a Baha'i gentleman was heard vehemently pronouncing that homosexuality was "anathema to all religions."

An unexpected curve ball came on Friday morning. During the final plenary, we were listening to the various reports of what each region had accomplished and intended to do during the next year. Feeling emotionally exhausted and mentally numb from all the words, I tuned out for most of that session. However, my body became alert and my ears perked up when the African delegation began their report. An older gentleman, a Christian minister, proceeded to read a statement, a portion of which I include here:

> Whereas we affirm the principle of listening and speaking freely with respect to deepen[ing] our mutual understanding and trust, we are concerned that [an] important principle is being violated, namely "Deliberations and decisions are to be made openly and reflect diversity. They are not to be dominated by any single view or interest."
>
> We recommend that a procedure or mechanism be put in place to sieve out individual or group interests which have the potential to destroy what we are seeking to build.
>
> We felt rather betrayed yesterday to be forced to deal [with or] support what we consider to be a foreign agenda to our continent.
>
> We deeply resent the way the gay-lesbian issue was introduced and how it claimed to have been supported by the majority of the delegates.
>
> We request strongly that the issue does not become part of the agenda and outcome of the Global Summit of the URI.

I was stunned. I was hurt. I felt confused, angry, and defeated. The facilitators quickly moved us into the final process, in which everyone queued up to the center of the room, and, mirroring the opening process, shared one word to symbolize what they took from the summit. As I listened to the same litany of "love, peace, inclusion," and the like, I was overcome with anger and disgust and could not bring myself to participate. I stood up and moved back to the outside of the group.

Later I wished I had had the presence of mind to speak the words "Nelson Mandela," pointing to that universal symbol of freedom, and to the irony that post-apartheid South Africa is the only nation in the entire world which includes constitutional protection for gays and lesbians. I was also struck by the irony that it was the African delegation who had regularly used the Q-Spirit portable stereo (which we had lent to the conference organizers for the summit) during their morning meditations. That such intolerance was being shown by people who experience discrimination in many parts of the world because of their skin color was a painful paradox.

Subsequently, I was informed that not all African delegates had been involved in or were even aware of the resolution's drafting. I was assured by three of them—all in their twenties or thirties, incidentally—that they certainly did not share those feelings. The following week I called Godwin Hlatshwayo, one of the conference facilitators who is African, and asked him to help me understand what had transpired. His perception was that to some delegates, the problem had been my disregard for the process; many expressed their objection to public pronouncements in general, and did not think "individual or personal agendas" were appropriate. For several of those who objected, he said, it was the first time they had ever heard the topic of homosexuality discussed in public, and they had been offended by that. While they may have sympathized with my pain, my actions had also generated doubts about whether they had been endorsed by the URI staff or conference facilitators. Apparently, some had already been feeling that the summit was "too Western and quite exclusive." Because of the long and violent history of colonialism, many Africans are understandably sensitive to being coopted into a Western agenda.

Hlatshwayo also expressed that from his perspective the whole experience was a positive thing, even if it had been personally painful for me, for the Africans, for the URI staff and conference facilitators, and for others present. He mentioned that it was a positive sign of the Africans' commitment to the process, since their normal modus operandi might be to remain quiet, then never show up again. In that sense, they were implicitly agreeing to continue to participate, and that in itself was progress. He also felt that it was an important first step toward the possibility of discussing the issue next year; a couple of delegates had privately said that they sympathized and would like to learn and understand more about the issue.

Obviously, from a queer perspective, the view is somewhat grim. My actions crystallized the strong opposition and repulsion that homosexuality still evokes in many people, from a variety of cultures and religions. The experience was painfully eye-opening and educational. It made me realize my naïveté and inexperience as an activist. After a few days of licking my wounds, it became clear to me that I was not about to go away, nor stand idly by. I remain convinced that if there is any chance for such an effort as the United Religions to succeed, is has to be based on truth—not on pretense, or lies—and it has to include everyone. It cannot be about having nice conversations about the common things shared by the different religions, while ignoring the difficult issues.

An important point to emphasize about my URI experience is the sense of hope I received from the youth assembled there. My impression is that, regardless of their place of origin, the younger generations are much more open and accepting than their older counterparts. To many of them, sexual orientation is a nonissue. I was also impressed by the depth of their spirituality, their creativity, and their commitment and dedication. Many thanked me for "bringing in the truth," and making the whole week real for them: "Before, it was only words," said a youth from Malaysia. As I was leaving on Friday, I approached a group of them and told them that I was not sure I would be returning but wanted to thank them for the hope they gave me. Their response was, "Thank *you*. You give us strength."

A Call for Compassion

Over the few months following the '98 URI experience I found myself reluctant to even talk about it. It took some time for me to integrate the feelings of vulnerability, anger, failure, and confusion generated by both my interaction with the Muslim philosopher and the strongly worded and unequivocal response to my statement from the African delegation, which, incidentally, was composed mostly of Christians and Muslims.

What was I thinking? How naïve could I be? Did I not realize that such a strong action would elicit an opposite and equal reaction—a basic universal law of physics? For weeks, I felt vulnerable and stupid; I fluctuated from feelings of failure to ones of anger and planning what action I would take next year—the old "I'll show them" reactive routine. I lay low on the issue for a time, telling only a few people about the experience. Although I was advised by an activist friend to contact the International Gay And Lesbian Human Rights Commission, I did not follow up after an initial round of phone tag. Obviously, I felt ambivalent about how to proceed.

As old feelings and insecurities came up, I began feeling like a fool for making myself so vulnerable in front of my opponents. "They probably think I'm weak and a sissy for crying; real men don't cry," I caught myself thinking. In that flashback of neurosis I also caught myself feeling: "No way; I can't go back next year. How humiliating!" Besides making myself wrong, I also found myself making *them* wrong: "To hell with this. It is just too difficult, and maybe we should just write off the older generations; change will have to come from the younger ones. These are primitive societies and backward religious institutions. I won't waste my time on them any more. Some of these cultures are just barely up to talking about the inclusion of women. In some, women are still forced to walk behind men, their bodies covered and their faces veiled. In parts of Africa, thousands of young women still routinely experience genital mutilation. How can we expect these cultures to begin to understand about us?"

Eventually, though, I was able to make a kind of peace with myself. I had approached my action with a great deal of consciousness, and from a place of truth and courage, I reminded myself. That is always honorable, regardless of the consequences. I was able to feel compassion for myself.

Having opened my heart, I was also able to feel forgiveness and compassion for my adversaries. For how long had it taken me—and most queer people—to come to a place of self-acceptance? For many of us it is a matter of emotional, psychological, spiritual—and sometimes physical—survival. We have no choice about it; our very difference, our queerness, compels us to undertake the difficult work of reevaluating cultural and religious mores and rejecting beliefs and attitudes that deny or demonize who we are. It takes most of us years to counteract the effects of our internalized homophobia and to dismantle old habits of thinking and adopt new ones. How much more difficult it must be, then, to change these prejudices in those for whom it is not a matter of self-preservation?

Without slowing down one bit our individual and collective activist efforts towards queer equality and freedom in all arenas, we need to develop an attitude of compassion for our families and friends, and even toward our opponents. The challenge is in moving beyond the kind of separation thinking that has been ingrained in us and putting into practice what probably all spiritual systems tell us in one way or another—that we are all one. Thus, I find the following technique, which I learned from Maia Dhyan, very useful in bridging the ego's experience of separation and making wrong. In the heat of the moment, when someone has just hurt us or insulted us or cut us off on the highway, it helps to remind ourselves that "I, too, have been that way," or "I have done that in the past," or "Given a certain set of conditions and situations, I too could have been that way or acted in that manner." This nullifies or cancels out our self-righteous attitude of superiority, the inherently dichotomous "I am right, and they are wrong," which is at the core of all anger. It helps bridge the gap between people that stems from the ego's illusion of separateness. If we really do believe that we are all one, and that these are not just nice, fluffy words we use to feel good about ourselves, here is a real opportunity to move that belief out of the realm of theory and into practice.

Deborah Johnson agrees that it is important to be aware of the law of action and reaction in our activist work. "As society's balances are shifting, there is a role and responsibility that the ones who are rising up into power have in helping the other people adjust to their new stations in life. Every time there's a shift, it involves more than just us, and that requires a certain amount of compassion." She explains that in our society, women have had to work hard to help men adjust and understand that they are not losing any of their masculinity by sharing equal status with women. Likewise, she says, "Black folk have had to work really hard with white folk on this issue." Because of her long-time involvement with the gay and lesbian rights movement, Johnson feels like she has "earned enough stripes" to be able to say that "as queer people we lack compassion for straight people. We lack compassion for what they are going through; we lack compassion for their struggles, and we are not doing anything to help them adjust, to try to bridge that gap. And, too often, we lack compassion for our own allies—those who cross the lines, those who come over and help, many times paying a heavy price for doing so."

When his book *Stranger at the Gate* first came out, Mel White found himself suddenly thrust in the midst of a war being waged against queer people by powerful religious forces, some of whom were his former clients. One of the first strategies he attempted was to contact some of the people for whom he had worked as a ghostwriter—Jerry Falwell, Pat Robertson, and James Kennedy—hoping to show them the harm their words and actions were inflicting on real human lives. He was met with that same deadening silence many of us have encountered in comparable situations. White, who had no training or experience in activism, "didn't know there were rules for doing justice nonviolently, rules established in the heat of battle by leaders of the great nonviolent justice movements." At one point, he sent out a letter to friends expressing his frustration and hopelessness. In response, he received a note from Lynn Cothren, Coretta King's personal assistant, teaching him one of the first rules of nonviolence: "Giving up on one's adversary is in itself an act of violence." The principles and techniques for doing justice nonviolently were used by Martin Luther King, Jr., who was inspired by Gandhi, whose philosophy was in turn influenced by the example and teachings of Jesus.

White states that the "soul force" principles of Jesus, Gandhi, and King are intended to both "develop our souls and transform our society." The most relevant of these principles to our discussion on service and compassion are: *I believe that I am most likely to find God while I am serving others. I believe that I will not discover the purpose of my life or the power in my life until I seek God by serving others. I believe that when I seek God in serving others, my own life will be renewed, empowered, and made more meaningful.* Finally, White brings up another challenging concept: Our opponent is not our enemy, "but a victim of misinformation" just as we have been.

In the ultimate analysis, we don't need to fear the fundamentalists. No doubt we need to keep a respectful and watchful eye on them; they still represent a threat to our movement. But they are a small minority, albeit a loud, well-funded, well-organized, and media-savvy one that has effectively crept into the corridors of power. When we take a long-term historical and evolutionary perspective, however, it seems to me that they are on their way out, and, deep down inside, they know it. They are fighting their last battle, which does make them dangerous, particularly because of their deeply held convictions. But their limited and limiting world view cannot survive much longer and will ultimately go the way of the dinosaurs. They are people, just like us. Terrified of change, their vitriol is fueled by ignorance. They are the ones holding on the tightest to the pebbles and twigs on the river bottom. Having compassion for them, even loving them—if nothing else because they are sharing the human experience in these times of dramatic change—does not mean we have to like them, their anachronistic beliefs, or their pernicious methodologies. But viewed from a detached perspective, they are in most need of help right now, for they are the most fearful of the changes that are now happening and those inevitable ones that have yet to come. And maybe, just maybe, given a certain combination of factors—if we had been born into their situations, and if we had not been blessed with our liberating status of sexual outsiders—we would feel the same way.

Coming Out Is Letting Go

Coming out is a profoundly spiritual act. Coming out means letting go—letting go of fear; letting go of limitation; letting go of anything and everything that has held us back, or anything we have been grabbing on to. It's about rejecting the lies, and embracing the truth, whatever the consequences. Coming out is an act of courage, and an act of love; it means relinquishing our self-protection, casting off the illusion of "security," and allowing ourselves to be who we are, regardless of what anyone else says or thinks we should be or do. Although it can be easy for others to see when we are not being ourselves, no one but ourselves can tell us who we are. Coming out also means renouncing our futile attempts to control ourselves and our emotions—and all the conditioning to which we have been subjected: that it's wrong to feel emotions, or enjoy sex, or laugh too loudly, or display affection in public.

Coming out is about letting go of victim consciousness and assuming active responsibility for our lives. It means giving up the self-consciousness that has held us back for way too long. Who cares what anyone thinks of us? What matters is that we become who we are, that we let our true selves *come out.* In the ultimate sense, coming out is about being ourselves. If that means coming out as a gay, lesbian, bisexual, or transgendered person, then go for it. If it means coming out as an artist, or a poet, when everyone around you thinks you should go to medical school or law school or trade school, then go for what you really want. It may mean coming out as a spiritual person.

Coming out spiritually is also about letting go. It means rejecting feelings of shame or embarrassment because we are on a conscious spiritual path, whatever that may be. For queer people, it includes and presumes coming out, and all the shedding that entails. It's about coming out of the quagmire of our lives—freeing ourselves from our neurotic patterns—and emerging as liberated whole beings. It involves emancipating ourselves from the expectations others have of us, and our expectations of them. Coming out spiritually also means "letting go and letting God," as they say in recovery circles.

It is time for us to come out as gay, lesbian, bisexual, transgendered, or queer within the spiritual communities we are a part of. It is also time for us to come out as spiritual beings to our gay friends. In both cases, exemplars are sorely needed.

By letting go, trusting that we will not be alone, we release our fearful, white-knuckled hold on our lives. After tumbling and getting thrown and tossed about a bit—and if only we will resist long enough the urge to grab on again, to hold on for dear life to the illusion of safety and security—then the current will lift us up. As we stabilize, pretty soon we are able to glide in unison with the current. We learn how to use its force. But "using it" implies too much separation, because as we use "The Force," we also give ourselves up to it. We put ourselves in its hands. We trust that it knows where we are going. We stop fearing and resisting the current and become one with it.

Beyond Labels

Many spiritual teachers say that eventually we must let go of our identities. Gay Vedanta teacher Jim Gilman went through a transformational process in which everything he had held on to was "ripped away so that even being *iden-*

tified as my sexual orientation had to go." Clearly, he explains, "That does not mean being straight but simply letting go of anything we hang on to."

For gay or lesbian people, transcending personal identities may present an additional challenge. Many of us have struggled long and hard to develop a sense of identity, one that is often inextricably tied in to our sexual orientation, and may find that identity difficult to give up. Warning about the spiritual trap all labels can hold, Ram Dass explains that if gay people will "sit down and examine their own minds in a systematic way, they may experience the freedom to take more delight in life and in their gay expression of it. And they will see that who they are isn't gay, and it's not not-gay, and it's not anything—it's just awareness."[10] We can see this happening in the younger generations of queers and "post-queers" who increasingly reject labels and seem to be more fluid in their sexuality. With less boundaries, less limitation, and less rigidity, they may have an advantage in working toward transcendence.

In a challenging essay titled "The Pit and the Pendulum," Gavin Geoffrey Dillard, poet, former porn actor, and author of *In the Flesh,* drew from his study of the Advaita Vedanta tradition to speak of how the "Universal Force . . . recognizes no boundaries and adheres to no definitions. . . . Love acknowledges no 'ghettos'—because our entire social fabric appears to be made up of a gazillion specific words and catch-phrases, like *ghetto, Castro clone, foot-stomping dyke, lipstick lezzie, leather faerie.* . . . And most of us know that we're in one ghetto or another. We choose these ghettos—these walls to hide behind—because we feel safe there; it is how we've been conditioned, it is how we have learned to hold that loving mistreated baby at bay. . . . So now I've become a homosexual, or gay, or queer, or a reluctant top, or a dubious polygamist, or a mister in search of a master, or whatever bumfuck handkerchief I'm wearing today. But I am not these things." While clarifying that he is not necessarily knocking any of these things, and that he is just fulfilling his job as poet and iconoclast, Dillard concludes that "the awakened soul recognizes no dichotomies—no goods and bads, rights and wrongs, blacks and whites. But these bubbles of pride, of identity, are all limitations. And limitations are not a quality of Awareness. They therefore are our suffering. They are missing the mark. These swings of the pendulum keep us in the pit of ignorance."

In the ultimate sense, I agree with the reality these men are addressing. But perhaps as a group the queer community is not there yet. I suspect that we need to develop a real sense of identity before we can move beyond it. We need to remember who we are. We need to reclaim our sacred roles. If we are already fulfilling them, we need to recognize and own and name them. There is power in recognizing and naming—both personal and communal. We can then consciously tap into particular archetypes and "download" instructions, inspiration, and resolution, both in the sense of resolving inner conflicts caused by years of hiding, and in the sense of resolving to do something—to decide, at a deep level, to act. Like gratitude, resolution is a state of being. When we achieve it, we become unstoppable, because we are divinely inspired, informed, and empowered.

A Time to Cultivate, a Time to Soar

Voltaire concludes his brilliant work *Candide* with the words: *"Il faut cultiver notre jardin"* (We must cultivate our garden). What do you need to do to cultivate your own garden? What parts of your life need grooming, weeding, or clearing? What steps are you willing to take to facilitate your growth, your healing process, your evolution? What might your next step be? What support do you need to actually take it? From whom should you elicit that support; or with whom might you at least share your concerns, your fears, your dreams? What obstacles to loving can you eliminate? How can you help dissolve whatever is blocking you from truly loving and accepting yourself—and therefore others—more fully? What is impeding your progress? Where are you lacking compassion? Where are you falling short of the mark? What will you commit to doing this year? This month? This week? Today?

Is there a class or workshop you've been meaning to take, or a practice you've felt drawn to, perhaps yoga, meditation, or breathwork? Is there a book you've been meaning to read, or finish? You need to find your own path and commit to it; to find your own particular set of skills, strengths, interests, and passions—and develop those. If you are not clear about what your path—or your next step—may be, ask for help. Ask the universe, or Spirit, or your Higher Self: "How can I help?"

What if you committed one evening, or one day, each week to your own self-discovery? Sacrificing one night a week of going out or watching TV or talking on the phone or working, and devoting it to yourself will be well worth it. Your actions toward that end will be supported—of that I have no doubt, as I have discovered in my own life. The universe has a vested interest in our becoming fully ourselves. As long as we are coming from a place of truth, of passion, of vision, of generosity, our efforts will be supported.

Consider taking more responsibility for one another. Try listening to our gay elders, and capturing their life experience and wisdom. Listen to the voices of our youth as well and discover the freshness and optimism they offer. For it will take all of us to effect real change. It is also important that we affirm each other more, instead of taking each other down or diminishing each other. Extending each other the benefit of the doubt and cutting each other some slack will facilitate dialogue and cooperation. We must allow room for all the diverse voices which comprise our movement. The competitive and mean-spirited infighting which has too often characterized our dealings with each other is not helpful and is not productive behavior. It is dysfunctional, and most likely the result of internalized homophobia, the remnants of self-hatred and self-degradation. We need to move beyond that now.

Cheryl Rosenthal, a film producer, agrees that we need to develop a *real* sense of community. "The only reason we call ourselves a gay community is because we have alternative sexual practices to heterosexuals. Go figure. I think that if we could get past our genitalia and be about the purpose for which we are here on the planet, these powerful individual tribes—lesbians, gay men, bisexuals, transgendered people—*together* have what it takes to stand up and make a difference in this world. . . . We just haven't taken responsibility for who we are. The most important thing is that we need to come together as a community and take action in the world that reaches beyond the magnificent job we've done with AIDS. AIDS really brought us together as a community and we showed up behind it. We need to take the world on as our next cause."

When we fully reclaim our identity, our power, our unique roles, when we connect with our truth and our purpose, magic will be commonplace in our lives, individually and as a *community.* In order to assist this process in your own life, open yourself to, allow, even welcome, change. Stop for a moment and look around you. What is working in your life, and what isn't? Deep inside, you know the answer, even if you don't want to look at it, or it is hard to accept. Even if it saddens or upsets you. Do whatever you need do to get right with yourself, and with Spirit. By Spirit I don't mean a separate, authoritarian, punitive entity, but the very current of life itself, God, the Tao. Learn to work with the flow. Allow the current to take you. What do you have to lose? Take a chance. Take a leap. There will be others waiting on the other side, others who have already leapt into the great and wonder-filled abyss of the unknown. Take a deep breath and soar.

Just Do It!

Holly Boswell is the founder of Kindred Spirits, a grassroots national network for transgendered spirituality based in North Carolina. With approximately our dreams of change and freedom are impeded by plain old inertia or laziness. And that is what I appreciate about Nike's directive to "Just Do It!" Often, action, any action, even a simple first step, is all that is needed. So I was somewhat disappointed when Nike changed their slogan in an effort to boost sagging sales. Their new slogan, "I Can," is all right. However, in spiritual terms it almost seems like taking a step backwards. "I Can" risks remaining stuck in the realm of possibility, unlike "Just Do It," which clearly prompts us to move from potentiality into the realm of cause.

Besides the few mentioned in this chapter, there are many other actions you can take to make a contribution. A myriad of causes and organizations could use your help. Support those you feel are doing good work on our behalf, as well as those that are striving to save the environment, or working on behalf of women, children, the homeless, or whatever you feel drawn to. They could use your contributions of time as well as money.

Rabbi Sharon Kleinbaum, head of New York's Congregation Beth Simchat Torah, was one of eighteen lesbians and gay men invited by *Out Magazine* in 1997 to set our "agenda" for the new millennium.[11] Her suggestion was a "two-pronged approach to religion: 1) At the national and grassroots level we must directly confront the bigotry that is spread in the name of God. We must deny the right wing a monopoly on the interpretation of God's will. 2) We must deepen our own spirituality, our own 'soul force' (as Gandhi called it), fed by the enduring truths of our religious traditions and our personal journeys and communal revelations." In order to accomplish those goals, she recommends that we do two things: join specifically queer religious communities and support progressive activist groups within existing denominations. Joining and supporting your local queer-friendly church may both serve your spiritual development and give you a sense of community. These usually offer plenty of opportunities for volunteering and contributing. Whatever form of service you feel drawn to, just do it.

It is also important that we express gratitude to and show support for our straight allies, those who have been putting their necks on the line on our behalf, in the name of truth, justice, and equality, sometimes suffering deleterious consequences. Among them are Rev. Jimmy Creech; Episcopal Bishops John Spong (New Jersey), William Swing (California), and Richard Grein (New York); Catholic Bishop Thomas Gumbleton of Detroit; Archbishop Desmond Tutu; Rev. Jesse Jackson; Rabbi Janet Marder, the first rabbi of Los Angeles' gay/lesbian synagogue, Beth Chayim Chadashim; Rev. Toni Cook of St. Paul's United Methodist Church in Denver; Rev. Cecil Williams and Janice Mirikitani of Glide Memorial Methodist Church in San Francisco; Rev.

two hundred members, the group's goal is to "awaken people's potential." Boswell believes that because queer people have been excluded from most of contemporary culture, "that is one of the reasons why things are so off-kilter. Our culture will continue to ail as long as our voices are not honored and integrated. It is important to honor ourselves in that way and then reclaim our place at the table. For us, it's too easy to become involved with ourselves and ghettoized. Kindred Spirits wants to bring our gifts back to the whole of humanity." As an artist, Boswell acts out the time-honored queer function of creating beauty. For her, "the creative process is very much akin to the spiritual process." She also embodies the spiritual archetype of social activist. "Sometimes my friends ask why I'm spending so many hours maintaining lists, or sending out newsletters. I respond: 'What else would I do?' This is who I am and what I'm about. For me it's all about serving each other; it's about answering a spiritual call, and I just do it."

When we pay attention and tune in to the world around us, we notice that the universe is constantly speaking to us. Signals come to us from unexpected sources: a stranger at the grocery line, billboards, license plates. Sometimes we turn on the radio and a certain song is playing with just the right message that we need to hear at that moment. Lately, it seems to me, as the world's slumbering but undeniable process of awakening continues to unfold, the messages are increasing both in frequency and directness. Each day, innumerable films and TV programs expose millions of people all over the world to messages of increased expansion, compassion, and understanding. They open us up to new possibilities and expand the way we view ourselves and our role in the universe.

Even advertising slogans are conduits for spiritually minded messages. Not long ago I was sitting alone on a quiet beach in Miami, pondering what course of action to take in a specific area of my life. I kept going back and forth, exploring the issue from different angles, when I looked up and saw one of those single-engine propeller planes dragging a promotional banner behind it. An advertisement for CK, Calvin Klein's perfume, this one read simply: "Just Be," a wise and fitting suggestion which I followed.

In recent television commercials both Italian nuns and Tibetan monks communicating telepathically were used to extol the virtues of computers, and a class-full of yoga practitioners to sell breath mints. One of the more familiar slogans has been Nike's exhortation to "Just Do It!" Most of us are well acquainted with the tendency among human beings to think, talk, or dream about how our lives will change once we do X or get Y. Too often, those wonderful and inspired ideas remain just that—thoughts, plans, and ideas—because of our own fear and resistance to disturbing the status quo. Sometimes

Jim DeLange of San Francisco's St. Francis Lutheran Church; Rev. Rodney Romney of First Baptist Church of Seattle; Chris and Barbara Purdom of the Interfaith Group; Laura Montgomery-Rutt, founder of the Alliance for Tolerance and Freedom; and many others too numerous to mention here.

Too often we hear complaints about the well-organized and well-funded efforts of the Christian Right or other homophobic groups whose agenda is our oppression. Words are easy; there is no intrinsic challenge in bitching and complaining. It is through acting that we really define ourselves in the world. Our pioneering efforts now could not only benefit us all but also the many others to follow, who have yet to come out. By our actions, we help make their world less antagonistic and more tolerant than ours. As we embark on new lives filled with heartfelt intentions and the commitment to improve our lot and make a contribution, remember that "We Can" is a given: the truth is that in the depths of ourselves we already know that we can accomplish whatever we really set our minds and hearts to do. What is important (and often missing) is simply getting off our butts and *just doing it.*

The Lavender Wave

We all have gifts to share. All humans do. But as gay people we have something special and unique to contribute. Our pain and our sense of alienation are often transmuted into contribution. Pain has deepened us. It has made us able to understand the pain of others. It promotes compassion. We *are* different, in the sense that our perspective is different. We do stand outside of the mainstream. We do reflect things back to and serve as a mirror for society. We are artists and we are healers. We create, promote, and support beauty—we bring beauty, color, texture, sound, music, and sensual delight to the world. We have a sense of joy, fun, and celebration to share with the world.

We have overcome the worst of adversities yet still managed to thrive and create amazing beauty in spite of it all. The art and beauty we have contributed throughout the ages, and which we continue to produce, is staggering. That we have accomplished this under hostile conditions—often in hiding, or while persecuted—in unfavorable situations in which we were not able to be fully and openly ourselves, is mind-boggling.

For those of us living today, a new opportunity exists. For the first time in the history of civilization, large numbers of people can identify themselves as gay or lesbian or bisexual or transgendered or queer or whatever. Never before has there really existed a visible gay community-in-the-making. Never before have we been able to live so openly, to be freely ourselves, to work and live and create as whole beings—as integrated beings who need not conceal entire parts of our humanity.

The genie's out of the bottle. I suspect we "ain't seen nothing yet" from our fledgling community. What art, what discoveries, what inventions, what music, what new fashions and trends, what social change and innovations, will we produce and create now—as we continue to unleash ourselves and set ourselves free?

There are no limits to what we can do or accomplish. There are no limits to who we can be. What beauty is brewing in *you* as you read these very words? Why not let go *now* whatever has held you back? What do you have to lose—except fear, limitation, mediocrity, unfulfillment, and lies? Why not go for excellence, in whatever way or form you choose to express it?

We can draw strength, creativity, and inspiration from our gender-bending and sexually fluid ancestors: Michelangelo. Sappho. Leonardo. Walt Whitman. Gertrude Stein. Tennessee Williams. Emily Dickinson. Oscar Wilde. Eleanor Roosevelt. Randy Shilts. Margaret Mead. Harvey Milk. Hastíín Klah. We'wha. Wu Tsao. Alexander the Great. Rikki Streicher. Marlon Riggs. Audre Lorde. Edward Carpenter. Josephine Baker. Plato. And all the others, including those whose names we don't know—the artists, the shamans, the priestesses, and the priests, the Native American Two-Spirits—revered for the sacred functions they fulfilled. Listen now to the voices of our ancestors, as they call out encouragement to us. We can be, and do, and accomplish, and experience, all they did and all they could not. Why not excel also for all those who are no longer able do it—our lovers, family members, and friends who have left their bodies due to AIDS, or breast cancer, or suicide, or drug addiction? Or for those who still lack the freedom to be themselves in other parts of the world? Through us they will be enjoying the gift of liberty, and the unique opportunity this time presents.

We owe it to them. We owe it to ourselves. We owe it to those who follow. For, in truth, we are those who go first. In particular, we are the generations of dramatic change, the "queers of the parentheses," to adapt Jean Houston's phrase. We are those who are in the midst of the transition, helping to bring about the metamorphosis. Already we can see in the younger generation of humans a more fluid, more relaxed state of being, and less hang-ups about sexuality. To them, it is not such a big deal whom one sleeps with. It's like, so what? We must involve ourselves, seek contact with, mentor the next generation—and our own elders.

Let us break the mold once again. For that, too, is our destined role: explorers of consciousness, expanders of boundaries, pushers of the envelope.

Let us make an irreversible difference in this world, at this most crucial turn on our collective road.

The best way to combat or counteract the effect of those who would do away with us or throw us back in the closet, lock the door, and throw away the key, is for each one of us to shine, to strive for nothing less than excellence, to go for it, holding nothing back. Only we can turn the key to our own closets and let ourselves out. No one can do it for us, but neither can they keep us in there against our will. The human spirit is irrepressible, and, obviously, so is the lavender spirit.

We must shine. We must all shine now—not out of rebelliousness or to prove anything to anybody—but because being us to the best of our capacity is the only thing that will really fulfill us. Life truly is about becoming all that we can be, to reclaim the army's slogan. As Tom Waddell, founder of the Gay Games, once said, "To do one's personal best is the ultimate of all human achievement." That is the goal toward which to stretch, step by step, or leap by leap, in our own time, at our own pace. As our beauty unfolds and our hearts open, we become gentler and more compassionate, yet brighter, more empowered, and fearless.

We have been holding on, holding back, playing small, hiding our light under a bushel. Enough of that. It is time to let go. We are needed now—all of us. That means each one of us completely, without holding anything back, with as much wholeness and integrity as we can muster. It also means all of us together—all those who feel a calling to do something, to be who we are to the fullest, to make a difference, to give it all we've got, regardless of the consequences.

It is time to show our true colors, time to let ourselves be seen, time to emerge in our best outfits. It is time to let the light out, let it through, and let it shine. It is time to feel our beauty inside, under all the blockages, all the lies, all the conditioning, underneath our pasts. It is there beneath the rage, the hatred—toward self and others—the anger, the disappointment, the confusion, the loneliness, the pain, the tears, the rejection, the tragedy of life. It is time to come out now in all our radiant magnificence.

In the words of Marianne Williamson, "Our deepest fear is not that we are inadequate. Our deepest fear is that we are powerful beyond measure. It is our light, not our darkness, that most frightens us. We ask ourselves, 'Who am I to be brilliant, gorgeous, talented and fabulous?' Actually, who are you *not* to be? You are the child of God. Your playing small does not serve the world. There is nothing enlightened about shrinking so that others won't feel insecure around you. We were born to make manifest the glory of God that is within us. It's not just in some of us; it's in everyone. And as we let our own light shine, we unconsciously give other people the permission to do the same. As we are liberated from our own fear, our presence automatically liberates others."[12]

By reclaiming our spiritual heritage, and consciously enacting the roles and functions which we have always played, we become empowered and develop a deep sense of self. We discover the pot of gold at the end of the rainbow: personal fulfillment, a life of purpose, peace, and passion. As we queer people reclaim those traditional roles, the world at large will also benefit. Humanity has been running off-balance, incomplete, the same way we do whenever we suppress or exclude any other group, whether it is women, or blacks, or Latinos, or whoever. What will it take for us to get it—to understand that we need all of us—all of our talents and gifts and skills? We need to work together to heal ourselves, heal our country, heal our ailing planet. It will not happen if we continue to demonize and scapegoat each other.

Because we come from all corners of the world, from all ethnic backgrounds, and all spiritual traditions, queer people can be exemplars for the rest of the world. We can show them how to work together to heal ourselves and our community. Let us join forces; combine energies, talents, and resources; deepen existing alliances and form new ones. Let us reach out to others, to all those who share a progressive vision of humanity, all those who are struggling to support change, and who are taking a stand for freedom, for truth, for justice, for the rights of women and minorities, for the environment. Let us join hands with all those who share a vision of a better world.

The effect we can have on the world is unimaginable. The world needs us now. The Earth needs us. Spirit needs us. We need us. Will you help heal our community? Will you help change the world?

Think of the supernovas, exploding, completely giving themselves away, holding nothing back, so that life could happen. That same generosity is in our blood and genetic materials. Holding nothing back as we give ourselves away, let us give until there is nothing left to give, and then give some more. Let us forgive, even when we think it is beyond our capabilities to do so. Let us love until it hurts, and then love some more, as we are filled with sacred fire. For passion is fire. Whether it is sexual passion or the passion for our children, our art, our work, or our causes, it is fire. Let us choose to offer ourselves to that sacred fire.

It is time to let go. The world calls out for us to leap. There is a spiritual awakening happening in this country, and all over this world. We can support it by coming out of the spiritual closet, by acknowledging that it is taking place, by talking about it to our friends and co-workers, by being an active, conscious part of this phenomenon that is sweeping the world.

I see a queer community healed, made whole, stronger, more empowered, more unified, more integrated, more compassionate, happier, better adjusted, more accepting of self and others, more content, more brilliant, more successful, more creative, more liberated. I see a queer community awakening to our potential to transform the world.

I see a wave. Slowly at first, but surely, unstoppably, irreversibly, gathering momentum. I see it sweeping across this country, across the world: a wave of lavender light, a wave of beauty, a wave of creativity, a wave of courage, a wave of truth, a wave of selfless service, compassion, and generosity, a wave of freedom, a wave of Spirit—a gay wave, a queer wave.

A Quick Guide to the World's Spiritual Traditions for Queer Seekers

Organized religion—in any form—brings up conflict and challenges for many people, not just queers. Given the wide range of religious denominations, and the differences in their decision-making mechanisms, how do we, as GLBT people, make sense of it all? Where do we stand, according to these varied, and to many, sacred belief systems, and better yet, why should we even care? Why should we want anything to do with traditions which, to many of us, are at best anachronistic remnants of a different era, and at worst fear-based and hate-filled organizations which have our exclusion and condemnation as a goal?

We need to care because the roots of homophobia are inextricably bound up in these same religions. Concerning ourselves with and working toward change within these organizations, is of crucial importance. In addition, many queer people believe that we have much to teach organized religion about traditional religious values of tolerance, acceptance, unconditional love, forgiveness, and the celebration of creation in all of its glorious diversity.

Clearly, queer people will always exhibit that same diversity in the spiritual paths we choose to follow. For, in truth, we *are* present everywhere—in Christianity, Judaism, and Islam, in Buddhism and Hinduism, in the Radical Faeries and other Earth-based, Goddess-based, and neo-pagan groups, as well as the New Age and New Thought movements. In the search for transcendence, we can be found preaching from the pulpit garbed in priestly vestments or a white collar; in nature rituals and shamanic drumming circles; in Bible study, yoga classes, breathwork groups, and Zen meditation; in twelve-step groups, Hindu chanting, and Taoist Tantric practices— and in various permutations of the above.

An analysis of the major religions uncovers a wide variance in regard to homosexuality even within individual denominations. However, some general conclusions can be made. We shall begin with the major traditions of the Far East (Hinduism, Buddhism, Taoism), followed by those originating in the Middle East (Judaism, Christianity, Islam). Then we will look at Earth-based traditions, the New Thought movement, and other alternative paths.

Hinduism

Many people claim that India is the spiritual heart of the planet, and that makes sense. Both Hinduism and Buddhism were born there; with its earliest archaeological findings dating to around 5000 B.C.E., Hinduism is considered the oldest of the world's extant major religions, influencing many of the others. In India today, Hinduism is practiced by a majority of the population. Worldwide, it encompasses an estimated seven hundred million adherents. The Vedas, or sacred Hindu scriptures, include the Upanishads and the two great Sanskrit epics, the Mahabharata and the Ramayana.

Of the many deities composing the Hindu pantheon, there are several that exhibit dual or fluid gender. Half man and half woman, Ardhanarishvara, a manifestation of Shiva, represents the blending of the male and female cosmic principles—"unity in diversity." Ardhanarishvara is also identified with communication, and serves as an intermediary who bridges the worlds of women and men as well as the human and divine realities.[1]

One of the most popular deities of Hinduism, Ganesha is also associated with androgyny. Half-elephant and half human, Ganesha is the remover of obstacles to new undertakings and the deity of prosperity and thresholds. His head is often depicted as that of a female elephant and his body as a human male, which, depicted as plump and soft—a standard for beauty in India—also reflects androgyny. In *Shiva and Dionysus: The Religion of Nature and Eros,* gay scholar Alain Daniélou describes Ganesha as "the guardian of the gate which leads to the coiled snake-goddess (Kundalini). . . . In the human body, the strait gate leading to the earth-center, or snake-goddess, is the anus. It is here that the center of Ganesha is found, the guardian of gates and mysteries, and servant of the Goddess."[2]

Ganesha's brother Skanda, also known as Ayappan, is considered the god of homosexuals.[3] The god of beauty and perpetual youth—two of the spiritual functions we visited earlier—he is also referred to as an eternal bachelor.

Other stories involving androgyny abound in Hinduism. For example, in the Mahabharata, we learn the story of Arjuna, the warrior-prince who at one point is cursed by the nymph Urvashi, whose advances he has rejected, to live as a harem dancer and "eunuch." When Arjuna's father intercedes, the hero's punishment is reduced to one year. Referring to this story, Will Roscoe notes in *Queer Spirit* that "the disguised Arjuna is described as a 'fire within a well'—fire being a male element and water female. What strikes me most about the . . . account is the almost campy way in which Arjuna's hypermasculinity is juxtaposed to his third-sex costume. When I try to picture this, I get the image of a body builder wearing see-through harem pants—a very sexy androgyne."[4]

Controversy exists concerning Hindu attitudes toward homosexuality. In contrast to classical Hinduism, where homosexuality seems to have been treated with neutral interest, in modern-day India the practice of homosexuality is frowned upon and condemned. There is no dogma in Hinduism against homosexuality, and, as we have indicated, it certainly displays considerable androgynous and homoerotic mythology. Vedanta teacher Jim Gilman states that like all the major religions, Hinduism has a "terrible track record when it comes to sexuality." Gilman, though, points out that if we go back to the early sources, we find a "very natural, earthy relationship to sexuality." According to Ozmo Piedmont, the fourth-century Kama Sutra has a section with detailed instructions for the maximizing of pleasure through fellatio between two men, and also has references to lesbian sex. "Both are understood to be normal proclivities when sexist and homophobic translations are eliminated." He further reports that when gay scholar Daniélou returned to the original sources of the Kama Sutra, he found references to homosexual unions—"marriages that were socially sanctioned in parts of India."

A somewhat surprising finding reported in *Cassell's Encyclopedia of Queer Myth, Symbol and Spirit* is that the great Mohandas Gandhi, revered in India as well as in the West, actually launched a campaign to destroy historical evidence of homosexuality in Hindu temples. Its purpose was to foster the perception that homosexuality had been brought to India by the corrupting influence of British colonialism; until it was eventually blocked by writer Rabindranath Tagore, the crusade of denial was continued by Nehru's government. In fact, there are reports that Nehru was quite upset when his friend Daniélou published photographs of ancient temples displaying homoerotic images.[5]

In his doctoral dissertation, *The Veils of Arjuna: Androgyny in Gay Spirituality, East and West,* Ozmo Piedmont reports that on one hand, there is more intimacy, including physical affection and public displays of affection, among males in India than in liberated and politically organized gay America. "Yet the evidence of homophobia is undeniable," he states, adding that "a lot of denial exists concerning homosexuality."

According to Piedmont, India's third-gender people are spoken of as eunuchs, a collective term not unlike our use of the word "queer" to encompass lesbians, gay men, bisexuals, and transgendered people. To Hindus, he writes, because "homosexuals imply gender integration and transcendence"—they represent an ideal. "In addition, homosexuals as androgynes have a special role as intermediaries between the sexes and connectors to the Divine."[6] Most "eunuchs" are considered to have spiritual power, and to serve a purpose in society and the cosmic plan. Among them we find the priests of the Ramanandi monastic order, which call themselves *rakis* when in service to the God Rama, and *sakhis* when serving the goddess Rita. As *sakhis* they consider themselves women, dressing in feminine garb, and even observing Hindu menstruation taboos.[7]

The *hijras* mentioned in Part 1 are probably the best-known example of the eunuch class. Many of them, having experienced ritual castration as the ultimate act of sacrifice to the Goddess, dress and identify as women. They live in communes and are thought to have the power to bestow both blessings and curses; their presence is thus particularly welcome at events such as marriage ceremonies, festivals, and at the birth of male children, where their special dances are thought to impart good fortune. *Hijras* often engage in prostitution to support themselves. Like the *hijras,* the *jogappas* also engage in religious transvestism and perform at special functions such as marriage and birth ceremonies. They are also considered sacred and are regarded with a mixture of fear and respect. In contrast, however, they identify as males "who have become vehicles for divine female energy;" they do not castrate themselves, and do not engage in prostitution. Most of them are thought to be homosexual.[8]

Buddhism

One of the world's major religions, Buddhism is based on the life and teachings of Siddhartha Gautama, a prince who became known as the Buddha, meaning the "one who is awakened." Born in 563 B.C.E. in Lumbini, a small kingdom in what is today Nepal, Siddhartha lived a sheltered and privileged life of wealth and luxury until age twenty-nine, when, after being exposed to humanity's suffering and misery—and distressed about the meaning of old age, sickness, and death—he walked away from his wife, son, and royal future in search of answers and enlightenment. After an unsuccessful search in the ascetic path and with a variety of teachers, he sat in meditation under the famous Bodhi tree, determined not to get up until he had fully discovered the meaning of reality. Moving through progressively higher states of consciousness, he finally attained the enlightenment for which he had been searching. Buddha then began to travel and teach; as increasing numbers of people began to follow him, he eventually created a monastic community, or *sangha.* His prolific teachings were passed on in the oral tradition and were finally recorded about four hundred years after his death.

The two basic branches of Buddhism, the Theraveda (The Way of the Elders) and the Mahayana (the Great Vehicle), contain many different sects. In America, Zen and Tibetan Buddhism are the most popular forms.

In its relationship to homosexuality, it is important to remember that because of Buddhism's inherent flexibility and adaptability, it is easily influenced by the culture of which it is a part. Thus, Buddhism in different countries will exhibit different attitudes toward homosexuality; moreover, differences may be evidenced in the same country at different time periods.[9] Gay Buddhist scholar José Ignacio Cabezón concludes that even though there has been wide disparity in what Buddhism has had to say about homosexuality, the prevalent attitude has been one of neutrality. Furthermore, he points out that in those instances where it was condemned, the issue had more to do with sexuality in general, as opposed to specific concerns about same-sex relations.[10] Cabezón concludes that in those cases where homosexuality is condemned it is either because monastic celibacy vows have been broken or men have transgressed the social order by assuming a female role.[11]

For the most part, according to experts, Chinese Buddhism exhibits tolerance toward same-sex relations. In *Cassell's Encyclopedia,* we find several instances of this, including the "Ten Sisters Society," which, between the sixteenth and the nineteenth centuries, "embraced resistance to heterosexual marriage, passionate friendship and lesbian intimacy and held ceremonies of same-sex unions."[12] The Golden Orchid Association, a women's organization with similar goals, surfaced closer to the twentieth century. Its members married each other and even adopted children; they were ejected from the group if they ever married a male. Attributing the change in attitudes to Christian influence from the West, Cabezón further points out that it was not until the twentieth century that sentiments toward homosexuality in China turned from neutral to hostile.

Japanese Buddhism, in contrast, breaks out of the neutrality pattern with quite a flare. There are moments in Japanese history when same-sex relationships were celebrated as sacred and as the ideal, even launching a literary movement (the *Chigo Monogatari*). Starting in the fourteenth century, we begin to see literature devoted to the celebration of male love.

Historians also provide amusing instances describing how passionately the Japanese defended their homosexual relations. When Spanish Jesuit missionary Saint

Francis Xavier arrived in Japan in the sixteenth century, he was appalled by the "ab-horrent" practices of Buddhist monks, to the point of eventually describing sodomy as the "Japanese vice." In one case, a group of missionaries encountered a group of young men who, having identified them as the ones condemning homosexuality, chased the Jesuits down the street while throwing their shoes at them. After receiving a typically Japanese respectful welcome, Francis Xavier and his cohorts were likewise banished from the court of a duke and from a monastery after he began reading in "a loud, hostile voice, the story of Sodom and Gomorrah."[13]

John Giorno, a poet, performer, and founder of the AIDS Treatment Project, says that homosexuality is "rampant" in Tibetan monasteries. A practicing Buddhist in the Nyingma Tibetan tradition, Giorno is also author of *American Book of the Dead* and *Balling Buddha,* among other books. A delightfully honest and informative interview with Giorno, conducted by Winston Leyland, appears in *Queer Dharma.* In it he recalls being in Tibetan monasteries in the '70s and discovering young monks sleeping in each others' arms: "They may not call it gay, but they were lovers. They loved each other, their hearts were open and their bodies were open. I really liked this vibe, a great deal of love from the heart center in a completely male world."[14] How-ever, gay Buddhist scholar Roger Corless qualifies that persons of the same sex sleep-ing together is a common practice in Asia, where privacy, and having one's own bed, is unusual and not valued.

Lesbian Buddhist Sandy Boucher, author of *Opening the Lotus: A Woman's Guide to Buddhism,* says that same-sex relationships are just as valid within most Buddhist settings as their heterosexual counterparts. Boucher acknowledges that homophobia is occasionally encountered among American Buddhist circles, but is quick to point out that nowhere in Buddhist doctrine are there specific condemnations of homosex-uality. All relationships are measured by the degree to which they "promote the well-being of both parties"; the Buddhist principle of "not harming" is also an important guide in gauging relationships.[15]

A controversy was recently sparked in the gay Buddhist world due to confusing and contradictory remarks by the Dalai Lama. In a 1994 *Out* interview, the Dalai Lama said that if a person does not have religious vows, and assuming mutual con-sent, it would be acceptable to have same-sex relations as long as no one was being harmed. However, in his 1996 book, *Beyond Dogma,* he seemed to reverse himself and began speaking in terms of "sexual misconduct" and "inappropriate" body parts. He wrote that sexual behavior involving the mouth or the anus, as well as masturba-tion, were considered "sexual misconduct," regardless of the participants' gender.

The controversy captured the gay community's and the media's attention be-cause of the well-loved and highly respected exiled leader's impending visit to San Francisco to attend an international peace conference. The Dalai Lama, who, by all accounts, is not homophobic, agreed to meet with representatives of the queer Bud-dhist community. According to Dennis Conkin, who followed the story for the *Bay Area Reporter* and later summarized the series of events in *Queer Dharma,* the meet-ing was "warm and candid," and the Dalai Lama readily admitted that he did not know the ultimate origin of the teachings in question. Among other things, he clarified that for non-Buddhists, "there is no harm in mutually agreeable sexual acts"; he asserted his unequivocal opposition to discrimination based on sexual orientation, and expressed support for gay and lesbian efforts to attain equal rights. Furthermore, he acknowledged that because Buddhism takes into account the cultural and societal context of its teachings, it is possible that if the precepts in question were considered within the context of a culture in which homosexuality was "part of accepted norms," it would then be found acceptable in Buddhism. Recognizing that neither he nor any other Buddhist teacher has the authority to unilaterally reinterpret these teachings, he recommended that discussions be taken up with other Buddhist *sanghas*. Although he adhered to his view that—for Buddhists—the practices in question consist of sexual misconduct, he said that it was important to consider these issues within their context, and that it is preferable to engage in prohibited sexual activities than to suppress them, if deprivation would lead to frustration, aggression, or other negative consequences.[16]

Regardless of the controversy, Buddhism is experiencing rising popularity among queer people, mostly due to its predominant neutrality and silence concerning sexual orientation. Queer people, so often alienated by the authoritarian and judgmental attitudes of other religions, tend to find solace in Buddhism's practical approach, its lack of dogma, and its emphasis on compassion.

Taoism

According to most scholars, Taoism was brought forth by the Chinese philosopher Lao Tzu, born around 604 B.C.E. The fundamental precepts of Taoism are contained within the *Tao Te Ching* (*The Way and Its Power*). The word *Tao* literally means "the way," or "the path."

The goal of Taoism is mastering the Tao—learning how to manage its flow. One of the ways to do this is through the practice of *wu wei,* usually translated as "nonaction," but more accurately meaning "effortless action." Modern sayings like "don't fight it; just flow with it" or "just ride the wave" embody Taoist concepts. Taoism emphasizes simplicity, humility, selflessness, respect for Nature, and the impermanence of things.

One of the best examples of the Taoist attitude toward life is the story of the farmer whose horse runs away. When a neighbor comes over to express his sympathy, the farmer responds, "Who knows what's good or bad?" The next day the horse returns, bringing with it a herd of wild horses. The neighbor comes over to congratulate the farmer, whose response is, "Who knows what's good or bad?" The following day the farmer's son, attempting to tame one of the wild horses, takes a fall and breaks his leg. Again, the neighbor comes over to commiserate, and the farmer's response remains the same, "Who knows what's good or bad?" The next day a group of soldiers comes by to recruit young men for an upcoming battle, and the farmer's son is spared because of his injury.

As the background and source of all life, the Tao is beyond gender. Taoists, however, believe that it is made up of both *yin* (feminine, or receptive) and *yang* (masculine, or active) energies. As part of the Tao, all humans contain both yin and yang energies, although in women, according to Taoist beliefs, *yin* is stronger, while in men *yang* is more prevalent.

Essentially, Taoism is silent and/or neutral about homosexuality, although negative attitudes can be found in some teachers' writings. These are mostly attributed to cultural influences, although some are encapsulated within the belief that same-sex relations are not conducive to the conservation or expansion of *chi* because they fail to balance yin and yang forces. Sa Wei-Dao, one of the founding members of Queer Taoists in San Francisco, reports that although one of the basic precepts of Taoism is withholding judgment, members of the group have encountered undeniable discomfort among heterosexual Taoists.

Sandra A. Wawrytko, in an essay published in *Homosexuality and World Religions,* concludes that although some Taoist teachers believe that homosexuality is in disharmony with the Tao, and even question its naturalness, when pressed, they seem to revert to Taoism's basic principle of openness. In the following passage, she quotes Master Mantak Chia's response to the question of whether homosexuality could impede spiritual growth:

> The Taoists are too wise to condemn anything outright, as everything leads back to the Tao. So the question really is how can it be against nature, or the Tao, if the Tao created it? Homosexuality is not against the Tao, but it is also not the highest experience of the Tao possible. It's impossible to experience the full balance of male-female polarity with homosexual love.[17]

Chia goes on to explain that the problem is compounded for gay men, "because their double yang energy is too expansive and more easily leads to conflict," while the double yin energy of a lesbian couple can be more "harmonious, because yin is yielding." According to Sa Wei-Dao, the belief is that a relationship between two women would be imbued with so much yin energy that it would "either quickly run out of whatever passion brought them together or they would analyze and deconstruct it into nothingness." Could this be one explanation for "lesbian bed death"? And could this be a reason why gay male relationships seem shorter lived than lesbian ones?

Obviously, this is an oversimplification of complex human behavior, and, as several queer writers have observed, this model ignores the fact that all humans contain both yin and yang energy within themselves. Furthermore, R. H. Van Gulik points out that according to Taoist alchemy, sexual relations between two men do not necessarily result in a reduction of chi, but could instead produce an "exchange of yang energy." And lesbian writer Elsa Gidlow, author of *Elsa: I Come with My Songs,* ventures that lesbians "increase their yang energies while fully living their yin, thus inwardly harmonizing these aspects of themselves and of the universe."[18]

As we saw earlier, in his more recent book, *The Multi-Orgasmic Man,* Chia actually devotes an entire chapter to gay sexuality.

Judaism

Half of humanity has been directly influenced by Judaism, because of its having given birth to Christianity and its shared ancestry with Islam. By some estimates, the combined numbers of Christians and Muslims (about 2.7 billion people) account for approximately half of today's world population. In comparison, as of the early 1990s there were about 12.8 million Jews in the world, the majority of them living in the United States (5.5 million) and Israel (3.9 million).[19] The revelations given to the Jews by God are recorded in the Torah, which means literally "law" or "doctrine," and which is the foundation on which Jewish religion and law stand.

The Jewish religious tradition is unequivocal in its condemnation of homosexuality. Based on the prohibitions made explicit in Leviticus (18:22 and 20:13), the traditional Jewish law (*halachah*) clearly condemns homosexual acts. Openly gay rabbi Yoel Kahn observes that in spite of recent scholarly interpretations which have questioned the meaning of ancient biblical invectives condemning homosexuality—suggesting, for example, that they referred to idolatrous cultic prostitution, or a violation of the ancient Middle-Eastern code of hospitality (as we will summarize later)—the interpretation of the passages in question by Jewish scholars has been consistent throughout history.[20]

The *halachah* is harsh in its prohibition of male same-sex behavior, which, at one point, was treated as a capital offense punishable by stoning. In *Que(e)rying Religion,* Ellen Umansky explains that Judaism is much more lenient when it comes to lesbianism because it is not directly condemned in the Hebrew Bible, and because it does not entail the "wasting of procreative seed." Instead, it is rebuked as an "unseemly, immoral act"—an *issur* (a general religious violation)—instead of a *to'evah* (an abomination, which male homosexuality was considered), or even an *arayot* (specific sexual sin).[21] These days not even the most conservative Jewish scholars endorse capital punishment for homosexuality, and almost all are clearly intent in separating the "sin" from the "sinner," stating that homosexuals should be treated with compassion and should be allowed to become members of congregations.

Dramatic differences become evident as we consider the different branches of Judaism, although, as Kahn points out, there are liberal and fundamentalist factions within each. In non-Orthodox Judaism, the trend in recent decades has been toward increasing support of gay and lesbian Jews. Reform Judaism has explicitly opposed legal discrimination based on sexual orientation. In 1975, the Central Conference of American Rabbis (CCAR) passed a resolution affirming civil rights for gay people. In 1990, they reaffirmed the equality of all members, regardless of sexual orientation, and expressed support for gay and lesbian rabbis. Presently, Reform Judaism does not discriminate on the basis of either gender or sexual orientation when ordaining rabbis, of whom celibacy is not required. In 1996, the CCAR passed a resolution in support of gay civil marriage—as opposed to religious ceremonies involving rabbinical officiation. Thus, although many Reform rabbis will perform same-sex commitment ceremonies, they tend to discourage the use of the word "marriage."[22] An official discussion of *kiddushin* (religious marriage ceremonies) for same-sex couples is anticipated by some in the near future.

The Union of American Hebrew Congregations (UAHC) has also adopted comparable gay civil rights resolutions, officially stating that "in accordance with the teaching of Reform Judaism, all human beings are created '*Betselem elohim*' (in the divine image)."[23] In 1993, UAHC also expressed support for the legal recognition of lesbian and gay relationships. Since 1973, when UAHC accepted into its membership Beth Chayim Chadashim, the gay and lesbian-outreach synagogue in Los Angeles, more than twenty gay synagogues have flourished in the United States. Among them are Bet Havarim in Atlanta, Am Tikva in Boston, and Beth Simchat Torah in New York City, the largest gay and lesbian Jewish congregation in the world with eight hundred members. Under the leadership of Rabbi Sharon Kleinbaum, Beth Simchat Torah draws close to three thousand congregants during the high holidays. The World Congress of Gay and Lesbian Jewish Organizations orchestrates many of these synagogues and other organizations. Besides the twenty synagogues, there are another twenty cultural or social groups in the U.S., and an additional twenty-three worldwide, including Mexico, Hungary, Israel, and Australia.

In Conservative Judaism, which maintains a tradition of halachic authority, there is ongoing debate on the meaning of the law pertaining to homosexuality. While the Rabbinical Assembly came out in support of civil rights for gays and lesbians, and welcomes homosexuals into their synagogues and related organizations, gays and lesbians are not accepted as rabbis or cantors, and same-sex commitment ceremonies are unsanctioned.[24]

In some ways the most liberal, the Reconstructionist movement grew out of the Conservative movement in the 1930s; it promulgates the adaptation of Jewish teachings to the circumstances of modern life. The Jewish Reconstructionist Federation has stated that it opposes "all forms of discrimination on the basis of sexual orientation and actively supports legislation designed to prohibit such discrimination." The Reconstructionist Rabbinical College has an official policy of nondiscrimination in their school.[25] For some time now, the Reconstructionist Rabbinical Association has upheld rabbis who opt to officiate at same-sex commitment ceremonies. The Reconstructionist branch is making steadfast progress toward full acceptance of gay and lesbian Jews.

Most traditional, and encompassing a wide array of factions, is the Orthodox branch, of which the Hasidic sect represents the more conservative end of the spectrum. Unlike the former two, the Orthodox movement (which only accounts for an estimated 3 percent of American Jews) does not have a national unifying organization. The majority of Orthodox Jews still consider homosexuality an "abomination." Others, however, regard homosexual behavior as *anoos* (compelled) and thus not morally culpable, in spite of the fact that their actions are condemned. Many Orthodox synagogues will accept gay members but withhold certain privileges if they are out. According to Rabbi Allen Bennett, founder of Congregation Sha'ar Zahav in San Francisco and the first openly gay rabbi in Jewish tradition, some Orthodox rabbis, notably Eli Finkelman of Berkeley, have publicly argued for gay and lesbian inclusion in Judaism.

Several Jewish scholars suggest that their religion's condemnation of homosexuality stems from two major sources. Besides the cultural taboo against "wasting the seed" (originating from the emphasis on procreation), there was the second, and related, need for the ancient Israelites to differentiate themselves from neighboring cultures. Hence the prohibitions on such practices as cultic prostitution, common among the Canaanite people whose land the Israelites conquered. This dual emphasis on maintaining a separate identity and on ensuring the survival of the Jewish race has colored much of its culture, history, and thought.

In response to concerns that sanctioning homosexuality will result in the obliteration of the Jewish family, Umansky writes that "rather than bemoaning the dissolution of the traditional Jewish family, we might work to create a new family life that affords all members—women as well as men, homosexuals as well as heterosexuals—the sense of dignity, equality, and worth which, according to the Talmud, is our common possession."[26] Similarly, Kahn argues that the inability, or even the unwillingness, to reproduce does not prevent the marriage of heterosexual Jewish couples. Adding that more and more lesbian and gay couples are having children and raising families, he concludes that "it is not the homosexual who is not interested in fulfilling the covenant responsibility, as much as it is the community that stands in her or his way."[27]

Reform Rabbi Janet Ross Marder writes that "Jewish condemnation of homosexuality is the work of human beings—limited, imperfect, fearful of what is different, and, above all, concerned with ensuring tribal survival. In short, I think our ancestors were wrong about a number of things, and homosexuality is one of them."[28]

And yet it is important to keep in mind that it was only in 1972 that Sally J. Presiand became the first female rabbi in Jewish history. That means that it's only been in the last three decades of the last three thousand years that women have been allowed in the rabbinate. Unquestionably, progress is being made. As a final note, in 1988 the Knesset, the Israeli Parliament, legalized sexual relationships between men. One of the effects of the law was allowing openly gay men to serve in the Israeli army, considered one of the essential requisites of Israeli society. As a secular institution, the Knesset is not bound by the *halachah,* and, conversely, its decrees do not constitute part of traditional Jewish law. In spite of this, the Knesset's actions are extremely significant in the evolution of Jewish attitudes vis-à-vis homosexuality.[29]

Comprising Judaism's mystical tradition, in recent years the Kabbalah is finding renewed interest and increasing popularity. Some believe that, compared to traditional Judaism, it exhibits more flexibility regarding gender and sexual variance. *Cassell's Encyclopedia,* for example, mentions several instances of the Kabbalah's links to homosexuality, androgyny, and transgenderism.[30]

Islam

The Arabic word *islam* derives from *salam* which means "peace," or "surrender."[31] "To surrender to God or the law of God" is its more precise religious meaning.[32] Founded by the Prophet Muhammad in Arabia in 622 C.E., the religion now includes an estimated one billion followers (called Muslims) worldwide. Besides its prevailing presence in the Arab and Turkish world, as well as in Africa and Southeast Asia, Islam is the second most populous religion in Europe and is experiencing dramatic growth in North America.

The main source of Islamic belief is the Koran (the word *Qur'ān* means "recitation"), a compilation of revelations said to have been given by God directly to Muhammad during the twenty-two years which encompass his time as prophet (610–632 C.E.). As the literal transcription of God's messages to Muhammad, the Koran is considered to be infallible.

Like Judaism and Christianity, Islam places strong emphasis on the family and encourages reproduction. Social acceptability plays a commanding role in Islamic culture. Islam's condemnation of homosexuality stems from the story of Lot which is mentioned five times in the Koran, although without reference to the city of Sodom. The sin of "Lot's people," however, was made clear, and, according to Khalid Duran, leaves no room for interpretation or theological concessions when it comes to homosexuality. The Koran (26:165-166) says, "How can you lust for males, of all creatures in the world, and leave those whom God has created for you as your mates. You are really going beyond all limits." And to the Prophet himself are attributed the following words: "Doomed by God is he who does what Lot's people did"; "No man should look at the private parts of another man, and no woman should look at the private parts of another woman"; "Whoever has intercourse with a woman and penetrates her rectum, or with a man, or with a boy, will appear on the Last Day stinking worse than a corpse; people will find him unbearable until he enter hell fire, and God will cancel all his good deeds."[33]

At twenty-one, Faisal Alam is the founder of Gay Muslims, a Boston-based group which began in 1997 as an Internet listserve. With over two hundred members from twenty countries, the group had its first international gathering in 1998. Alam believes that there are variances in the translations of the Koran passages which specifically refer to male-to-male sexuality, and that further research is necessary to clarify exactly what was being prohibited. "There are indications that the punishment was not for homosexuality as we now know it, but for the practice of perverted, lustful desires, or for adultery, inhospitality, or the looting of caravans. There is also no evidence that the Prophet punished anyone for same-sex behavior; it was not until the second Caliph that we find records of that."

Anti-sodomy legislation varies among Islamic countries, and is harshest in those still ruled exclusively by the *Shari'a* (the code of law derived from the Koran), and most lenient in those influenced by secular law and, in particular, the Napoleonic Code.[34] Legal punishments range anywhere from two-months' to fifteen-years' imprisonment, to death by stoning (in Saudi Arabia, Iran, and Afghanistan). However, capital punishment is not commonly enforced and the system is designed to discourage accusations. In the Middle East, Turkey stands alone as having no anti-sodomy regulations; Indonesia, the single most populous Islamic country in the world, also has no anti-sodomy laws.

While the Koran unequivocally condemns homosexuality, many Muslim cultures exhibit a double standard when it comes to its actual practice. As is the case in some Latin American cultures, it is ignored as long as it is not flaunted openly.[35] A closer inspection of cultural mores reveals that homosexuality is socially objectionable only if a male is the recipient of penetration. Active insertion is not considered homosexuality. Its rejection is therefore associated to the perceived loss of masculine status in a highly misogynistic society. It is no surprise, then, that research into the sexual practices of women—not to mention lesbianism—are practically nonexistent.[36] Needless to say, the concept of same-sex unions is not even a blip on the Islamic consciousness radar.

Sufism, Islam's mystical tradition, is this religion's only branch presenting a positive image of same-sex love. According to scholars, Sufism developed about a century after the death of Muhammad, when, as a demonstration against the excessive worldliness—exemplified by the sultans' expensive silks and satins—which they felt was corroding Islam, a group of Muslims began wearing rough woolen apparel, from which the name *Sufi* derives (*suf* means wool).[37] However, openly gay Sufi Sheikh Muiz Brinkerhoff reports that other experts trace the roots of Sufism back to the Egyptian mystery schools.

Emphasizing the internal, rather than the external, the Sufis pursued transcendence and ecstatic union with God, a direct experience of the divine. By the twelfth century they were assembling in communities clustered around spiritual teachers, or *sheikhs*. Sufis are known for their passionate poetry, which beautifully expresses the pain of separation from and a deep longing for God. Because of its emphasis on the internal, in Sufism one's sexual orientation is not as important: "the only thing that counts is union with the Divine through mystic exaltation."[38] Much of Sufi poetry is replete with homoerotic descriptions. It should not be surprising that Sufis have experienced repression at the hands of fundamentalist Muslims, who find even the concept of *shahêd*—that the image of God can be evidenced in a male beloved—offensive and heretical.[39]

The best known exemplar of the Sufi tradition is Rumi, considered by many to be Islam's greatest mystic poet. His relationship with Shams-ad-din Tabrizi—his *shahêd*—is well documented. Falling passionately in love with Shams, Rumi abandoned his community of disciples and went off to live in the desert with his beloved. Increasingly jealous, the disciples persecuted Shams, who was eventually forced to escape their desert hideaway. When he was found murdered, Rumi was said to enter a profound state of grieving, which lasted forty days; it was during this time that he began to dance—acting out his pain, mourning, and longing in the same garden where Shams's corpse was found. Out of this whirling, passionate lamentation emerged the tradition of the *sama,* the spinning trance dance for which the Sufi Whirling Dervishes of the Mevlevi Order are known.[40] As he turned, he entered into a trance state, and the quatrains for which he is now famous would begin to pour forth; they were then copied down by students. It should be noted that some scholars refute the homoerotic elements of this relationship, insisting that the poetic language employed was characteristic of the genre and symbolic of divine, not human, love.

In 1910, Sufism was brought to the West by Inayat Khan, who introduced certain innovations and distillations of the traditional teachings from India. Even in modern-day America, gay and lesbian Sufis encounter homophobia within their tradition. Brinkerhoff, who was initiated into the Sufi Islamia Ruhaniat Society, explains that if an order has adopted Islam as its outer manifestation, then there will be problems. He reports, however, that a substantial number of the those within his order's teaching circle identify as "nonheterosexual," although they are not quite open about it.

All in all, the outlook for gays and lesbians in Islam is not very promising, at least for the foreseeable future. Because so many Muslim countries are just emerging from colonialism, gay civil rights are at the bottom of their scale of priorities. Analogous to Maslow's hierarchy of individual needs, many of the third-world cultures in question have pressing, survival-level, social and economic problems which must be addressed first. One of these complex social dilemmas is the abyss between the genders, caused by the imposed separation of the sexes.

If there is any hope for change, according to Duran, it will have to come from one of the exiled communities, because no Islamic secular government would dare risk the repercussions of being labeled "decadent" or "depraved" by fundamentalist factions seeking absolute theocratic control. Islam is a theocratic religion attempting to attain "God's rule on Earth," an absolute system with no separation between social, spiritual, economic, and political arenas.[41]

It is probably no coincidence that of all the religions, Islam and Christianity are the two most homophobic ones, and the two which historically have exhibited the greatest militaristic tendencies. Barring developments in Protestantism during the past few decades, they are also the two most oppressive of women. No other religions have engaged in more violence or have engaged in such zealous efforts to attain converts. The Islamic *jihads,* or "holy wars," are analogous to Christianity's Inquisition, its Crusades, and its early colonization of America (and the subsequent decimation of the Indigenous inhabitants).

Christianity

With an estimated 1.7 billion members, and a considerable presence in every inhabited continent, Christianity has the largest following of all the major religions. Its influence on Western culture has been and continues to be immeasurable. Even our calendar is set on the date attributed to Jesus' birth (even though his actual birth is now believed to have taken place closer to 4 B.C.E.).

Christian intolerance of homosexuality basically stems from six biblical passages. Because extensive work has been done in this area, only brief mention will be made of them here, and the reader is referred to other sources for a more complete discussion.[42]

Traditionally interpreted as a condemnation of homosexuality, the Sodom story in Genesis 19: 1–11 has been re-explained by recent biblical scholarship. New interpretations question the translation of certain words and suggest instead that inhospitality to strangers, not homosexuality as we understand it today, was the intended transgression. Basically, the story goes that God sends two angels to Sodom, where they are offered shelter by Lot. All the neighboring people then surround Lot's house and demand that he release the visitors so that they "might know them." It is the mistaken interpretation of the Hebrew verb *yada* (to know) as carnal knowledge—one of its least frequent uses in the Bible—that has given meaning to this passage. Biblical scholars, such as John Boswell, Daniel Helminiak and others, now believe that it is more likely that its intended meaning was "to have thorough knowledge of," or the inspection of the visitor's identifying documentation. They also point out that Sodom and Gomorrah had already been singled out as being in hot water before the incident in question, and that since all of Sodom's inhabitants (other than Lot's family) participated in the event and were later destroyed, it is unrealistic to think that they were *all* intent on homosexual rape. And, if that was the intention, why would Lot offer them his *daughters?* Scholars further question Lot's exemption from a sexual infraction when he then turns around and engages in incestuous relations with his daughters. Finally, they point out that of all the other biblical passages which mention the story of Sodom and Gomorrah, not a single one contains any allusion to homosexuality.

The Book of Leviticus, also called the "Priests' Manual," was a manual of rituals and ethical behavior for the ancient Hebrews. Chapters 17–26 are often referred to as the Holiness Code, because they summoned the Hebrew people to become holy in the same way God is holy. From Leviticus 18:22 we get the infamous "abomination" invective: "You shall not lie with a male as with a woman; it is an abomination"; and Leviticus 20:13 doles out the punishment for the aforementioned infraction: death. Experts have reexamined these texts and suggest that they refer to uncleanliness, not "abomination" in the sense of an intrinsic moral evil. Moreover, these scholars point out, the rules constituting the Holiness Code were intended to distinguish Jewish identity from that of the pagan people surrounding them. In particular, they sought to prohibit the religious practices of the Canaanites, such as idolatry and sexual fertility rites. Therefore, many now believe that the prohibition was not of homosexuality per se but of the idolatrous practice of ritual/cultic sexuality. Besides, to uphold only some of the Levitican prohibitions while arbitrarily dismissing others which are now considered archaic, irrelevant, or absurd—such as prohibitions against cutting one's hair or shaving, eating pork and shellfish, having sex with a menstruating woman, the hybridization of seeds, and the mixing of fabrics in clothing—is undeniably hypocritical.

The only allusions to homosexuality in the New Testament, or Christian Bible, are found in the letters of St. Paul. Experts now believe that the interpretation of Romans 1:18–32 referring to homosexuality as "a violation of natural law" was inaccurate, and that Paul's intended meaning was more likely "unusual," or "out of the ordinary."[43] This would make homosexuality "socially unacceptable," as opposed to "unnatural," "sinful," or "morally wrong."[44] Again, they point out that Paul's admonitions must be taken within the context of the sexual excesses of the Greco-Roman world in which the early Christians were trying to establish themselves, and that he was probably referring to the "uncleanliness of Gentiles" and their idolatrous sexual acts.

The same applies to the other two references in Paul's epistles—1 Corinthians 6:9–10 and 1 Timothy 1:9–10. In both of these passages, translations such as "effeminate," "abusers of themselves with mankind," and "homosexuals" are considered by some experts to be unwarranted. Besides, as already mentioned, they are being taken out of their cultural and historical context and more likely were intended to prohibit male cultic prostitution or abusive male-male sexual practices, such as rape.

Other experts are not convinced by these etymological analyses. Conner et al. suggest instead that more research be done on other biblical passages which possibly present same-sex relationships in a positive light. Certain passages describing, for example, the relationship between Jonathan, son of King Saul, and David, legendary warrior/king/poet/prophet/healer/slayer of Goliath, are suggestive of homoerotic content. As they bid each other good-bye prior to Jonathan's final battle, they were said to have "kissed each other and wept together."[45] And, once he heard of Jonathan's death, David was disconsolate, professing that his love for Jonathan was "wonderful, more wonderful than that of women."[46] Likewise, writers like Nancy Wilson, author of *Our Tribe,* have seen intimations of same-sex love in Ruth's adamant refusal to leave her mother-in-law (Naomi, David's great-grandmother) once Naomi's husband and two sons were killed: "Don't urge me to leave you or to turn back from you. Where you go I will go, and where you stay I will stay. Your people will be my people and your God my God. Where you die I will die, and there I will be buried."[47] And for the European medieval period, John Boswell has successfully demonstrated the ubiquity of homoerotic literature, and the existence of same-sex unions.[48]

From what little we know of Jesus' actual life, it is clear that he was not one to mince words or withhold his thoughts; time after time, he spoke his truth regardless of the consequences. Is it not telling, then, that not one single admonition was pronounced by him about homosexuality? What about Jesus' example of hanging out with the "lowest of the low," the "sinners," and the disenfranchised? If he were alive today, he would be found, as Jallen Rix sings in "Down at Stonewall," at a gay bar, for who are considered the lowest of the low, the outcasts, in today's culture?[49] And what "lepers" would he be healing, if not those afflicted by AIDS, regardless of their sexual orientation?

Admittedly, there is a vast range of interpretations about what it means to be a Christian. People claiming that appellation run the gamut from very progressive, as evidenced by the number of churches involved in the civil rights and other social justice movements, to the extreme fundamentalism of the Christian Right. There is also a wide range of opinions among Christian denominations concerning homosexuality.

Roman Catholicism

The official stance of the Roman Catholic Church on homosexuality is crystal clear: it is forbidden. Possibly in response to declarations by the American Medical Association and the American Psychological Association in the early '70s, which removed homosexuality from their lists of illnesses, the Church's 1975 *Declaration on Certain Questions Concerning Sexual Ethics* warns of "those who, basing themselves on observations in the psychological order have begun to judge indulgently, and even to excuse completely, homosexual relations between certain people."

Another example is the 1992 Vatican letter to the American bishops mandating their opposition to all gay rights legislation, even if it exempted the churches. In effect, the document endorsed anti-gay discrimination in employment, housing, and adoption. Comparing homosexuality to a contagious disease or mental illness, it asserted that the state has a duty to limit people's civil rights if the common good of society is involved.

Also in 1994, the Church released its *Catechism of the Catholic Church*, in which homosexual acts were described as acts of "grave depravity," "intrinsically disordered," and "contrary to the natural law." It did, however, advise that homosexuals be "accepted with respect, compassion, and sensitivity," and that "every sign of unjust discrimination in their regard should be avoided." It also called homosexual people to chastity—described as "self-mastery" through which they would reach inner freedom, and "approach Christian perfection."

A possible opening was signaled by a 1997 letter from the U.S. bishops called "Always Our Children." Acknowledging the inherent nature of sexual orientation, and advocating tolerance and support for gay Catholics, the letter encouraged Catholic parents to "do everything possible to continue demonstrating love for your child," and cautioned against outright rejection or severing relations. Although the letter certainly indicated progress, and was unprecedented in its positive tone and content, it still fell short of the mark by upholding "homosexual activity" as objectionable, and by neglecting to voice the need for a softening in the Church's staunch and condemning doctrine. However, any positive feelings or sense of gain generated by the bishops' letter were counteracted when, later that same year, the pope publicly denounced same-sex marriages for the first time, as he directed Catholics to resist legal attempts to change marriage laws. Speaking of the dangers in allowing "other forms of unions of couples contrary to the initial plan of God for the human race, he warned that gay unions threaten the future and "society at its very foundations."[50]

Even so, Jim Schexnayder, a Catholic priest, finds reason for optimism. As executive director for the National Association of Catholic Diocesan Lesbian and Gay Ministries, Schexnayder frequently comes up against the struggle between the Church's official teachings and pastoral practice—between Rome and the local community. His hope lies on the local level. Schexnayder reports that more and more parishes and dioceses are evolving welcoming ministries; in his own diocese of Oakland, two Catholic high schools have gay and lesbian support groups.

A group for GLBT Catholics, Dignity was founded in 1969 in Los Angeles by Fr. Patrick Nidorf, becoming established as a national organization in 1973. It now has seventy-five chapters across the United States, with its main offices in Washington. In addition to worshiping together as openly gay or lesbian Catholics, Dignity members enjoy social occasions and work together in support of social change.

Orthodox

The word "orthodox" stems from the Greek word for "right belief." As such, the Orthodox Church, with an estimated two hundred and fifty million members worldwide, considers itself the only one with a legitimate claim to an unbroken link to the early Christian church. This continuity of faith, of teaching, and of community is of critical importance to the Orthodox, who view themselves as the "One Holy Catholic and Apostolic Church." Furthermore, they contend that all historical offshoots of Christianity (including the Roman Catholic Church) were caused by splits from the "right beliefs" of Orthodoxy. The great schism between the Eastern Orthodox and Roman Catholic churches occurred in 1054, both branches excommunicating each other and blaming the other for the split. Rejecting papal authority, the Eastern church lacks the centralization of the Roman church, and has a much more democratic philosophy (for instance, its lay people actually elect their clergy, and their parish priests are permitted to marry).

The Orthodox Church of America's official website clearly delineates its stand on homosexuality. After referencing some of the same "texts of terror" discussed earlier, including Paul and Leviticus, one passage, based on the latter, actually states: "Homosexual acts, like adulterous and incestuous behavior, are condemned in the law of Moses. Those who do these things, both men and women, are, according to God's law of the old covenant, to be put to death." Other phrases include more of the same about giving up "natural relations," being "consumed with passion," "dishonoring . . . their bodies," "committing shameless acts," "refus(ing) to acknowledge God . . . and obey his divine teachings."

The Orthodox Church teaches that "homosexuality is the result of humanity's rebellion against God" and is therefore "against its own nature and well-being." It does, however, assert that homosexuals are to be treated with "the understanding, acceptance, love, justice and mercy due to all human beings." The Church also recommends that assistance be given us "to admit these [homosexual] feelings to [our]selves and to others who will not reject or harm [us]," to discover the "specific causes" of our orientation, and to work toward "overcoming its harmful effects." Finally, the Church draws a line between those "struggling with homosexuality who accept the Orthodox faith and strive to fulfill the Orthodox way of life" and those "instructed and counseled in Orthodox Christian doctrine and ascetical life who still want to justify their behavior." Like other believers struggling with their own challenges, the former are allowed to be "communicants of the Church." The latter, however, are clearly not to "participate in the Church's sacramental mysteries, since to do so would not help, but harm them."

Founded in Los Angeles in 1980, AXIOS—a word derived from the Greek liturgy which means a "truly worthy and deserving person"—is an organization of gays and lesbians belonging to, having been raised in, or having converted to Eastern rites. AXIOS members include several clergy and even some bishops.

Protestantism

The next major schism in Christianity came about in the sixteenth century in the form of the Protestant Reformation. These series of splits were generated by complex and still-debated causes, including social, political, and economic changes—the rise of nationalism, of cities, of the middle class, of capitalism, and of an individualism triggered by Renaissance thought.[51] Additionally, it was fueled by the infractions, abuses, and corruption of the Church's hierarchy, such as the selling of "papal indulgences," or pardons. The Protestants also objected to the concept of papal infallibility and replaced it instead with the ultimate authority of the Bible. Of course, as history has attested, the risk inherent in this individualistic approach is the likelihood of multiple biblical interpretations resulting in a myriad of splits within Protestantism.

While Protestantism's rejection of Mary and the Catholic saints deprives it of Christianity's only feminine aspect in what is otherwise a very patriarchal entity, several of the Protestant denominations have been advocating and implementing the ordination of women during the last three decades.

Anglican/Episcopalian

Of all the Protestant denominations, the Anglican Church most closely resembles Catholicism. It was established around 1530, when King Henry VIII became infuriated by Pope Clement VII's unwillingness to annul his marriage from Catherine of Aragon (who had failed to produce a male heir), thus preventing his marriage to Anne Boleyn, one of the queen's ladies-in-waiting.

According to Louie Crew, founder of Integrity, the Episcopalian gay and lesbian national association, over the last two decades the Episcopal Church has experienced parallel internal struggles over the ordination of women and the inclusion of lesbians and gays. For example, Integrity was founded in 1974, and in response, the House of Bishops created a "Task Force on Homophiles and the Ministry." That same year marked the ordination of "The Philadelphia Eleven"—the first women priests in the Episcopal Church, although they were deemed "irregular" because the ordination of women had not been officially sanctioned.

In 1976, Church canons were finally changed to allow the ordination of women, and earlier ordinations were "regularized." That same year the General Convention enacted a resolution which stated that "homosexual persons are children of God who have a full and equal claim with all other persons upon the love, acceptance, and pastoral concern and care of the Church." Resolutions in support of gay civil rights were also passed (and subsequently reaffirmed in 1979 and 1983).

Due to growing opposition within the House of Bishops, in 1979 the General Convention passed a compromise resolution declaring that no one who was sexually active outside the bonds of heterosexual marriage should be ordained. Several bishops strongly dissented. Theologian Carter Heyward, one of the Philadelphia Eleven and author of several books including *Touching Our Strength,* came out as a lesbian shortly thereafter. In spite of the resolution, since 1979 several bishops have quietly (for the most part) ordained openly gay lesbians and gays.

In the 1985 General Convention, the growing schism concerning gay issues began to make itself more evident. In a speech, the Presiding Bishop declared that, "There will be no outcasts in this Church of ours." The next year saw the establishment of a group which has led a powerful and concerted campaign against the ordination of lesbians and gays and the blessing of same-sex unions. In 1989, John

Spong, Bishop of Newark, well-known supporter of gay rights and author of *Rescuing the Bible from Fundamentalism,* ordained openly gay Robert Williams in a highly publicized event, appointing him to head Oasis, a newly formed ministry for lesbians and gays.

A significant development occurred in 1996, when Bishop Walter Righter was cleared of heresy charges for ordaining a gay man as a deacon. Setting the stage for subsequent events, the Church court affirmed that gay ordination was not a violation of the Church's "core doctrine." In July of 1997, a historic General Assembly repealed an amendment prohibiting sexual relations for non-married clergy, and just barely—by one vote—lost the effort to approve same-sex unions. Then, in August of 1997, the Episcopal Church issued an official apology to gays and lesbians for the rejection and mistreatment they had experienced in the Church, yet another unprecedented occurrence.

These accomplishments, however, also had an undesired effect: they served to energize and unify the adverse forces. By the summer of 1998, a collusion of sorts had cemented between Western conservative and evangelical elements and bishops from underdeveloped countries. After uncharacteristic, widely publicized, and at times, vitriolic infighting, the bishops of the Lambeth Conference, a decennial gathering of the leaders of the worldwide Anglican Communion, voted decisively in favor of a resolution declaring the practice of homosexuality to be "incompatible with Scripture." Adopted by a margin of 526 to 70, the resolution also recommended against gay and lesbian ordination.

Although visibly stunned by the successful conservative counteroffensive, progressive bishops were able to put a positive spin on the debacle. Spong, for example, said, "I think the victory is this: this issue is on the front-burner of every province in the world. Lambeth is where the Episcopal Church was twenty years ago."[52]

Methodist

The Methodist movement originated in England's Oxford University in 1729, when a group of students led by John Wesley began to meet for prayer and worship. Because of the methodical way in which they conducted their rituals and practices, they received the derogatory name of "Methodists." Methodism caught on strongly with the British working classes, for whom the formal nature of Anglicanism was off-putting. Methodist meetings grew and were eventually held in open fields, triggering a religious revival among the poorer classes. The denomination's emphasis on social consciousness stems from its humble beginnings.

In 1972, a statement was presented for inclusion in the Church's Social Principles, which affirmed that "homosexuals . . . are persons of sacred worth," and recommended the Church's support of gay civil rights. However, the statement also clarified that the Church does not "condone the practice of homosexuality" and considers its practice "incompatible with Christian teaching." Although attempts were later made at a 1976 General Conference to repeal this negative language, they not only failed but further prohibitions were added, preventing the use of Church funds to promote in any way the acceptance of homosexuality. Furthermore, in 1984, the General

Conference explicitly laid out a commitment to "fidelity in marriage and celibacy in singleness," thereby prohibiting the ordination of open, practicing homosexuals.

In 1996, a sentence was added to the Church's Social Principles section which read: "Ceremonies that celebrate homosexual unions shall not be conducted by our ministers and shall not be conducted by our churches."

As with the Episcopalians, 1998 proved to be a crucial and contentious year for the Methodists, and for the same reason: the issue of homosexuality. In March, the Methodist Church was rocked by the church trial of Rev. Jimmy Creech at the First Methodist Church in Kearney, Nebraska. Creech faced the possibility of having his career as a minister destroyed because he had conducted a commitment ceremony for two lesbians. He was found guilty by a jury of his peers of "conducting a homosexual union," but innocent—by a single vote—of "disobeying the Order and Discipline of the United Methodist Church." Essentially, the jury determined that although Creech had broken the letter of the 1996 law against same-sex covenant ceremonies, "by meeting the pastoral needs of two women in his congregation he had fulfilled the spirit of Christ upon which the laws of the United Methodist Church are based." In the wake of the trial, demonstrations were held by conservative members of the Methodist Church protesting the "crisis" and the "liberal agenda" of certain elements within the Church.[53] Months later, Creech was forced to relocate to North Carolina when his bishop unilaterally removed him from his post.

In August 1998, the controversy came to a head. In heated reaction to the Creech victory, conservatives took their case to the Church's highest court, the Judicial Council. Creech's defense was based on the contention that the controversial sentence added to the Methodist Book of Discipline in 1996 was not binding because it had been placed in the social principles section and not in the section dealing with church structure and regulations. The court's ruling was unequivocal: regardless of its placement, the sentence in question was deemed to be not merely "advisory" but "binding." What that means is that any minister performing same-sex unions is now in undisputed violation of church law and subject to its discipline, including suspension and expulsion from the Methodist Church.

In 1984, Affirmation: United Methodists for Lesbian/Gay Concerns created the Reconciling Congregation Program for congregations supporting inclusion for gays and lesbians. Of the approximately forty-two thousand Methodist congregations worldwide, only about ninety-two are Reconciling.

Presbyterian

The word "presbyterian" originates from the Greek *presbyteros,* or elder. Presbyterianism was begun by John Calvin, one of the most important champions of the Protestant Reformation. Originating in Geneva, Switzerland, the Presbyterian or Reformed tradition became one of the fastest growing of the Protestant branches, and one of the most international. Churches in continental Europe were generally called Reformed, whereas those in the United Kingdom and North America were called Presbyterian.

In the U.S., the Presbyterian Church (U.S.A.), whose northern and southern branches split as a result of the Civil War, and were subsequently reunited in 1983, has approximately three million members. Presbyterians are known for their emphasis on education and were responsible for the founding of Princeton University as well as other educational institutions. They tend to be highly committed to the ecumenical movement and were critically involved in the creation of the World Council of Churches.

According to openly lesbian Donna Riley, the Presbyterian Church does not have an official (that is, constitutional) stand on homosexuality, and there is vehement disagreement among its members about this issue.

In 1976, the Church reaffirmed its position that "the practice of homosexuality is a sin," then turned around and expressed official support for gay civil rights the next year. In 1996, Presbyterian delegates to the General Assembly ratified an amendment to the Church constitution limiting ordination to those who maintain "fidelity in the covenant of marriage of a man and a woman, or chastity in singleness," thus significantly tightening the rules against ordination of gays and lesbians.[54] In 1997's highly politicized General Assembly, the "fidelity and chastity amendment" was again ratified, still requiring celibacy of all non-married clergy and effectively banning openly gay clergy. However, the language was somewhat toned down to include "fidelity and integrity in marriage or singleness, and in all relationships of life."

Riley clarifies that the amendment has yet to be interpreted, and that there will likely be dissenting interpretations of the meaning of "chastity," some Presbyterians maintaining that it is not the same thing as celibacy. Furthermore, others believe that to "be guided" by the constitutional standards of the Church does not necessarily mean living "in conformity" with them.

Other contradictory messages are evident within the Church's teachings. On one hand, for example, the youth sexuality curriculum officially teaches that homophobia is a sin and that discrimination against gays and lesbians is wrong, while on the other hand, the Church itself discriminates against gays and lesbians in ordained leadership roles. Similarly, the General Assembly voted in 1997 to write a brief in support of the Hawaii same-sex marriage civil case, a seeming contradiction to an earlier 1994 amendment that would have banned all ministers from participating in same-sex union ceremonies (but which ultimately failed to gain ratification by the regional bodies). While affirming the traditional definition of marriage as a "contract between a man and a woman," the compromise language acknowledged that same-sex couples in committed relationships "seek equal civil liberties in a contractual relationship with all the civil rights of married couples."

The More Light Churches Network is a coalition of congregations of the Presbyterian Church (U.S.A.) that affirms the inclusion of all people, regardless of sexual orientation, at all levels, including membership and ordination. As of March 1998, the network included eighty-seven churches.

Lutheran

Worldwide, Lutheranism is the largest Protestant denomination, with an estimated eighty million members. It was started by Augustinian monk Martin Luther, whose actions in protest of the papacy and of church excesses effectively catalyzed the

Protestant Reformation in 1517. Luther rejected the authority of the pope, believing instead in each person's ability to develop a personal relationship with God. Like other Protestant traditions, Lutheranism asserts the ultimate authority of the Bible, and the doctrine of salvation through faith. Lutherans ordain women priests and their clergy are allowed to marry.

Concerning homosexuality, the Lutherans have no specific prohibitions against the ordination of gay clergy; however, celibacy is obligatory for all non-married clergy, regardless of sexual orientation. In the Evangelical Lutheran Church of America (ELCA), gays and lesbians are allowed to be church members. In 1991, the ELCA Assembly passed a resolution affirming that "gay and lesbian people, as individuals created by God, are welcome to participate fully in the life of the congregations." In 1993, the ELCA Assembly took an official stand in support of civil rights for gays and lesbians, expressing "strong opposition to all forms of verbal or physical harassment or assault of persons because of their sexual orientation." And in 1995, the ELCA Assembly expressed the need for the Conference of Bishops to speak "words of prayer and pastoral concern for gay and lesbian persons and repudiate all words and acts of hatred toward such persons in our Church and in our communities." However, that same year the Lutheran Church Worldwide Assembly rejected findings and recommendations of a committee attempting to redefine and modernize issues of sexuality, including teachings about homosexuality. The following year, two San Francisco Lutheran congregations—St. Francis Lutheran and First United Lutheran Church—were expelled for ordaining openly lesbian and gay clergy who openly rejected the requirement for celibacy.

In 1997, lesbian pastor Deb Click was presented with a "Sophie's Choice" ultimatum by her bishop: she could either abandon her partner and their children or resign her position as associate pastor of the St. Paul Lutheran Church in Newark, Ohio. After she chose to resign, an intruder broke into Click's office, leaving her confidential counseling files scattered all over her desk and her personal belongings packed up and left outside her office.[55]

In 1984, Lutherans Concerned, an outreach ministry for GLBT people, created the Reconciling in Christ program to acknowledge congregations welcoming queer seekers. It consists of over one hundred Lutheran congregations in North America.

Baptist

The Baptists originated in 1609, when John Smyth and Thomas Helwys broke away from the Church of England. In the early seventeenth century, the Baptists came to the New World where they settled originally in what is now Rhode Island. Like other Protestant denominations, they experienced a schism over the issue of slavery, resulting in the formation of the Southern Baptist Convention in 1845, now the largest Protestant denomination in the U.S. with over 15.4 million members. Evolving out of the Northern Baptist Convention, the American Baptist Churches, U.S.A. has about 1.5 million members. The twenty-two Baptist denominations in the U.S. account for approximately two-fifths of all Protestants. Worldwide, there are about thirty-four million members.

Like other Protestants, Baptists uphold the Bible as the ultimate source of authority. Unlike other Protestants, they believe in a Church of converted, or "regenerated," individuals, people who have freely repented of their sins and accepted Jesus as their savior. As a result, they oppose infant baptism (because they have no concept of repentance or faith); they also practice baptism by immersion rather than by sprinkling.

In regard to homosexuality, in 1987 the Southern Baptist Convention explicitly condemned homosexuality as "a manifestation of a depraved nature and a perversion of divine standards." The American Baptist Church issued a similar if more sedate statement of doctrine in 1991: "Homosexual practice is incompatible with Christianity."

In 1992, the Southern Baptist Convention expelled two congregations, one for ordaining a gay man, and another for conducting a same-sex union ceremony. When a third church, the Pullen Memorial Church, was ousted the following year for blessing another gay union, the Southern Baptist Convention changed one of its core principles—that of the autonomy of individual congregations—by dictating homosexuality as the single issue where individual congregations are obligated to follow the Convention's rules.

In her award-winning series on "Religion and Homosexuality" for the *Pensacola News Journal,* Alice Crann tells the story of the 1995 expulsion of the First Baptist Church of Granville, Ohio, from both local and state organizations because of their support of homosexuality. In a significant development, the church experienced a 60 percent increase in membership following their expulsion.

In 1997, the Southern Baptist Convention declared its infamous boycott against Disney because of the company's pro-gay practices: domestic partner benefits, TV shows such as *Ellen* on Disney-owned ABC, and "Gay Days" at the Disney theme parks. The 1998 Convention reviewed the Baptist "Faith and Message" and added a section on the family in which marriage was defined as "the uniting of one man and one woman in covenant commitment for a lifetime." It also made headlines for its language advocating that a wife "submit herself graciously to the servant leadership of her husband."

Tim Phillips is an openly gay Baptist minister. A member of the American Baptist Church, he explains that the A.B.C. is considerably more tolerant than the Southern Baptist Convention. It did not join the boycott against Disney, for instance. Nevertheless, the University Baptist Church in Seattle, where he is minister, is currently under siege from the denomination's conservative element for its open and accepting policy.

Founded in 1991, the Association of Welcoming and Affirming Baptists is made up of churches, organizations, and individuals who are willing to go on record as welcoming lesbian, gay, and bisexual Christians into full membership and participation.

Mormons

With an estimated ten million members worldwide, the Mormon Church, properly identified as The Church of Jesus Christ of Latter-Day Saints (LDS), was founded in 1830 by Joseph Smith, known to his followers as "the prophet." From its comparatively recent beginnings, the movement grew rapidly due to its aggressive evangelization practices and above average rates of birth. Besides having a revolving corps of approximately forty-five thousand missionaries, former members report that there is a high degree of fear-induced pressure to proselytize; they are allegedly told that they won't "make it into heaven" if even one person passes them by whom they did not attempt to "save."

Because of their political strategy of voting as a unit through a single Church party, and their practice of polygamy, among other things, the Mormons generated quite a bit of controversy among their neighbors. To avoid persecution, they left upstate New York and moved westward, settling first in Illinois, where Smith was killed by a mob. They eventually established their headquarters in Utah, where they were led by Brigham Young, the Church's second great leader. After persistent conflicts with the federal government, they eventually abolished the practice of polygamy (more accurately, polygyny, since only men were entitled to more than one spouse) in 1890.

In their conservative moral teachings and social practices, Mormons resemble their fundamentalist Protestant counterparts. (Theologically, however, they have fundamental differences, concerning such beliefs as, for instance, the nature of the Trinity as three separate entities.) Both groups oppose abortion and birth control, share a distrust of ecumenical efforts, and place women in secondary and subservient roles. To this day, Mormon women cannot be ordained as priests, nor are they allowed to play an official role in the Church's elaborate hierarchy. In contrast, all Mormon males over age twelve are generally ordained, although it was not until 1978 that ordination was permitted for black men. Women were not even allowed to attend temple unaccompanied by their husbands until 1988. And, of course, both groups are vehemently homophobic.

According to Church doctrine, "the Lord's law of moral conduct is abstinence outside of lawful marriage and fidelity within marriage"; therefore, sexual relations are only acceptable "between husband and wife appropriately expressed within the bonds of marriage." Anything outside of that, including fornication, adultery, and homosexual behavior, is considered sinful, and subject to Church discipline. Church writings emphasize the use of the word "behavior" when discussing homosexuality; their incontestable belief is that homosexuality is a choice, not an innate condition. Engaging in homosexual behavior "violates the commandments of God, is contrary to the purpose of human sexuality, distorts loving relationships and deprives people of the blessings that can be found in family life and in the saving ordinances of the gospel," according to a Church booklet titled *Understanding and Helping Those Who Have Homosexual Problems.* A guide to assist Church leaders in dealing with those afflicted with the "homosexual problem," the booklet asserts that "regardless of the causes, these problems can be controlled and eventually overcome." It further beseeches Church leaders to reassure those struggling with homosexual feelings that "they can be healed from their afflictions through the atonement of the Savior." Another troubling segment unabashedly declares that "members of the Church are *commanded* to control their sexual thoughts and desires . . . (and) are expected to obey the Lord's law of sexual purity."

In 1976, Church rules were amended to add "homosexual feelings," not just homosexual acts, as sufficient reason for excommunication. Masturbation and pornography (including all forms of "vulgar, immoral, or perverse entertainment") are said to "always accompany homosexual transgressions," and are considered "deviant practices," "very dangerous," and "addictive." And, to add insult to injury, the Mormon Church in Hawaii (unsuccessfully) requested to be made a co-defendant in the state's suit against gay marriages.

There are two organizations which minister to GLBT Mormons: Affirmation and GALA (Gay and Lesbian Acceptance), which is part of the Reorganized Church of Jesus Christ of Latter Day Saints (a much smaller, Missouri-based church founded by the son of Joseph Smith).

United Church of Christ

The United Church of Christ (UCC) was created in 1957 as a result of the merger between two churches: the Congregational Christian Churches and the Evangelical and Reformed Church (a Presbyterian church). The UCC has about 1.5 million members.

Both of the UCC parent churches shared a strong tradition of social justice. The Congregationalists, for instance, were quite active in the anti-slavery movement, and were the first of the mainline American churches to ordain both a black man (in 1785) and a woman (in 1853).

Without a doubt, of all the mainstream Christian denominations, the UCC has the best record when it comes to gay and lesbian people. As early as 1969, the UCC Council for Christian Social Action declared its opposition to anti-gay discrimination and the exclusion of gays from the military. In 1972, the UCC was the first to ordain openly gay William Johnson.

In 1973, the UCC Executive Council officially declared that sexual orientation should not interfere with the ordination of qualified candidates. That same year, the UCC Gay Caucus, later the United Church Coalition for Lesbian/Gay Concerns, was officially recognized at General Synod. In 1975, the UCC expressed support of gay civil liberties, and the first out lesbian (Anne Holmes) was ordained in 1977. The 1991 General Synod released one of the most positively phrased statements yet from a church concerning homosexuality, stating that it "boldly affirms, celebrates and embraces the gifts of ministry of lesbian, gay and bisexual persons." Besides participating in the 1993 March on Washington for Lesbian, Gay and Bisexual Equal Rights and Liberation, UCC leadership officially testified at the House Armed Services Committee, denouncing the ban on military service for gays and lesbians. Later that year, it published the first (and perhaps, still the only) exhaustive curriculum for AIDS education and prevention designed specifically for a Christian audience. In 1994, Peter Ilgenfritz and David Shull were elected as associate ministers of the University Congregational Church in Seattle, the first openly gay couple in history to serve a mainline Christian congregation. To date, UCC remains the only Christian denomination that officially sanctions same-sex unions.

Christina Hutchins is an openly lesbian UCC minister. When asked what it was about her religion that nurtured her and allowed her to stay within its fold, she acknowledged that she still "struggled at the edge of Christianity." However, she continued, "I stay because in it I find an embodiment of God's love. Jesus was a person who made love in every act. To me, that's the connection between my spirituality and my sexuality, and my energy for the world. The other word is probably grace, and I experience that when I lie with my lover, when we make love, when I put my head on her chest and rest there, when I sing hymns in church, when I dance."

Of the two hundred and twenty-three "Open and Affirming" churches in the UCC, four serve a predominantly lesbian and gay congregation: City of Refuge UCC in San Francisco, Liberation UCC in Cleveland, Spirit of the Lakes UCC in Minneapolis, and Phoenix UCC in Kalamazoo, Michigan.

Quakers

Formally known as the Society of Friends, the Quakers are a Christian-based group originating in seventeenth-century England during the Protestant Reformation. Unlike other Protestants, however, they did not begin as a formal organization. Attracted by the novel ideas of lay preacher George Fox, followers began to congregate informally, and were eventually called "Quakers" because of the tremors their bodies experienced prior to receiving a divine message.

In America, they settled initially in New Jersey in the 1660s. At first persecuted, they later earned the respect of other colonists because of their integrity and proven leadership in social reform. Almost two hundred years before the Civil War, they were condemning the practice of slavery; they were also known for their friendly relations with the Native Americans. Worldwide, there are about three hundred thousand Quakers, with a majority in the U.S.

Some of their core beliefs are unique compared to other Christian denominations. Most significant is the concept of divine revelation as immediate and individual; Quakers believe that all persons—regardless of gender, race, or even sexual orientation—are able to perceive the word of God within themselves. They refer to this as the "Christ within," or the "inner light."

Because every person is a potential conduit for the word of God, the Quakers have no formal creed, liturgy, or clergy, and up until recently did not have structured services. Their worship services were instead based on silence. Today, some of the Friends meetings have more formal or semi-structured meetings, which can be led by a paid clergy person.

Basic to Quaker philosophy is the innate goodness of humanity; they strive to honor truth, sincerity, simplicity, tolerance, and nonviolence. In terms of membership and other privileges, there are no differences between the sexes.

At the 1985 annual assembly of the Pacific Meetings, the Society of Friends eliminated all gender-specific vocabulary from their guidebook, *Faith and Practice*, thereby authorizing individual meetings to offer same-sex union ceremonies.

A member of the Society of Friends for fifteen years, transman Jason Cromwell says his spirituality is "very inward, and deeply personal." When asked to speak about his spirituality, Cromwell admits he has difficulty separating the secular from the spiritual. "I am a deeply spiritual person; it's just a part of my life—it's just what I do. I am often described as an activist but consider myself an educator. If the work that I do motivates others to action, great. I do what I do because it leads me."

Friends For Lesbian and Gay Concerns is an association of lesbian, gay, bisexual, transgender, and non-gay Friends who seek spiritual community within the Religious Society of Friends.

MCC

It's been a long road since twelve people showed up at Troy Perry's living room in October 1968 for the first meeting of what was to become the Metropolitan Community Church (MCC). Obviously filling a vacuum in the gay community, one year later MCC services were filling Los Angeles' 385-seat Encore Theater. And by its thirtieth anniversary, the Universal Fellowship of Metropolitan Community Churches (UFMCC) is by far the world's largest religious organization for gays and lesbians.

The author of several books, including *The Lord Is My Shepherd, and He Knows I'm Gay,* Perry was born in Tallahassee, Florida. From an early age he was drawn to religion; in a *Los Angeles Times* feature, his younger brother Jimmy remembered how Perry used to "baptize" his younger siblings in a fifty-five-gallon drum in their backyard. He would also have Jimmy kill bugs so that he could officiate at their funerals.[56]

In a disturbing, yet somehow not surprising development, as a young man Perry ended up marrying the daughter of the very same Church mentor he had approached with concerns about his budding homosexuality. Hoping against hope, Perry believed what the Church told him: marrying a good woman would cure him.

The next time he would confide in a Church official—in 1963, as the twenty-three-year-old pastor of a Pentecostal church in Santa Ana, California—the results would be dramatically different. Suddenly, Perry found himself twice excommunicated: from the Church which had been his life and spiritual source, and from his family, when his wife left him, refusing to allow any further contact with their two infant sons.

The next five years would prove to be both a time for self-discovery, as Perry dove in with a vengeance to explore the gay life he had been resisting, and a dark night of the soul, as he struggled unsuccessfully to reconcile his spirituality with his sexuality. At one point, he attempted suicide, surviving only because his roommate discovered him bleeding to death in the bathtub—both his wrists slashed.

When he finally came out of his existential slump, both his mother and a local psychic independently conveyed the same message—to start his own church. Soon thereafter he placed an ad in a Los Angeles gay publication. The rest is history.

Ministering predominantly to queer people, MCC unwaveringly advocates that homosexuality is not a sin and that it is not condemned by the Bible. Openly gay, noncelibate gays, lesbians, bisexuals, and transsexuals are welcome as members and can be ordained as clergy. MCC churches annually conduct over five thousand commitment ceremonies for gay couples.

Not surprisingly, such a radical stance was liable to generate fear and resistance from established powers. For years, MCC has been trying to obtain membership in the National Council of Churches—to no avail. In recent years, eighteen MCC churches have been destroyed by arson and others have been vandalized. In Stockton, California, an MCC minister was violently and mysteriously stabbed to death—all the blood drained from his body.[57] Perry himself has had to resort to traveling with bodyguards, and Church conventions require security procedures such as metal detectors.

Nevertheless, MCC epitomizes the rising interest in spirituality in the gay community. Considered one of the ten fastest-growing denominations (of any type) in America, its membership and popularity have been steadily climbing.[58] In 1997, North American members contributed in excess of fifteen million dollars to Church coffers. When compared to donations to MCC, individual contributions during the same time period to the Human Rights Campaign (about seven million dollars) and the National Gay and Lesbian Task Force (about one and a half million dollars) dwarf in comparison. Its largest Church, the Cathedral of Hope in Dallas, is in the midst of a capital campaign to build a multi-million-dollar new structure designed by internationally renowned gay architect Philip Johnson. It is conceived as a symbolic spiritual center for gay and lesbian Christians all over the world. Further evidence of MCC's flourishing success is that in 1996, thanks to a one-million-dollar down payment generated through Church collections, the denomination was able to purchase a $3.8 million complex for their worldwide headquarters in West Hollywood—to include a sanctuary, a visitors center, archives, and a museum.

Perry has been invited to meet with such luminaries as Archbishop Desmond Tutu in South Africa, which is home to one of the largest MCC churches. A tireless advocate for gay rights, he was also invited to participate in White House conferences on AIDS and hate crimes. In addition to Perry, other lesbians and gay men shine from within the MCC structure. Nancy Wilson is the pastor of the Los Angeles church and author of *Our Tribe.* Michael Piazza, the pastor at the Cathedral of Hope, is also author of *Holy Homosexuals.* And since 1994, Mel White, author of *Stranger at the Gate,* has been MCC's minister of justice.

Alternative Paths

Having taken a look at the major religious traditions of the world, we will now consider other spiritual traditions which are important either because of their rising popularity, or because of their inherent openness to queer people. Some are ancient and some are new. Some, like the Unitarian Universalists, grew out of or were influenced by Christianity but decidedly require separate categorization. Others, such as Unity and Religious Science, have a basis in or contain elements of Christianity but are best categorized as New Thought. We will also consider the bourgeoning New Age movement.

The major, organized religions are also called the historical religions because they are based on written records. But as Huston Smith points out, in terms of human history, these encompass only the last four thousand years. In contrast, what can alternatively be called Earth-based, nature-based, primal, tribal, or oral religions span the preceding three million years. Remnants of these traditions can still be found in Australia, Africa, Siberia, parts of Southeast Asia, and among the Indigenous people of the Americas.[59]

Many Westerners have attempted to recapture the Indigenous people's sense of connectedness with the universe, reverence for nature, respect for all life, and celebration of the body and sexuality. Some refer to it in terms of a neopagan revival, a return to pre-Christian, pre-modern beliefs and practices, a rebirth in interest in the traditions of those people who were called "pagans" by the rapidly proliferating Christian movement. These were the traditions which—whether because of religious convictions or political and economic appetite—Christians felt compelled to eradicate.

Tens of thousands of Western seekers have read and been inspired by *Mutant Message,* Marlo Morgan's chronicle of her walkabout with the Australian aborigines, even though it was subsequently classified as fictional when she refused to account for its factual accuracy, ostensibly to protect the privacy of the tribe with whom she had journeyed. Many others have found meaning in the works of Carlos Castañeda, Dan Millman, or Gabrielle Roth, all of which draw from the wisdom and spirit of Indigenous people.

Unitarian Universalists

The Unitarian Universalist Association (U.U.A.) is the result of the 1961 merger of the American Unitarian Association and the Universalist Church of America. Both traditions shared liberal leanings and humanitarian concerns.

The Unitarians obtained their name because of their rejection of the concept of the Trinity. They also did not believe in such traditional Christian doctrines as original sin, everlasting punishment, or the divinity of Jesus Christ. Although not exclusively Christian, Universalism incorporated many Christian beliefs. Their name stems from the belief in universal salvation, or "the eternal progress of all souls."

U.U.A. members are not required to subscribe to any particular religious belief—there is no official statement of faith. With an estimated 172,000 members in the U.S., the organization has headquarters in Boston and an annual general assembly.

The U.U. Church does not teach that life's ultimate truth has been revealed in some scripture but instead holds that together humans must seek to understand the meaning of our lives. They incorporate reason and scientific evidence and value a person's life experience, intuition, and inner creative capabilities.

As early as 1970, Unitarian Universalists declared their opposition to discrimination against gays; in 1973, they created the Office of Gay Concerns (now the Office of Bisexual, Gay, Lesbian, and Transgender Concerns). Its purpose is to work for acceptance of BGLT persons among U.U. congregations. In 1980, the U.U.A. General Assembly called for member churches to assist in the settlement of openly-gay ministers, passing a resolution in support of same-sex unions in 1984. In 1987, it called for its members to oppose "sodomy" laws, urging congregations not to do business with companies that discriminate. In 1996, it called for Church-wide support of the legalization of same-sex marriage.

In addition, the U.U.A. has also come out in opposition to AIDS discrimination, and has advocated against anti-gay discrimination in employment, housing, the military, and marriage; it has publicly opposed anti-gay initiatives in Oregon and Colorado, and Church leadership and thousands of members participated in the 1993 March on Washington.

Their literature claims that U.U. has the largest percentage of women and openly queer ministers of all religious organizations. They have not only called for the full inclusion of gays and lesbians in the Church and in society but have implemented an affirmative action program to place queer ministers in their churches. Same-sex unions are frequently performed in U.U. churches.

Considered a "membership organization affiliated with U.U.A.," Interweave is a group for BGLT individuals and friends with chapters throughout North America. Not all congregations have Interweave chapters, and whether or not a congregation is considered welcoming is independent of the presence of an Interweave chapter.

Unity

More than a century old, the New Thought movement is a modern spiritual philosophy based on premises such as constructive thinking—the idea that our thoughts and attitudes affect our experience. In his book *The Varieties of Religious Experience,* William James referred to it as the religion of "healthy-mindedness." Arising out of a Christian background, New Thought has no one creed but instead draws from different philosophical and religious traditions. The Unity Church and the Church of Religious Science are its two most prominent examples.

A nondenominational, Christian-based, religious fellowship, Unity was cofounded in 1889 by Charles and Myrtle Fillmore, in Kansas City, Missouri, where church headquarters are still located. Founded on basic Christian principles and spiritual values, its teachings were synthesized from a variety of sources, including Theosophy, Hinduism, Christian Science, and New Thought. To many, Unity is not so much a religion as a way of life, a spiritual resource for daily living. At one point, Unity followers even referred to their system of beliefs as "Practical Christianity." Unity claims to offer a "practical, nondogmatic approach . . . that helps people of all faiths lead happier, healthier, and more prosperous lives."

Acknowledging that Church dogma and group ritual can often restrict the individual's experience, the basic purpose of Unity's teachings is to support people to establish a personal connection with God. Unity teaches that as children of God, human beings are "heirs to all that God is and all that God provides." They believe that God is present in every person, and that through prayer and meditation, God's presence can be felt directly in one's daily life. Sherryl Hodgins, a lesbian lay minister, is active at her Unity Church, where she does volunteer work with children. What she appreciates about Unity is "that there's not a lot about concept or theory but much about bringing the divinity down to the practical nature. To me, that's what Unity is about."

In accord with the growing social and legal movement toward increasing equality for gays and lesbians, the Unity Church does not hold sexual orientation as an impediment to church membership, employment, or ordination.

Regardless of the partners' gender, the main questions Unity teachings pose of any relationship are the same: Is it healthy? That is, is it a reflection of God's love; and does it help to make the partners better people and the world a better place? Although some churches honor same-sex union celebrations or rituals for gays or lesbians, others do not.

Kevin Rice is a thirty-year-old former Southern Baptist and Assemblies of God minister who desperately tried everything within his means to rid himself of his homosexuality—including exorcism, a traumatic and disconcerting experience. "I felt I was being condemned for being different; it was a very, very shameful experience for me; I felt like the scum on the bottom of a garbage can." Renouncing his ministry, which included a TV talk show, he eventually found a home at Unity Village in Kansas City. Rice says that "Unity provides a safe space—no judgment, shame, attack, or condemnation—for being just a different kind of expression of the nature of God. It is very inclusive, not exclusive. Everyone is free to be whoever they are."

Religious Science

Religious Science was founded by Dr. Ernest Holmes, whose 1927 book, *The Science of Mind,* encompasses the Church's main principles. Emerging out of a Christian background, Holmes was a self-taught student of the world's spiritual traditions who sought to distill their essential teachings from established dogma. In addition to the Eastern and Western spiritual teachings he extracted, he also synthesized elements of philosophy, psychology, and science. Like the Fillmores, Holmes never intended to start a new religion. Rather, his hope was that all the different religions would assimilate his method of thinking and adopt its practical teachings into their own. When this, however, failed to occur, he eventually agreed to support the creation of a new Church in order to ensure the survival of his teachings. That his philosophy sought to connect people's consciousness with their ultimate source helped him accept the appropriateness of calling it a religion.

Sometimes mistaken for Mary Baker Eddy's Christian Science, Religious Science teaches that more than mere surface thought, human consciousness is a mixture of thought and feeling. Its premise is that if a person's thoughts or deeply held beliefs are changed, the circumstances of their lives will also change. No substantial change in experience or circumstance can occur without a preceding change in consciousness. This mode of thinking places full responsibility for each person's life squarely on his or her own shoulders.

Religious Science emphasizes that its teachings are based on the age-old insights of various world's religions, albeit configured in a new and modern approach. Similar to Unity's message, Religious Science teaches that the truth—and one's divine connection—can only be found within. Although Religious Science does not reject the divinity of Jesus, it does affirm the divinity of all people. Because it teaches that God is present in, through, and as every individual, this inevitably results in a philosophy of intrinsic respect and tolerance toward all people.

David Bruner is an ordained minister in Religious Science and has officiated at many same-sex unions, as well as being "wed" himself in a Church of Religious Science to his same-sex partner several years ago. According to Bruner, both the Church's by-laws and the Ministerial Code of Ethics specifically address the issue of homosexuality. The latter document determines that ministers "dedicate (them)selves to the spiritual needs of those who call upon us regardless of race, gender, sexual/affectional preference, national origin, station in life, condition or physical challenge."

New Age

Although influenced by earlier developments, such as the teachings of Madame Blavatsky, Alice Bailey, and Edgar Cayce, the New Age movement originated in England in the 1960s, and quickly caught on in the United States. Gaining further popularity during the 1970s, New Age beliefs received a great deal of attention—not all of it positive—due to the high visibility of Shirley MacLaine, one of its better known proponents during the 1980s. These days New Age books regularly make it to the *New York Times* bestsellers list, some of them remaining there for inordinate, industry-defying lengths of time. To a significant degree, some have become part of the mainstream consciousness.

The term New Age stems from the belief that humanity is about to enter a new phase in our spiritual evolution—nothing less than a "New World Order," also referred to as the "Age of Aquarius." What is envisioned is a utopic society in which individual identity limited to ethnicity or national origin, for instance, will be supplanted by global consciousness. Theoretically, people will relate to each other as members of the human race; co-inhabitants of Planet Earth; manifestations of Gaia, the Earth Mother—in short, as one. Among other prophesied changes of the New Age are an end to the ravages of war, disease, famine, pollution, poverty, and discrimination in any of its present virulent forms (sexism, racism, homophobia, religious discrimination). The development of our ability to heal ourselves and others, and of our latent psychic powers, such as telepathy, and a heightened understanding of the universe, are other anticipated changes.

Though generalizations are difficult due to the wide variance and the inherent lack of dogma within the movement, many New Agers believe that the entire universe emanates from a single divine source, which can be witnessed everywhere around us. A logical corollary is the belief in the divine essence of all humans. Another prevalent theme is the belief that there is no one exclusive path to the Divine. Personal responsibility and personal choice are widely held values, and personal transformation is the goal of many. Because of its openness, many queer seekers are attracted to the movement.

Creation Spirituality

Creation Spirituality is an ancient tradition experiencing renewed interest in great part due to the efforts of theologian and spiritual revolutionary Matthew Fox, author of *Original Blessing, The Coming of the Cosmic Christ, The Reinvention of Work,* and many other books. For decades a thorn in the side of the Vatican, Fox was repeatedly (though unsuccessfully) silenced because of his radical views on feminism and homosexuality, among other teachings. Eventually Fox was asked to leave the Dominican Order, at which point he converted to the Episcopalian Church. In 1996, he founded the University of Creation Spirituality in Oakland, evolving out of another program he had founded twenty years earlier.

Instead of original sin, Creation Spirituality emphasizes "original blessing"—the belief that the true nature of all things, including humanity, is good. It seeks to nullify "us versus them" dichotomies between white and black, men and women, gays and straights, Christians and "pagans." Essentially egalitarian, it celebrates the diversity inherent in creation. Creation Spirituality also advocates eco-spirituality, liberation theology, and a holistic and healthy sexuality rather than its puritanical repression or wanton, market-driven exploitation.

According to Fox, the University of Creation Spirituality is philosophically modeled after the original twelfth-century universities, when—true to their name—these institutions strove to give people a real sense of their place within the universe. Similarly, one of the goals of Creation Spirituality is rekindling an experience of awe and reverence at our connectedness to all of creation. With all this in mind, it is almost unnecessary to state that the university fosters an environment which is very inclusive of women, minorities, and queer folk.

Native American

Disillusioned with strongly patriarchal and hierarchical religions, which too often have denied and suppressed nature, the body, and sexuality, increasing numbers of Westerners are seeking to reconnect with themselves and their world by attending shamanic workshops, sweat lodges, vision quests, and drumming circles. It is not surprising that so many thirst for reconnection, a real experience of Spirit in their bodies, and a nondual relationship with the world and the Divine. However, it should not be surprising either that certain segments of the Native American community are responding with protectiveness, fearing the further appropriation of their sacred rituals and traditions by an unknowing populace. I imagine some must feel something like, "Wasn't the appropriation of our land, the decimation of our people, and the destruction of our world, enough? Now you want to take our sacred rituals, too?"

Among most Native American tribes and other Indigenous peoples in the world, sexual mores were fluid, and most had no concept or word for homosexuality. As we have already seen, in many tribal systems people we now call gay, lesbian, bisexual, or transgendered were held in high esteem as the recipients of special gifts, powers, or blessings. These Two-Spirit people often assumed official roles as shamans and healers.

James Lord, who is a medicine person in training, enjoys a combination of Native American (Creek, Huesteck, and Blackfoot) as well as West African (Yoruba) ancestry. "The work we do as queer people is frequently breaking the static social codes that no longer work and discovering new ones that work. We discover these first for ourselves and then gift them to the rest of society. The Two-Spirit people were also known as bridge-builders because they were the only ones that knew what was going on in both the men's and the women's lodges. Many were also known for their prophetic abilities and were able to see the long-term actions necessary for the survival of the tribe."

According to Lord, some Native teachers are open to imparting some of their teachings to non-Indigenous people, while others are adamantly opposed to that practice. He compares the role of the Two-Spirit people to the "two eyes" of the African Hausa tribe and the Dagara gatekeepers, who were "basically allowed to do whatever they wished, because their exploration allowed society to be refreshed and renewed by the fruit of their discoveries."

African-based Traditions

The Yoruba religion was imported into the New World by Nigerian slaves. Its main derivatives are Santería, as it came to be known in Cuba and other parts of the Caribbean; Voodoo, which took hold mainly in Haiti, Trinidad, and Louisiana; and Candomblé, as the religion is called in Brazil. Although they all share the belief in a supreme deity called Olodumaré, most practitioners typically relate to its various manifestations, which are called *orishas*. Believers develop a special relationship with a particular *orisha*, who protects them and imbues them with *ashé*, or spiritual energy. During certain rituals and celebrations, the orisha often possesses the practitioner's body.

The word Santería derives from the Spanish word *santos* (saints). When forced to convert to Christianity, the slaves superimposed the identities of their *orishas* onto Catholic icons, thereby maintaining their traditional religion and culture while externally appearing to worship Catholic saints.

With the exile of approximately one and a half million Cubans to the U.S. after Castro's 1959 revolution, Santería eventually expanded its appeal beyond Cuban-American communities, wending its way into American culture. It now has many followers in cities such as Miami, New York, Los Angeles, and the Bay Area. On occasion, Santería adherents have found themselves embroiled in the American legal process. In 1987, the city of Hialeah, a predominantly Cuban-American suburb of Miami, passed a law prohibiting the practice of animal sacrifice. This decision, however, was reversed by a 1993 U.S. Supreme Court ruling, which decided that it was an unconstitutional violation of religious freedom.

Similarly, Voodoo blends elements of Yoruba religion with Catholicism. Besides the supreme deity called *Bon Dieu,* or the "good God," Voodoo practitioners also worship ancestors, the dead, and spirits called *loa,* or *lwa*. Voodoo rituals incorporate African dancing and drumming; its Catholic influence is seen in its adaptation of baptism and the sign of the cross, and its use of candles, bells, and crosses. A priestess (*mambo*) or priest (*houngan*) usually leads the rituals or feasts, in which a particular *loa* is summoned by means of singing, dancing, and drumming. Once an ecstatic trance is achieved, the dancers are taken over by the *loa* and are able to foretell the future, perform healings, and offer guidance.

Queer people in the Americas have found a place for themselves in the Yoruba tradition. With its myths of protective androgynous and homoerotic *orishas,* the Yoruba religion is appealing to many queer-identified individuals. Some of the *orishas* who are thought to be patrons of queer people are Oshún, Obatalá, Yemayá, Oya, and Babaluayé. In Brazil, lesbian Candomblé practitioners are called *monokó,* while queer male practitioners are categorized as *adé,* a general term parallel to our use of "gay," which includes a wide gamut of degrees of masculinity or gender variance. Thought to fulfill a specific sacred role, queer people are specifically referred to as *uma ponte dos Orixás,* meaning, "a bridge to/of the *orishas.*"[60]

In the Bay Area, artist and spiritual teacher AfraShe Asungi has created a group for women of African descent seeking to explore their creativity and spirituality. The MAMAROOTS: AJAMA-JEBI AfraKamaati Sistahood is a non-profit spiritual and cultural organization dedicated to the "AfraGoddess." The Sistahood is based on the principle that taking action requires a combination of *sheraa-t* (same as *ashé),* which the Yoruba people believe to be the Divine Breath of Life, and "MAMA, weaving her blessed life breath through us all." The group also advocates "Afro-saphism" as a way to reclaim the social and political power of bonding between African sisters.

Neopagan

Originating in the United Kingdom earlier this century, and catching on in America in the '60s, a neopagan revival has been occurring in the West. It refers to a return to those pre-Christian, mostly Goddess-based religions, which were eventually eradicated by Christianity as it ironically metamorphosed from persecuted into persecutor. Once Christianity became the state religion of the Roman Empire, it engaged in an official campaign to eradicate paganism, destroying temples and butchering countless non-Christians over the years.

At least part of the reason for this renaissance of neopagan religions is a reaction against the religions which have dominated the earth for the last several hundred years, religions which too often manifested as militaristic, imperialist, hierarchical, sexist, and homophobic. Increasing numbers of people are finding their spiritual needs unmet by these religions. Additionally, the worsening environmental crisis has triggered many to turn away from the dualism espoused by these religions (which often reject this world in favor of an anticipated, transcendent, future state) toward a more nature-based and holistic approach.

Modern-day neopagans comprise a wide variety of beliefs and practices. Generally, though, they share a reverence for nature and all its creatures. Believing in the interconnectedness of all life, many honor Gaia—the Earth—as a single, interdependent, living organism. Nature deities are worshipped in these traditions, and most neopagan rituals are held outdoors. Hand in hand with this reverence for nature is an honoring of sensuality, sexuality, and pleasure. Nudity is common in rituals and celebrations, and sex is considered by many as a sacrament.

The majority of neopagans are polytheistic, typically honoring a manifestation of the Goddess such as Diana/Artemis (goddess of nature, the moon, and the hunt), Aphrodite (goddess of love), or a version of the male fertility god, such as the horned god of the Celts, known as Cernunnos, or his counterpart in Greek mythology, Pan. Other deities are derived from Celtic, Egyptian, Norse, or Yoruba pantheons. Generally, they believe in "immanence," the concept that God/dess dwells in and can be found in all things. Nevertheless, some pagans are monotheistic and still others atheists, acknowledging the gods as human constructs or Jungian archetypes, or venerating the spirits contained in animals, mountains, or trees.

With their innate openness, augmented by the fact that the religion is in the midst of re-creation after centuries of persecution, neopagans tend to be eclectic and vehemently non-dogmatic. In fact, rather than a religion, some even view it as a movement or system of belief. In place of dogma and beliefs, neopagan religions emphasize experience and practice. They reject the structure, hierarchy, authoritarianism, centralization, and separation between laity and clerical elite evident in other religions. Consistent with its emphasis on the Goddess, neopagan groups are highly respectful of women. Most groups welcome queer people.

Wicca

Of the estimated two hundred thousand neopagans in the U.S., the largest and most influential group are the Wiccans, as modern witchcraft practitioners are called. Wicca is considered by some an initiatory form of Paganism. However, others disagree with that characterization. Although some neopagan practices do, in fact, derive from those of Wicca, others differ from them. Laine Lawless, lesbian founder of the Sisterhood of the Moon in San Francisco, explains that while witches are pagans, not all pagans are witches.

Whereas some sects formalize initiation, others, particularly solitary practitioners, forego this ritual. It should also be clarified that Wicca is only one among a variety of practices of folk-magic around the world which are considered witchcraft in our culture. In other words, there are many witches all over the world who do not identify as Wiccans.

Although witchcraft has been confused throughout history and is still identified with Satanism—a misperception that is perpetuated by Hollywood-induced images of wicked old witches stirring boiling cauldrons, or of deranged and sinister Satan worshipers stealing children for ritual sacrifice—it is a nature-based or fertility spiritual tradition. Because of its long history of persecution, which forced many practitioners to go underground, its origins remain mysterious. Some claim the origins of Wicca go back to ancient shamanic traditions, while others believe that it emerged in medieval Europe as surviving pagan groups intermingled. Still others feel that Wicca in its present form is really a twentieth-century development. Regardless of their genesis, in actuality most Wiccan rituals are benign, and include, for example, offerings to helpful spirits or the use of spells to promote health, financial abundance, a new lover or job, and the like. They do not inflict harm on others.

There is some disagreement as well pertaining to the etymology of the word *wicca*. While most believe that it stems from an old Anglo-Saxon word meaning "to bend or shape," others believe that the word stems from a different root meaning "wise one." For many practitioners, the word "witch," signifying the ability to effect changes, to bend or change reality, and to heal, symbolizes the reclaiming of an ancient tradition. Indeed, one Wiccan group, cofounded by bisexual author Starhawk, is called Reclaiming. Still others utterly reject the use of the word "witch," preferring instead "wicca," as a noun. Laine Lawless is one of those who dislikes the word "witch,"and she becomes very impatient with the question she is typically asked: "Are you a good witch or a bad witch?" She prefers instead the term "matriarchal Paganism."

With no single governing body, Wicca practitioners tend to be decentralized in organization. Their beliefs, practices, and rituals thus vary widely. That absence of rules is what Lawless appreciates about her tradition, which "puts the responsibility back on you, as well as the personal freedom to be who and what you are. You can't put the blame back on society and are responsible for yourself and for the consequences of your actions."

Although most Wiccans are solitary practitioners, many belong to covens, groves, and kindreds. In general, however, they share certain traditions, such as the celebration of nature and reverence for ancient deities like Diana or Hecate (goddess of witchcraft). Other beliefs include the celebration of the body and sexuality, and the equality of the genders. The majority of Wiccan groups are inclusive of people regardless of their sexual orientation, and several openly GLBT individuals have attained prominence within the movement. Among these are Z Budapest, Tom Cowan, Donald Engstrom, and Dr. Leo Martello.

Druidism

Druidism is the religious faith of the Celtic tribes that lived throughout ancient Europe. The Druids were a priestly and scholarly class or caste comparable to the Hindu Brahmans. Although scholars differ in their assessments of its etymology, the word "druid" is said to signify "wise man of the oak." The religion is Earth-centered, body-based, and immanent, as opposed to revealed or transcendent. Its wisdom is based in the Earth and all its inhabitants—in particular, the trees.

Originally established in 1717, the Order of Bards, Ovates and Druids (of which William Blake was an early chief) was reinstituted in 1988, and is now one of seven Druid orders based in the United Kingdom. In the United States, A Druid Fellowship is a national organization of Druids. Bards are poets and strive to become conduits for God/dess through their creative pursuits. Ovates are priests, and Druids are teachers. The process of becoming a Druid takes up to twenty years. Druids do not proselytize, and, in fact, are somewhat protective of their ancient teachings and mysteries. Theirs is not an exclusive tradition; it is possible, for example, to be a Christian or a Sufi Druid.

As we saw earlier, the ancient Celts had very open attitudes toward homosexuality. Dr. Rodney Karr, a gay therapist who facilitates the Golden Gate Seed Group of the Order of Bards, Ovates and Druids in San Francisco, reports that among Druids the gay issue is almost irrelevant, because of their belief both in the equality of all humans, and that we are all both male and female. Overall, he says, the order is "very positive toward gay people." Composed exclusively of gay men, the Golden Gate group regularly performs Druid rituals in the stone circle they have built next to the AIDS Grove (a national monument dedicated to those who have died from AIDS) in Golden Gate Park.

Radical Faeries

The Radical Faerie Fellowship was founded by Harry Hay and his partner John Burnside in the late '70s. Having started the Mattachine Society in the '50s, Hay was eventually removed from the organization's leadership because of his radical views and Communist links. Becoming more and more interested in issues of gay-centered spirituality, Hay and Burnside relocated to New Mexico, where their goal was to locate a living Native American Two-Spirit person. The first official gathering of Radical Faeries took place in 1979 in the Arizona desert near Benson. Among the two hundred men attending were Will Roscoe, Mitch Walker, Don Kilhefner, and Mark Thompson.

Utterly averse to hierarchy in any form, the Radical Faeries are gay men who share some basic neopagan beliefs such as the sacredness of nature and a respect for different paths to the Divine. With no dogma, doctrine, or central leadership, they are staunchly committed to group consensus as a decision-making process. The movement is flavored by Native American spirituality, and its members include a diverse bunch of Wiccans, Druids, and other traditions. Viewing themselves as stewards of the Earth, and respecting the sanctity of all life, they tend to be ecologically minded. In addition, they strive to live by Hay's teachings about subject-SUBJECT consciousness, and the interconnectedness of sexuality, spirituality, politics, and culture.

Faeries gather in circles and sanctuaries to celebrate gays as a "distinct and separate people," with our own culture, spirituality, and unique contributions to make. Rituals are varied and incorporate elements from different pagan traditions. The celebration of life is a common theme; rituals often involve dance, music, meditation, fire, prayer, ritual music, sweat lodges, drumming, mud pits, nudity, and, of course, camp and drag. Many Faeries also explore the use of magic. Sexuality and sensuality are honored and celebrated.

Joey Cain, who is writing a book about the Radical Faeries, confirms that the circle is the central ritual: "It's about speaking from the heart, and going to deeper levels of understanding of who we are. The process becomes a dynamo of exploration and going into deeper levels of self." Cain also believes that "gay men need to work together, outside of tradition and organized religion, to discover who we are—culturally, socially, and spiritually."

Available in most gay bookstores, the magazine *RFD* (Radical Faerie Digest) is the main Faerie publication, listing events and contacts in different areas of the country. There is a Faerie sanctuary in Wolf Creek, Oregon, and another one in the mountains near Liberty, Tennessee. Almost fifteen years ago, the Radical Faeries were granted church status by the IRS, under the name of the Church of Nomenus.

Women's Spirituality

Encompassing Goddess Reverence, feminism, eco-feminism, and a variety of spiritual paths, the Women's Spirituality movement emerged during the '70s. Honoring the lives, roles, and values of women, it is centered on the role of the Divine Feminine in all of her many forms. Besides the Goddess, Kuan Yin, and the Shekinah in Judaism, the lives and teachings of Christian female mystics such as St. Teresa of Avila, Hildergard of Bingen, and Julian of Norwich play important roles.

Because many of its founding mothers were women-loving women, the Women's Spirituality movement has been very inclusive of lesbians. Among the lesbian or bisexual leaders of the movement are Judy Grahn and Paula Gunn Allen, with a Native American and historical perspective, Z. Budapest, Vicky Noble, Hallie Iglehart Austen, and Starhawk, from the Goddess and/or Wicca tradition, Buddhist Diane Mariechild, Diane Stein, author of *Essential Reiki* and *The Women's Spirituality Book,* composers Kay Turner and Kay Gardner, and poets Audre Lorde and Adrienne Rich.

Based in Northern California, the Women's Spirituality Forum, founded by Z Budapest, presents biannual international festivals featuring workshops, spiritual rituals, and initiations, as well as cultural events such as music, dance, theater, and storytelling.

Queer Spirit

This movement, also referred to by some as "Gay Spirituality," a slightly less inclusive term, is based on the belief that many LGBT individuals have been spiritually inclined throughout history, often assuming important roles of spiritual leadership. The movement includes both those seeking to create a place for themselves within established, organized religions, as well as those seeking spiritual solace in alternative paths. As the name implies, a queer-centered spiritual path ponders, among other things, the spiritual value and unique contributions of being queer.

Inherently eclectic, its basic premise is that sexual and gender variance is encompassed by the Divine. Its advocates strive to identify homoerotic and transgendered deities, symbols, and images among the world's religions and mythologies, so as to provide sources of spiritual identification for queer people. Queer Spirit also recognizes the spiritual contributions made by many through the medium of art, particularly during times when they were excluded from explicit roles of spiritual leadership.

Many of its proponents have already been mentioned in these pages, and include Judy Grahn, Will Roscoe, Harry Hay, Paula Gunn Allen, Mark Thompson, Arthur Evans, Randy Conner, David Sparks, and Mariya Sparks.

Resource Guide

National Organizations

Affirmation
(Mormons)
P.O. Box 46022
Los Angeles, CA 90046-0022
http://www.affirmation.org

Affirmation
(Methodists)
P.O. Box 1021
Evanston, IL 60204
847-733-9590

AIDS National Interfaith Network
1400 I Street, NW, #1220
Washington, DC 20005
202-842-0010; 202-842-3323
thebody@aol.com

American Baptists Concerned
P.O. Box 3183
Walnut Creek, CA 94598-0183
925-439-4672
http://members.aol.com/ambaptists
ambaptists@aol.com

Association of Welcoming and Affirming
Baptists
P.O. Box 2596
Attleboro Falls, MA 02763-0894
508-226-1945; wabaptists@aol.com
http://users.aol.com/wabaptists/

Axios
(Eastern and Orthodox Christian)
P.O. Box 990 / Village Station
New York, NY 10014-0990
718-805-1952; AxiosUSA@aol.com

http://www.qrd.org/QRD/www/orgs/
axios

Brethren/Mennonite Council for L/G
Concerns
P.O. Box 6300
Minneapolis, MN 55406
612-722-6906; bmcouncil@aol.com
http://www.webcom.com/bmc/

Christian Lesbians OUT (CLOUT)
P.O. Box 5853
Athens, OH 45701
740-448-6424
clout@seorf.ohio.edu

Dignity
(Catholic)
1500 Massachusetts Ave., #11
Washington, DC 20005
dignity@aol.com
800-877-8797; 202-861-0017; 202-
429-9808 (fax); dignity@aol.com
www.dignityusa.org

Emergence International
(Christian Scientists)
P.O. Box 9161
San Rafael, CA 94912-9161
800-280-6653; billxls@aol.com

Evangelicals Concerned
311 East 72nd Street, #1-G
New York, NY 10021
212-517-3171

Friends for Lesbian/Gay Concerns
(Quakers)
143 Campbell Avenue
Ithaca, NY 14850
609-443-4706; jckelly@lightlink.com

Gay Buddhist Fellowship
2261 Market Street, #422
San Francisco, CA 94114
415-974-9878; www.gaybuddhist.org
(Men only)

Gay, Lesbian, and Affirming Disciples
Alliance (GLAD)
(Disciples of Christ)
P.O. Box 44400
Indianapolis, IN 46244
517-351-4780

Gay Muslims
686 Parker Street
Boston, MA 02120
617-685-4175; 617-373-8788 (fax);
falam@lynx.dac.neu.edu

HeartStrong
1011 Boren Avenue, #199
Seattle, WA 98104-1300
206-215-4536; MarcAdams@heart-
strong.org; www.heartstrong.org
(Support and resources for GLBT students in Christian schools)

Integrity
(Episcopalians)
P.O. Box 5255
New York, NY 10185-5255
202-462-9193; 202-588-1486 (fax);
http://www.integrityusa.org

Interweave
Unitarian Universalists for LBGT
Concerns
167 Milk St. #406

Boston, MA 02109-4339
SGoreTX@aol.com

Lutherans Concerned
2466 Sharondale Drive
Atlanta, GA 30305
404-266-9615; 404-266-9215 (fax);
luthcon@aol.com; www.lcna.org

More Light Presbyterians
P.O. Box 38
New Brunswick, NJ 08903-0038
732-932-7501; jda@scils.rutgers.edu
www.mlp.org

National Conference for Catholic
Lesbians
P.O. Box 436
Planetarium Station
New York, NY 10024

National Gay Pentecostal Alliance
P.O. Box 1391
Schenectady, NY 12301-1391
518-372-6001

New Ways Ministry
(Catholic)
4012 29th Street
Mt. Rainier, MD 20712
301-277-5674; 301-864-6948 (fax);
newways@juno.com
http://members.aol.com/NewWaysM

Q-Spirit
3739 Balboa Street, #211
San Francisco, CA 94121
415-281-9377; 415-386-3187 (fax);
qspirit1@aol.com; www.qspirit.org

Radical Faeries
Nomenus Wolf Creek Sanctuary
P. O. Box 312
Wolf Creek, OR 97497
nomenus@aol.com

Rainbow Wind
(Pagans)
P.O. Box 8275
Lexington, KY 40533-8275
RainboWind@aol.com
http://users.aol.com/RainboWind

Reformed Church in America Gay
Caucus
P.O. Box 8174
Philadelphia, PA 19101-8174

Seventh Day Adventist Kinship International
P.O. Box 7320
Laguna Niguel, CA 92607

ULGCS
(Christian Scientist)
P.O. Box 2171
Beverly Hills, CA 90213
213-876-1338

Unitarian Universalist Association
Office of BGLT Concerns
25 Beacon Street
Boston, MA 02108-2800
617-742-2100, x470; 617-742-7025
(fax); obgltc@uua.org

UCC Coalition for LGBT Concerns
(United Church of Christ)
800 Village Walk, #230
Guilford, CT 06437

800-653-0799; 203-789-6356 (fax);
mnecoalition@snet.net
www.coalition.simplenet.com

UCC Youth/Young Adult Program
Coalition for LGBT Concerns
1005 East 9th Avenue, #102
Broomfield, CO 80020
303-438-8475

Unity Fellowship Church
5148 W. Jefferson Blvd.
Los Angeles, CA 90016
323-936-4949; 323-938-8322

Universal Federation of Metropolitan
Community Churches
8704 Santa Monica Blvd., 2nd Floor
West Hollywood, CA 90069
310-360-8640; 310-360-8680 (fax);
UfmccHq@aol.com; www.ufmcc.com

Wesleyan Holiness Gay and Lesbian
Network
(Wesleyan Holiness Tradition)
3540 North Pennsylvania Street, #F
Indianapolis, IN 46205

World Congress of Gay, Lesbian, and
Bisexual Jewish Organizations
P.O. Box 23379
Washington, DC 20026-3379
info@wcgljo.org
www.wcgljo.org/wcgljo

Welcoming Church Programs

More Light Presbyterians
P.O. Box 38
New Brunswick, NJ 08903-0038
732-932-7501; jda@scils.rutgers.edu;
www.mlp.org

Oasis
(Episcopal)
31 Mulberry Street

Newark, NJ 07102
973-430-9909; TheOasisNJ@aol.com

Open and Affirming
(Disciples of Christ)
Park Avenue Christian Church
1010 Park Avenue
New York, NY 10028

Open and Affirming Program
UCC Coalition for LGBT Concerns
(United Church of Christ)
P.O. Box 403
Holden, MA 01520-0403
508-856-9316; 508-852-3559 (fax);
onaabday@aol.com

Reconciled in Christ Churches
(Lutheran)
2466 Sharondale Drive
Atlanta, GA 30305
404-266-9615; 404-266-9215 (fax);
luthconc@aol.com; www.lcna.org

Reconciling Congregation Program
(Methodists)
3801 N. Keeler Avenue
Chicago, IL 60641
773-736-5526; 773-736-5475;
mark@rcp.org; www.rcp.org

Supportive Congregations Network
(Brethren/Mennonite)
P.O. Box 6300
Minneapolis, MN 55406
612-722-6906; bmcouncil@aol.com
http://www.webcom.com/bmc/

Welcoming and Affirming Baptists
P.O. Box 2596
Attleboro Falls, MA 02763-0894
508-226-1945; wabaptists@aol.com
http://users.aol.com/wabaptists/

Welcoming Congregation Program
Unitarian Universalist Association
Office of BGLT Concerns
25 Beacon Street
Boston, MA 02108-2800
617-742-2100, x470; 617-742-7025
(fax); obgltc@uua.org

Regional Organizations

Oasis California
(Episcopal)
1661 15th Street
San Francisco, CA 94103-3511
415-522-0222; 800-419-0222; 415-
522-1198 (fax); oasiscalif@aol.com;
www.diocal.org/oasis

The Oasis
(Episcopal)

31 Mulberry Street
Newark, NJ 07102
973-430-9909; TheOasisNJ@aol.com
http//:members.aol.com/TheOasisNJ

United in Spirit/East Coast
55 Bethune Street, #642B
New York, NY 10014
212-463-0699

Retreat Centers/Conferences/Travel

Brothers Together
115 Newbury Street, #204
Boston, MA 02116-2935
800-462-9962; 617-247-3964;
bt@stasio.com; www.stasio.com
(Workshops and retreats for men)

California Men's Gathering
2215-R Market Street, #263
San Francisco, CA 94114
415-281-8336; cmg@webcom.com
www.thecmg.com

Camp Camp
P.O. Box 7806
Princeton, NJ 08543
888-924-8380; 609-683-1795 (fax);
info@campcamp.com;
http://www.campcamp.com
(Summer camp in Maine with some
spiritual activities)

Dawn Manor
621 Cattail Road
Livingston Manor, NY 12758-6726
914-439-5815; 914-439-8303 (fax);
dawnmanor@aol.com
(Gay-owned retreat center)

The Gathering
P.O. Box 25582
Albuquerque, NM 87125-0582
(GLBT Spiritual Gathering in NM)

Gay Spirit Visions
P.O. Box 339
Decatur, GA 30031-0339
770-972-8028;
gayspirit@mindspring.com
http://gayspirit.home.mindspring.com
e-mail reflector: gsv-list@listserv.aol.com
(Offer two yearly retreats for gay men)

Omega Institute
260 Lake Drive
Rhinebeck, NY 12572-3212
800-944-1001; 914-266-4828 (fax);
www.omega-inst.org
(Offers G/L programming)

Spirit Journeys
P.O. Box 3046
Asheville, NC 28802
704-258-8880; 704-281-0334 (fax);
spiritjourneys@worldnet.att.net
www.spiritjourneys.com
(Spiritually themed tours and workshops)

Spirit Rock
Box 909
Woodacre, CA 94973
415-488-0164, x381; 415-488-0170
(fax); www.spiritrock.org
(Offers Buddhist meditation retreats for
gays and lesbians)

Women's Spirituality Forum
P.O. Box 11363
Oakland, CA 94611
510-444-7724; silverzb@aol.com
www.netwiz.net/zbudapest
(Biannual "Goddess 2000," an International Goddess Festival)

Schools/Centers: Sexuality

Body Electric School
6527-A Telegraph Avenue
Oakland, CA 94609-1113
510-653-1594; 510-653-4991(fax);
bodyelec@aol.com
www.bodyelectric.org

Erospirit Research Institute
P.O. Box 3893
Oakland, CA 94609
510-428-9063; 510-652-4354 (fax);

kramer@erospirit.org
www.erospirit.org
(Joseph Kramer)

Gay-Tantra Institut
Kraustrasse b5
90443 Nürnberg, Germany
011-49-911-2-448-616;
arminchristoph.heining@t-online-de
(Based on Margo Anand's work)

Healing Tao Center
1205 O'Neill Highway
Dunmore, PA 18512
717-348-4310; 717-348-4313 (fax)
(Based on Matak Chia's work)

SCA
P.O. Box 1585
Old Chelsea Station
New York, NY 10011
800-977-HEAL; 212-606-3778;

info@sca-recovery.org
http://www.sca-recovery.org
(Sexual Compulsives Anonymous; 12-step recovery group)

SkyDancing Institute
20 Sunnyside Avenue, #A219
Mill Valley, CA 94941
415-927-2584; 415-924-6934
(Based on Margo Anand's work)

Transformational Seminars

The Experience
369 Montezuma Avenue, #123
Santa Fe, NM 87501-2626
800-966-3896; 505-820-7182; 505-820-7106 (fax); TheExperience@
TheExper.org; www.TheExperience.org

The Liberty Experience Training
2215-R Market Street, #182
San Francisco, CA 94114
415-863-4157

Books, Audio, Video

Christianity

Aarons, Leroy. *Prayers for Bobby: A Mother's Coming to Terms with the Suicide of Her Gay Son.* San Francisco: HarperSanFrancisco, 1995.

Bawer, Bruce. *Stealing Jesus: How Fundamentalism Betrays Christianity.* New York: Crown Publishers, 1997.

Boswell, John. *Christianity, Social Tolerance, and Religion: Gay People in Western Europe from the Beginning of the Christian Era to the Fourteenth Century.* Chicago: The University of Chicago Press, 1980.

Boyd, Malcolm. *Gay Priest: An Inner Journey.* New York: St. Martin's Press, 1986.

Brooten, Bernadette J. *Love Between Women: Early Christian Responses to Female Homoeroticism.* Chicago: The University of Chicago Press, 1996.

Curb, Rosemary, and Manahan, Nancy. *Lesbian Nuns: Breaking Silence.* Tallahassee, FL: Naiad Press, 1985.

Glaser, Chris. *Come Home! Reclaiming Spirituality and Community as Gay Men and Lesbians.* San Francisco: HarperSanFrancisco, 1990.

Gomes, Peter J. *The Good Book: Reading the Bible with Mind and Heart.* New York: William Morrow & Company, 1996.

Goss, Robert. *Jesus Acted Up: A Gay and Lesbian Manifesto.* San Francisco: HarperSanFrancisco, 1993.

Helminiak, Daniel A. *What the Bible Really Says About Homosexuality.* San Francisco: Alamo Square Press, 1994.

Heyward, Carter. *Our Passion for Justice.* New York: Pilgrim Press, 1984.

Kelly, Michael B. *The Erotic Contemplative: Reflections on the Spiritual Journey of the Gay/Lesbian Christian.* Oakland: EroSpirit Research Institute. (Video)

McNeil, John J. *Taking a Chance on God: Liberating Theology for Gays, Lesbians, and Their Lovers, Families, and Friends.* Boston: Beacon Press, 1988.

Mollenkott, Virginia Ramey. *Sensuous Spirituality: Out from Fundamentalism.* New York: Crossroad, 1993.

Perry, Troy D. *The Lord Is My Shepherd and He Knows I'm Gay.* Los Angeles: Universal Fellowship Press, 1972.

Piazza, Michael. *Holy Homosexuals: The Truth About Being Gay & Christian.* Dallas: Sources of Hope Publishing, 1995.

Rix, Jallen. *Ex-Gay? No Way: Recovery from Ex-Gay Ministries.* San Francisco: Triam Agency, 1998.

Scanzoni, Letha Dawson, and Mollenkott, Virginia Ramey. *Is the Homosexual My Neighbor?: A Positive Christian Response.* San Francisco: HarperSanFrancisco, 1994.

Spahr, Jane Adams; Poethig, Kathryn; Berry, Selisse; and McLain, Melinda V. *Called Out: The Voices & Gifts of Lesbian, Gay, Bisexual, and Transgendered Presbyterians.* Gaithersburg, MD: Chi Rho Press, 1995.

Spong, John Shelby. *Rescuing the Bible from Fundamentalism: A Bishop Rethinks the Meaning of Scripture.* San Francisco: HarperSanFrancisco, 1991.

White, Mel. *Stranger at the Gate: To Be Gay and Christian in America.* New York: Simon and Schuster, 1994.

Whitehead, Sally Lowe. *The Truth Shall Set You Free: A Family's Passage from Fundamentalism to a New Understanding of Faith, Love, and Sexual Identity.* San Francisco: HarperSanFrancisco, 1997.

Wilson, Nancy. *Our Tribe: Queer Folks, God, Jesus, and the Bible.* San Francisco: HarperSanFrancisco, 1995.

General Spirituality/Other Paths

Alpert, Rebecca. *Like Bread on the Seder Plate: Jewish Lesbians and the Transformation of Tradition.* New York: Columbia University Press, 1998.

Balka, Christine, and Rose, Andy, eds. *Twice Blessed: On Being Lesbian or Gay and Jewish.* Boston: Beacon Press, 1989.

Barzan, Bob. *Sex and Spirit: Exploring Gay Men's Spirituality.* San Francisco: White Crane Press, 1995.

Boucher, Sandy. *Opening the Lotus: A Woman's Guide to Buddhism.* Boston: Beacon Press, 1997.

Bouldrey, Brian, ed. *Wrestling with the Angel: Faith and Religion in the Lives of Gay Men.* New York: Riverhead Books, 1995.

Budapest, Zsuzsanna E. *Grandmother Moon: Lunar Magic in Our Lives—Spells, Rituals, Goddesses, Legends, and Emotions Under the Moon.* San Francisco: HarperSanFrancisco, 1991.

———. *The Grandmother of Time: A Women's Book of Celebrations, Spells, and Sacred Objects for Every Month of the Year.* San Francisco: HarperSanFrancisco, 1989.

Carpenter, Edward. *Intermediate Types Among Primitive Folk,* 2 ed. North Stratford, NH: Arno Press, 1975.

Comstock, Gary David, and Henking, Susan E., eds. *Que(e)rying Religion.* New York: Continuum, 1997.

Conner, Randy P. *Blossom of Bone: Reclaiming the Connection Between Homoeroticism and the Sacred.* San Francisco: HarperSanFrancisco, 1993.

Conner, Randy P., Sparks, David, and Sparks, Mariya. *Cassell's Encyclopedia of Queer Myth, Symbol and Spirit.* London: Cassell, 1997.

Evans, Arthur. *Witchcraft and the Gay Counterculture.* Boston: Fag Rag Books, 1978.

Grahn, Judy. *Another Mother Tongue: Gay Words, Gay Worlds.* Boston: Beacon Press, 1984.

Harvey, Andrew. *The Essential Gay Mystics.* San Francisco: HarperSanFrancisco, 1997.

Hasbany, Richard, ed. *Homosexuality and Religion.* Binghamton, NY: Harrington Park Press, 1989.

Herman, Bert. *Being, Being Happy, Being Gay: Pathways to a Rewarding Life for Lesbians and Gay Men.* San Francisco: Alamo Square Press, 1990.

Leyland, Winston, ed. *Queer Dharma: Voices of Gay Buddhists.* San Francisco: Gay Sunshine Press, 1998.

Matousek, Mark. *Sex, Death, Enlightenment.* New York: Riverhead Books, 1996.

McNaught, Brian. *Now That I'm Out, What Do I Do?* New York: St. Martin's Press, 1997.

Noble, Vicky. *Motherpeace: A Way to the Goddess Through Myth, Art, and Tarot.* San Francisco: HarperSanFrancisco, 1983.

———. *Shakti Woman: Feeling Our Fire, Healing Our World—The New Female Shamanism.* San Francisco: HarperSanFrancisco, 1991.

Raphael, Lev. *Journeys & Arrivals : On Being Gay and Jewish.* New York: Faber & Faber, 1996.

Ratti, Rakesh, ed. *A Lotus of Another Color: An Unfolding of the South Asian Gay and Lesbian Experience.* Los Angeles: Alyson Publications, 1993.

Roscoe, Will. *Changing Ones.* New York: St. Martin's Press, 1998.

———, ed. *Living the Spirit: A Gay American Indian Anthology.* New York: St. Martin's Press, 1988.

———. *Queer Spirits: A Gay Men's Myth Book.* Boston: Beacon Press, 1995.

———. *The Zuni Man-Woman.* Albuquerque: University of New Mexico Press, 1991.

Schmitt, Arno, and Sofer, Jehoeda, eds. *Sexuality and Eroticism Among Males in Moslem Societies,* New York: The Haworth Press, 1992.

Starhawk. *The Spiral Dance : A Rebirth of the Ancient Religion of the Great Goddess.* San Francisco: HarperSanFrancisco, 1989.

Sweasey, Peter. *From Queer to Eternity: Spirituality in the Lives of Lesbian, Gay & Bisexual People.* London: Cassell, 1997.

Swidler, Arlene, ed. *Homosexuality and World Religions.* Valley Forge, PA: Trinity Press International, 1993.

Thompson, Mark. *Gay Spirit: Myth and Meaning.* New York: St. Martin's Press, 1987.

———. *Gay Soul: Finding the Heart of Gay Spirit and Nature with Sixteen Writers, Healers, Teachers, and Visionaries.* San Francisco: HarperSanFrancisco, 1994.

Williams, Walter. *The Spirit and the Flesh: Sexual Diversity in American Indian Culture.* Boston: Beacon Press, 1986.

Spiritual Practices

Cohen, Ken. *QiGong: Traditional Exercises for Healing Body, Mind, and Spirit.* Boulder, CO: Sounds True, 1996. ((Video)

Dass, Ram. *Journey of Awakening: A Meditator's Guidebook.* New York: Bantam, 1978.

———. *On Spiritual Practice: Finding the Middle Way.* San Anselmo, CA: Hanuman Foundation. (Audio)

Forte, Robert, ed. *Entheogens and the Future of Religion.* San Francisco: Council on Spiritual Practices, 1997.

John-Roger. *Inner Worlds of Meditation: A Practical Guidebook for Exploring the Inner Levels of Consciousness.* Los Angeles: Mandeville Press, 1997.

Leonard, Jim, and Laut, Phil. *Rebirthing: The Science of Enjoying All of Your Life.* Cincinnati: Trinity Publications, 1983.

Moses, Johnny. *Medicine Path: Healing Songs and Stories of the Northwest Native Americans.* Boulder, CO: Sounds True, 1997. (Audio)

Ray, Sondra. *Celebration of Breath.* Berkeley: Celestial Arts, 1983.

Roth, Gabrielle. *Sweat Your Prayers: Movement as Spiritual Practice.* New York: Tarcher/Putnam, 1997.

Smith, Jean, ed. *Breath Sweeps Mind: A First Guide to Meditation Practice.* New York: Riverhead Books, 1998.

Yee, Rodney. *Yoga Journal's Yoga for Strength.* Healing Arts, 1992. (Video)

Work/Service

Dass, Ram, and Bush, Mirabai. *Compassion in Action: Setting Out on the Path of Service.* New York: Bell Tower, 1992.

Dass, Ram, and Gorman, Paul. *How Can I Help?: Stories and Reflections on Service.* New York: Knopf, 1985.

Fox, Matthew. *A Spirituality Named Compassion and the Healing of the Global Village, Humpty Dumpty and Us.* New York: Harper & Row, 1979.

———. *The Reinvention of Work: A New Vision of Livelihood for Our Time.* San Francisco: HarperSanFrancisco, 1994.

Williamson, Marianne. *The Healing of America.* New York: Simon & Schuster, 1997.

Sexuality and Relationships

Anand, Margo. *The Art of Sexual Ecstasy: The Path of Sacred Sexuality for Western Lovers.* New York: Tarcher/Putnam, 1989.

Bronski, Michael. *The Pleasure Principle: Sex, Backlash, and the Struggle for Gay Freedom.* New York: St. Martin's Press, 1998.

Chia, Mantak, and Arava, Douglas Abrams. *The Multi-Orgasmic Man.* San Francisco: HarperSanFrancisco, 1996.

Chia, Mantak, and Chia, Maneewan. *Healing Love Through the Tao: Cultivating Female Sexual Energy.* Dunmore, PA: Healing Tao, 1991.

Dass, Ram. *Sex and Spirituality.* San Anselmo, CA: Hanuman Foundation. (Audio)

———. *The Yoga of Relationships.* San Anselmo, CA: Hanuman Foundation. (Audio)

Hendricks, Gay. *The Ten-Second Miracle: Creating Relationship Breakthroughs.* San Francisco: HarperSanFrancisco, 1998.

Hopkins, Jeffrey. *Sex, Orgasm, and the Mind of Clear Light: The Sixty-four Arts of Gay Male Love.* Berkeley: North Atlantic Books, 1998.

Isensee, Rik. *Love Between Men: Enhancing Intimacy and Keeping Your Relationship Alive.* Los Angeles: Alyson Publications, 1990.

Keen, Sam. *To Love and Be Loved.* New York: Bantam, 1977.

Kramer, Joseph. *Evolutionary Masturbation: An Intimate Guide to Male Orgasm.* Oakland, CA: EroSpirit Research Institute. (Video)

———. *Fire on the Mountain: An Intimate Guide to Male Genital Massage.* Oakland, CA: EroSpirit Research Institute. (Video)

Levine, Stephen, and Levine, Ondrea. *Embracing the Beloved: Relationship as a Path of Awakening.* New York: Anchor, 1995.

Lowenthal, Michael, ed. *Gay Men at the Millennium: Sex, Spirit, Community.* New York: Tarcher/Putnam, 1997.

Mariechild, Diane. *Sacred Lesbian Sexuality.* Oakland, CA: Wingbow Press, 1995.

Moore, Thomas. *Soul of Sex: Cultivating Life as an Act of Love.* New York: HarperCollins, 1998.

Osho. *Tantra Spirituality & Sex.* Boulder, CO: Chidvilas, Inc., 1994.

Peck, Scott. *The Road Less Traveled: A New Psychology of Love, Traditional Values and Spiritual Growth.* New York: Touchstone, 1978.

Ray, Sondra. *Lasting Love Relationships.* New York: Sound Horizons, 1993. (Audio)

———. *Loving Relationships.* Berkeley: Celestial Arts, 1980.

Rotello, Gabriel. *Sexual Ecology: AIDS and the Destiny of Gay Men.* New York: Plume, 1997.

Signorile, Michelangelo. *Life Outside: The Signorile Report on Gay Men: Sex, Drugs, Muscles, and the Passages of Life.* New York: HarperCollins Publishers, 1997.

Somé, Sobonfu. *The Spirit of Intimacy: Ancient Teachings in the Way of Relationships.* Berkeley: Berkeley Hills, 1997.

Spencer, Colin. *The Gay Kama Sutra.* New York: St. Martin's Press, 1996.

Tessina, Tina. *Gay Relationships: For Men and Women.* New York: Tarcher/Putnam: 1989.

Thompson, Mark. *Gay Body: A Journey Through Shadow to Self.* New York: St. Martin's Press, 1997.

Williamson, Marianne. *A Return to Love: Reflections on the Principles of A Course in Miracles.* New York: HarperPaperbacks, 1993.

———. *The Relationships Workshop.* New York: Sound Horizons, 1992. (Audio)

Journals and Magazines

The Beltane Papers
2468 E. Pole
Everson, WA 98247
360-647-1264

FDR
P.O. Box 26807
Los Angeles, CA 90026

213-666-1350; FaeDishRag@aol.com
(Radical Faeries)

Gay Theological Journal
Bruce H. Joffe, Editor
8571-B Sudley Road
Manassas, VA 20110-3811

703-330-5600; 703-330-5357 (fax);
gaytheojrnl@pubpartners.com
http://www.pubpartners.com
gaytheojrnl.html

Menstuff
Gordon Clay, Publisher
P.O. Box 800
San Anselmo, CA 94979
415-453-2839
(Lists resources for men; gay inclusive)

Men's Voices
Bert H. Hoff, Editor
7552 31st Ave. N.E.
Seattle, WA 98115
Berthoff@wLn.com
http://www.vix.com/menmag
(Gay-friendly men's movement journal)

Of a Like Mind
Lynn Levy, Editor
P.O. Box 6530
Madison, WI 53716
608-257-5858; scgi@itis.com
(Lesbian-owned women's spirituality
magazine)

RFD
Box 68
Liberty, TN 37095
(Magazine for Radical Faeries and gay
men in rural areas)

Sage Woman Magazine
Anne Niven, Editor
P.O. Box 641
Point Arena, CA 95468
707-882-2052; 707-882-2793 (fax)
(Lesbian-friendly Goddess magazine)

Touching Body and Spirit
TBS Network
Sunfire, Editor
Box 957
Huntington, NY 11743-0957
800-248-3413; sunfire@idt.net
www.the-park.com/tbs
(Explores the relationship between body
and spirit)

White Crane Journal
Toby Johnson, Editor
P.O. Box 1018
Conifer, CO 80433-1018
TobyJohnso@aol.com
www.whitecranejournal.com
(Explores spirituality of gay men)

Women's Voices
Kate Scholl, Editor
P.O. Box 4448
Santa Rosa, CA 95402-4448
707-575-5654; ksholl@monitor.net
(Lesbian inclusive; mostly Northern
California)

Web Sites

Bridges Across the Divide
"Faith Communities and Homosexuality"
www.bridges-across.org/ba/faith.htm

Gay America
"Guide to GLBT Religion"
www.gayamerica.com/religion.htm

Gay and Lesbian Atheists and Humanists (GALAH)
www.serve.com/tgkindc/galah.html

Gay Christians.org
www.gaychristians.org

GayJews.org
www.gayjews.org

Gay Men's Spirituality
www.the-park.com/barzan/main.htm

Gays for God
www.gaysforgod.org

Interfaith Working Group
www.libertynet.org

Ontario Consultants on Religious Tolerance
"Religious groups' policies towards
homosexuality"
www.religioustolerance.org/
homosexu.htm

QMondo
Lifestyle/Culture: Religion
www.qmondo.com

Queer Muslims
www.angelfire.com/ca2/queermuslims

Rainbow Spirituality Ring
www.geocities.com/
westhollywood/3528/rainbow.html

Steps to Recover from Bible Abuse
www.truluck.com

Suite101.com
"Gay and Lesbian Spirituality"
www.suite101.com/welcome.cfm/
gay_lesbian_spirituality

The Park: One People, One Planet,
One Community
"Sex and Spirit"
www.the-park.com/sexspirit.htm

Whosoever, Online Magazine for GLBT
Christians
www.whosoever.org

BIBLIOGRAPHICAL NOTES

Part 1

1. Mark Thompson, *Gay Spirit: Myth and Meaning* (St. Martin's Press, 1987), p. 281.

2. Excerpted from *The American Heritage® Dictionary of the English Language, Third Edition* ©1996 by Houghton Mifflin Company. Electronic version licensed from INSO Corporation; further reproduction and distribution in accordance with the Copyright Law of the United States. All rights reserved.

3. Lynn Witt, Sherry Thomas, and Eric Marcus, *Out in All Directions: The Almanac of Gay and Lesbian America* (Warner Books, 1995), pp. 162–63.

4. Randy P. Conner, David Sparks, and Mariya Sparks, *Cassell's Encyclopedia of Queer Myth, Symbol and Spirit* (Cassell, 1997), p. 87.

5. Judy Grahn, *Another Mother Tongue: Gay Words, Gay Worlds* (Beacon, 1984), pp. 270–71.

6. Andrew Ramer, *Two Flutes Playing* (Alamo Square Press, 1997), p. 117.

7. Thompson, *Gay Spirit*, p. 207.

8. Ibid., p. 5.

9. Mark Thompson, *Gay Soul: Finding the Heart of Gay Spirit and Nature wit Sixteen Writers, Healers, Teachers, and Visionaries* (HarperSanFrancisco, 1994), p. 217.

10. Jamake Highwater, *The Mythology of Transgression: Homosexuality as Metaphor* (Oxford University Press, 1997), p. 21.

11. Ibid., p. 10.

12. Ibid., p. 19.

13. Thompson, *Gay Soul*, p. 44.

14. Edward Carpenter, *Intermediate Types Among Primitive Folk,* second edition (Arno Press, 1975), p. 58.

15. Ibid.

16. Ibid., pp. 59–60.

17. Thompson, *Gay Soul*, p. 70.

18. Ibid., p. 90.

19. Thompson, *Gay Spirit*, p. 206.

20. Thompson, *Gay Soul*, p. 23.

21. Personal communication.

22. Thompson, *Gay Spirit*, pp. 52–53.

23. Conner et al., *Cassell's Encyclopedia*, p. 306.

24. Thompson, *Gay Spirit*, pp. 60–61.

25. Thompson, *Gay Soul*, pp. 216–17.

26. Conner et al., *Cassell's Encyclopedia*, pp. 324–25.

27. Ibid., pp. 216–17.

28. Will Roscoe, ed., *Living the Spirit: A Gay American Indian Anthology* (St. Martin's Press, 1988), pp. 157–62.

29. Conner et al., *Cassell's Encyclopedia,* p. 114.

30. Ibid., p. 310.

31. Thompson, *Gay Spirit,* p. 204.

32. Thompson, *Gay Soul,* p. 16.

33. Mark Thompson, *Gay Body: A Journey Through Shadow to Self* (St. Martin's Press, 1997), p. 142.

34. Thompson, *Gay Spirit,* p. 206.

35. Don Kilhefner, "Gay People at a Critical Crossroad: Assimilation or Affirmation?," in Thompson, *Gay Spirit,* pp. 127–28.

36. Thompson, *Gay Body,* p. 143.

37. Thompson, *Gay Soul,* p. 127.

38. Ibid., p. 70.

39. Ibid., p. 90.

40. Grahn, *Another Mother Tongue,* pp. 226–28.

41. Thompson, *Gay Soul,* p. 175.

42. Ibid., pp. 70–71.

43. Ramer, *Two Flutes,* p. 112.

44. Thompson, *Gay Spirit,* p. xvi.

45. Grahn, *Another Mother Tongue,* p. 11.

46. Arthur Evans, *Witchcraft and the Gay Counterculture* (Fag Rag Books, 1978), p. 49.

47. Grahn, *Another Mother Tongue,* p. 47.

48. Walter Williams, *The Spirit and the Flesh: Sexual Diversity in American Indian Culture* (Beacon Press, 1986), pp. 41–42.

49. Will Roscoe, *Queer Spirits: A Gay Men's Myth Book* (Beacon Press, 1995), pp. 86–94.

50. Thompson, *Gay Soul,* p. 251.

51. Randy P. Conner, *Blossom of Bone: Reclaiming the Connection between Homoeroticism and the Sacred* (HarperSanFrancisco, 1993), p. 41.

52. Ibid., p. 43.

53. Grahn, *Another Mother Tongue,* p. 119.

54. Conner, *Blossom of Bone,* pp. 70–71.

55. Ibid., pp. 76–79.

56. Genesis: 41, *The Holy Bible: New International Version* (Zondervan Bible Publishers, 1973), pp. 60–61.

57. Conner, *Blossom of Bone,* pp. 88–89.

58. Conner et al., *Cassell's Encyclopedia,* pp. 91–92.

59. Ibid., p. 69.

60. Conner, *Blossom of Bone,* p. 94.

61. Grahn, *Another Mother Tongue,* p. 12.

62. Conner et al., *Cassell's Encyclopedia,* p. 49.

63. Ibid., pp. 129–31.

64. Ibid., p. 220.

65. Grahn, *Another Mother Tongue,* p. 119.

66. Conner, *Blossom of Bone,* pp. 150–51.

67. Ibid., pp. 53–57.

68. Conner et al., *Cassell's Encyclopedia,* p. 178.

69. Ibid., p. 225.

70. Thompson, *Gay Soul,* p. 103.

71. Williams, *Spirit and the Flesh,* p. 32.

72. Will Roscoe, *The Zuni Man-Woman* (University of New Mexico Press, 1991), p. 48.

73. Williams, *Spirit and the Flesh,* pp. 236–39.

74. Will Roscoe, "Living the Tradition: Gay American Indians," in Thompson, *Gay Spirit,* p. 75.

75. Ibid.

76. Will Roscoe, *Changing Ones* (St. Martin's Press, 1998), p. 26.

77. Thompson, *Gay Spirit,* pp. 59–60.

78. Grahn, *Another Mother Tongue,* p. 95.

79. Thompson, *Gay Soul,* p. 125.

80. Roscoe, *Changing Ones,* pp. 49–50.

81. Williams, *Spirit and the Flesh,* p. 315.

82. Kilhefner, *Gay People at a Critical Crossroad,* p. 127.

83. Carpenter, *Intermediate Types,* p. 63.

84. Edward Carpenter, "Selected Insights," in Thompson, *Gay Spirit,* pp. 154–55.

85. Gerald Heard, "A Future for the Isophyl," in Thompson, *Gay Spirit,* p. 178.

86. Jim Kepner, "I Should Have Been Listening: A Memory of Gerald Heard," in Thompson, *Gay Spirit,* p. 171.

87. Heard, "A Future for the Isophyl," p. 179.

88. Marvin Meyer, trans., *The Gospel of Thomas* (HarperSanFrancisco, 1992), p. 35.

89. Conner et al., *Cassell's Encyclopedia,* p. 325.

90. Thompson, *Gay Soul,* p. 56.

91. Bert H. Hoff, "Gays as Spiritual Gatekeepers: Indigenous Africans Celebrate the Gay Spirit," in Bob Barzan, *Sex and Spirit: Exploring Gay Men's Spirituality* (White Crane Press, 1995), pp. 16–19.

92. Sobonfu Somé, *The Spirit of Intimacy: Ancient Teachings in the Way of Relationships* (Berkeley Hills, 1997), pp. 133–38.

Part 2

1. *Webster's Ninth New Collegiate Dictionary* (Springfield, MA, 1989), p. 1137.

2. Matthew Fox, "Ask Matthew Fox," *Creation Spirituality,* Summer 1997.

3. Peter Sweasey, *From Queer to Eternity: Spirituality in the Lives of Lesbian, Gay & Bisexual People* (Cassell, 1997), pp. 11–13.

4. Gloria E. Anzaldúa, Foreword to Randy P. Conner, David Sparks, and

Mariya Sparks, *Cassell's Encyclopedia of Queer Myth, Symbol and Spirit* (Cassell, 1997), pp. vii–viii.

5. Thompson, *Gay Spirit,* p. 79.

6. Toby Johnson, "Joseph Campbell and the Lunar Vision," *White Crane Journal,* Number 31, Winter 1997, p. 13.

7. Thompson, *Gay Soul,* p. 255.

8. Ibid., p. 41.

9. Marian Jones, "Getting the Help You Need," *The Advocate,* May 26, 1998, pp. 55–56.

10. Sheppard Kominars and Kate Kominars, *Accepting Ourselves & Others: A Journey into Recovery from Addictive & Compulsive Behaviors for Gays, Lesbians & Bisexuals* (Hazelden, 1996), pp. 47–48.

11. Ibid., p. 57.

12. Timothy Pfaff, "Spirituality: The Community's Search for Wholeness," *San Francisco Frontiers,* Volume 14, Issue 15, November 23, 1995, p. 20.

13. Sogyal Rinpoche, "Bringing the Mind Home," in Jean Smith, ed., *Breath Sweeps Mind: A First Guide to Meditation Practice* (Riverhead Books, 1998), p. 7.

14. Ram Dass, *Journey of Awakening: A Meditator's Guidebook* (Bantam, 1978), p. 5.

15. Rinpoche, "Bringing the Mind Home," p. 7.

16. John Snelling, "Buddhist Traditions of Meditation," in Jean Smith, ed., *Breath Sweeps Mind,* p. 33.

17. Ram Dass, *Journey of Awakening,* p. 47.

18. Ibid., p. 51.

19. Ibid., p. 66.

20. Thynn Thynn, "Concentration and Meditation," in Jean Smith, ed., *Breath Sweeps Mind,* pp. 44–45.

21. Jack Kornfield, "The Art of Awakening," in Jean Smith, ed., *Breath Sweeps Mind,* p. 17.

22. Stephen Batchelor, "Going Against the Stream," in Jean Smith, ed., *Breath Sweeps Mind,* p. 28.

23. Snelling, "Buddhist Traditions," p. 29.

24. Thich Nhat Hahn, in Jean Smith, ed., *Breath Sweeps Mind,* p. 69.

25. Joseph Goldstein, "To Open, To Balance, To Explore," in Jean Smith, ed., *Breath Sweeps Mind,* p. 75.

26. Ibid., p. 79.

27. Henepola Gunaratana, "The Great Teacher," in Jean Smith, ed., *Breath Sweeps Mind,* pp. 61–62.

28. Sondra Ray, *Celebration of Breath* (Celestial Arts, 1983), pp. 10–11.

29. Excerpted from *The American Heritage® Dictionary of the English Language, Third Edition* © 1996 by Houghton Mifflin Company.

30. Robert Forte, ed., *Entheogens and the Future of Religion* (Council on Spiritual Practices, 1997), p. 1.

31. Ibid., p. 2.

Part 3

1. Michelangelo Signorile, *Life Outside: The Signorile Report on Gay Men: Sex, Drugs, Muscles, and the Passages of Life* (HarperCollins Publishers, 1997), p. 76.

2. This information is included here with permission from SCA. For a complete list, contact them at the address provided in the Resource Guide.

3. Clint Seiter, "Applying Buddhist Dharma to Casual Sex," in Leyland, ed., *Queer Dharma* (Gay Sunshine Press, 1998), p. 299.

4. Ibid., p. 300.

5. Margo Anand, *The Art of Sexual Ecstasy: The Path of Sacred Sexuality for Western Lovers* (Tarcher/Putnam, 1989), p. 4.

6. Ibid., p. 5.

7. Kamala Devi, *The Eastern Way of Love,* cited in Anand, *The Art of Sexual Ecstasy,* p. 39.

8. Anand, *Art of Sexual Ecstasy,* p. 40.

9. Ibid., p. 38.

10. Mantak Chia and Douglas Abrams Arava, *The Multi-Orgasmic Man* (HarperSanFrancisco, 1996), pp. xiii–xiv.

11. Ibid., p. 174.

12. Ibid., p. 178.

13. Ibid., p. 180.

14. Thomas Moore, *Soul of Sex: Cultivating Life as an Act of Love* (HarperCollins, 1998), p. 15.

15. Don Shewey, "Sexual Healing: Joe Kramer Sings the Body Electric," *Village Voice,* Vol. 37, No. 16, April 21, 1992, p. 37.

16. Bobby Gray, "Leathersex and Sexuality," *White Crane Journal,* Number 31, Winter 1997, p. 5.

17. Ibid.

18. Jim Leonard and Phil Laut, *Rebirthing: The Science of Enjoying All of Your Life* (Trinity Publications, 1983), p. 28.

19. Thompson, *Gay Body,* p. 189.

20. Ibid., p. 201.

21. Diane Mariechild, *Sacred Lesbian Sexuality* (Wingbow Press, 1995), pp. 56 and 31.

22. Scott Peck, *The Road Less Traveled: A New Psychology of Love, Traditional Values and Spiritual Growth* (Touchstone, 1978), p. 81.

23. *A Course in Miracles* (Foundation for Inner Peace, 1975), p. 315.

24. Thompson, *Gay Spirit,* p. 203.

25. Mariechild, *Sacred Lesbian Sexuality,* p. 56.

26. Anand, *Art of Sexual Ecstasy,* p. 41.

27. Chia and Arava, *Multi-Orgasmic Man,* p. 222.

Part 4

1. Torie Osborn, *Coming Home to America: A Roadmap to Gay & Lesbian Empowerment* (St. Martin's Press, 1996), pp. 52–53.

2. Richard Bach, *Illusions: The Adventures of a Reluctant Messiah* (Dell Publishing Group, 1977), pp. 9–24.

3. James Allen, *As You Think* (New World Library, 1998), p. 77.

4. Brian Swimme, *The Universe Is a Green Dragon* (Bear & Co., 1984), pp. 39–40.

5. Ram Dass and Mirabai Bush, *Compassion in Action: Setting Out on the Path of Service* (Bell Tower, 1992), pp. 134–35.

6. Swimme, *Universe Is a Green Dragon,* p. 146.

7. Christine Wicker, "A Lesson in Kindness: Bar Company Provides Support, Gifts for Adopted Grade School," *The Dallas Morning News,* August 30,1998.

8. Robert Goss, *Jesus Acted Up: A Gay and Lesbian Manifesto* (HarperSanFrancisco, 1993), p. 154.

9. During the public forum, a group of young men planted themselves strategically throughout the Stanford Chapel, where the event was held. Once the proceedings began, one by one they arose and began screaming mostly unintelligible words, among which "Jesus" featured prominently. As one was escorted out, the next would stand and take his place.

10. Thompson, *Gay Soul,* p. 167.

11. Sharon Kleinbaum, "Religion: Our Soulforce," in "Staring Down 2000," *Out,* February 1997, p. 71.

12. Marianne Williamson, *A Return to Love: Reflections on the Principles of A Course in Miracles* (HarperPaperbacks, 1993), pp. 188–89.

Appendix 1

1. Ozmo Piedmont, Ph.D., *The Veils of Arjuna: Androgyny in Gay Spirituality, East and West* (doctoral dissertation), p. 230.

2. Alain Daniélou, *Shiva and Dionysus: The Religion of Nature and Eros,* cited in Conner et al., *Cassell's Encyclopedia of Queer Myth,* p. 154.

3. Piedmont, *Veils of Arjuna,* p. 316.

4. Roscoe, *Queer Spirits,* p.119.

5. Conner et al., *Cassell's Encyclopedia,* p. 19.

6. Piedmont, *Veils of Arjuna,* p. 262.

7. Ibid., p. 278.

8. Ibid., p. 283.

9. José Ignacio Cabezón, "Homosexuality and Buddhism," in Leyland, ed., *Queer Dharma,* p. 30.

10. Ibid., p. 34.

11. Ibid., p. 38.

12. Conner et al., *Cassell's Encyclopedia,* p. 8.

13. Ibid.

14. Leyland, *Queer Dharma,* p. 281.

15. Sandy Boucher, *Opening the Lotus: A Woman's Guide to Buddhism* (Beacon Press, 1997), pp. 119–20.

16. Dennis Conkin, "The Dalai Lama and Gay Love," in Leyland, *Queer Dharma,* p. 354.

17. Sandra A. Wawrytko, "Homosexuality and Chinese and Japanese Religions," in Arlene Swidler, ed., *Homosexuality and World Religions* (Trinity Press International, 1993), p. 210.

18. Conner et al., *Cassell's Encyclopedia,* p. 354.

19. "Judaism," *Microsoft® Encarta® 98 Encyclopedia.* © 1993–1997 Microsoft Corporation. All rights reserved.

20. Rabbi Yoel H. Kahn, "Judaism and Homosexuality: The Traditionalist/Progressive Debate," in Richard Hasbany, ed., *Homosexuality and Religion* (Harrington Park Press, 1989), p. 49.

21. Ellen M. Umansky, "Jewish Attitudes Towards Homosexuality: A Review of Contemporary Sources," in Gary David Comstock and Susan E. Henking, eds., *Que(e)rying Religion* (Continuum, 1997), p. 183.

22. Kahn, "Judaism and Homosexuality," p. 75.

23. Ontario Centre for Religious Tolerance (http://web.canlink.com/ocrt/ocrt_hp.htm).

24. Lewis John Eron, "Homosexuality and Judaism," in Arlene Swidler, ed., *Homosexuality and World Religions,* p. 126.

25. Ibid., p. 125.

26. Umansky, "Jewish Attitudes," p. 186.

27. Khan, "Judaism and Homosexuality," p. 73.

28. Janet R. Marder, "Getting to Know the Gay and Lesbian Shul," *Reconstructionist,* cited in Swidler, *Homosexuality and World Religions,* p. 126.

29. Eron, "Homosexuality and Judaism," p. 104.

30. Conner et al., *Cassell's Encyclopedia,* pp. 273–74.

31. Huston Smith, *The Illustrated World's Religions: A Guide to Our Wisdom Traditions* (HarperSanFrancisco, 1991), p. 146.

32. "Islam," *Microsoft® Encarta® 98 Encyclopedia.* © 1993–1997 Microsoft Corporation. All rights reserved.

33. Khalid Duran, "Homosexuality and Islam," in Arlene Swidler, ed., *Homosexuality and World Religions,* pp. 181–82.

34. Jehoeda Sofer, "Sodomy in the Law of Muslim States," in Arno Schmitt and Jehoeda Sofer, eds., *Sexuality and Eroticism Among Males in Moslem Societies* (The Haworth Press, 1992), pp. 131–46.

35. Duran, "Homosexuality and Islam," pp. 190–91.

36. Arno Schmitt, "Different Approaches to Male–Male Sexuality/Eroticism from Morocco to Usbekistān," in Arno Schmitt and Jehoeda Sofer, eds., *Sexuality and Eroticism,* pp. 1–21.

37. Huston Smith, *Illustrated World's Religions,* p. 170.

38. Duran, "Homosexuality and Islam," p. 196.

39. Conner et al., *Cassell's Encyclopedia,* p. 20.

40. Ibid., p. 303.

41. "Islam," *Microsoft® Encarta® 98 Encyclopedia.*

42. John Boswell, *Christianity, Social Tolerance, and Homosexuality;* Daniel Helminiak, *What the Bible Really Says About Homosexuality;* Nancy Wilson, *Our Tribe;* Michael Piazza, *Holy Homosexuals;* Rembert Truluck, *Steps to Recovery from Bible Use.*

43. Daniel A. Helminiak, *What the Bible Really Says about Homosexuality* (Alamo Square Press, 1994), pp. 64–65.

44. Ibid., p. 74.

45. 1 Samuel 20:41, *The Holy Bible: New International Version* (Zondervan Bible Publishers, 1973), p. 269.

46. 2 Samuel 1:26, *The Holy Bible: New International Version,* p. 280.

47. Ruth 1:16, *The Holy Bible: New International Version,* p. 247.

48. John Boswell, *Christianity, Social Tolerance, and Homosexuality* (The University of Chicago Press, 1980).

49. Jallen Rix, "Down at Stonewall," *The Sacred and the Queer* (Triam Music, 1996).

50. *San Francisco Frontiers,* December 12, 1997.

51. Huston Smith, *Illustrated World's Religions,* p. 228.

52. Gustav Niebuhr, "Anglican Conference Takes Tough Line on Homosexuals," *The New York Times,* August 6, 1998, p. A-1.

53. Bob Reeves, "United Methodists Plan to Rally to Uphold Traditional Doctrines," *Lincoln Journal Star,* April 23, 1998, pp. 1B, 3B.

54. Don Lattin, "Gay Issues Emerge at Church Sessions," *San Francisco Chronicle,* June 24, 1997.

55. *The Mission,* Newsletter of the Lutheran Lesbian & Gay Ministries, October 1997.

56. John M. Glionna, "A Path Less Traveled," *Los Angeles Times,* March 16, 1998, p. 1-Metro.

57. Brad Gooch, "Divine Design," *Out Magazine,* No. 32, May 1996, p. 70.

58. Ibid., pp. 66–68.

59. Huston Smith, *Illustrated World's Religions,* p. 232.

60. Conner et al., *Cassell's Encyclopedia,* p. 5.

INDEX

Index

COMING OUT SPIRITUALLY:
ABOUT Q-SPIRIT

Q-Spirit is an international network of gay/lesbian/queer people who wish to connect with others sharing an interest in personal growth, spirituality, and the many expressions of each. Honoring all paths and traditions, our goals include helping our community reclaim its spiritual heritage; exploring and redefining the expressions of our spirituality; and discovering how we can make a difference together in ways we could not do alone. At present, Q-Spirit offers individual monthly gatherings in the Bay Area, featuring guest speakers, ritual, meditation, discussion, entertainment, community service, and the opportunity to meet fellow journeyers.

For inclusion in our forthcoming Lavender Healers' Network, featuring GLBT healers of all modalities, or to receive our monthly newsletter, *Q-Spirit Matters*, please send to the address below your

Name:
Address:
Telephone:
Fax:
Email:
How did you hear about Q-Spirit?:
Gender (optional):
For Lavender Healer's Network, include brief (20-word max.) description of your work:

Q-Spirit
3739 Balboa Street, #211
San Francisco, CA 94121
(415)281-9377; (415)386-3187 fax
info@qspirit.org; www.qspirit.org

ABOUT THE AUTHOR

Christian de la Huerta is founder and Executive Director of Q-Spirit, an international network of gays and lesbians interested in spirituality. He is also owner of Mercurio Communications, a publicity and promotions firm specializing in gay and lesbian authors as well as the psychology/self-help/spirituality genre. Christian is the host of "Spirit Wave," an Internet radio program heard weekly at www.GAYBC.com. A seminar leader and group facilitator, he graduated with honors from Tulane University with a degree in psychology. As a Certified Rebirther (Breathwork Practitioner), Christian leads groups and has a private practice, in which he serves as spiritual coach and counselor.